Western 1975

# PERSONAL AND INTERPERSONAL COMMUNICATION

# PERSONAL AND INTERPERSONAL COMMUNICATION

## Dialogue with the Self and with Others

John J. Makay
*The Ohio State University*

Beverly A. Gaw
*Wright State University*

Charles E. Merrill Publishing Company
*A Bell & Howell Company*
Columbus, Ohio

Photo credits:

page 2:   top — Linda Briscoe
          middle — Saundra Woodruff
          bottom — Linda Briscoe

page 54:  top — Saundra Woodruff
          middle — Eugene Luttenberg, EPA, Inc.
          bottom — Dan O'Neill, EPA, Inc.

page 116: top — Yohannes Besserat, EPA, Inc.
          middle — Saundra Woodruff
          bottom — Dan O'Neill, EPA, Inc.

page 176: top — Linda Briscoe
          middle — Saundra Woodruff
          bottom — Linda Briscoe

Published by
Charles E. Merrill Publishing Company
*A Bell & Howell Company*
Columbus, Ohio 43216

*This book was set in Times Roman.*
*The production editor was Beverly Kolz.*
*Cover photo was by Linda Briscoe.*

Library of Congress Catalog Card Number: 74-26371

ISBN: 0-675-08719-8

1 2 3 4 5 6 7 8 9 10—80 79 78 77 76 75

Printed in the United States of America

*To my friend Charlotte
who introduced me to this approach
in her communication with me and
helped show me the way.*

J.J.M.


*To my teacher and my friend,
John.*

B.A.G.

# Contents

# Preface

This book is intended for a first course in interpersonal communication, for those instructors and students who desire to explore the quality of human interaction as well as the fact of it. Our focus is essentially a humanistic one, at least in the sense that we examine personal meaning and individual personal growth at the same time we survey those social, psychological, and environmental factors which can be more or less empirically tested and elucidated.

In less than one decade, the beginning courses in speech communication departments have grown and changed. More than ever before our discipline is now introducing students to the broad scope of human communication, to communication wherever it occurs—within the individual and in one-to-one or small group encounters, as well as in one-to-many situations. And more than ever before, we believe, students are eager to discover the relationships between their own personal meanings and growth and the messages in their transactions. Personal meaning, albeit elusive of empirical, scientific experimentation, nevertheless merits the effort of our struggling to understand it better. We need to see more clearly and fully the relationships between meaning and other valuable elements in human communication.

For these reasons, the reader may expect to find, in addition to the source-perceiver models of communication, more in this book on the self, or meaning, personal growth, trust, and dialogue than in many other introductory texts on communication. An entire section, for example (three chapters), explores the relationship between meaning and messages; another section contains three full chapters on dialogue —both with the self and with others. These two sections are framed by two others. Three introductory chapters in the first section describe the basic concepts and theories of both intra- and interpersonal communication, and a final section relates routine, dyadic, and group experiences to what has been examined in the first three-quarters of the book.

This plan for the book, and the words which make up our message, are ours and we take full responsibility for them. But they are far richer and more readable in their present form because of the insights and critical suggestions offered by William E. King of St. Petersburg Junior College, Richard L. Johannesen of Northern Illinois University, and especially Virginia Kidd of California State University, Sacramento. Their helpful reviews contributed much to the revision and editing of the manuscript. Likewise, the careful and judicious editing of Bev Kolz, Series Editor at Merrill, refined and polished our efforts, and we are grateful for her invaluable help. The photographs which extend and amplify our message throughout the text were in part supplied by Saundra Woodruff and Linda Briscoe. Finally, we recognize the book would not have been completed without the support of our editor Tom Hutchinson and the encouragement of our mates, Mary Makay and Bruce Gaw.

John J. Makay
Beverly A. Gaw

# PART ONE

# Introduction to Interpersonal Communication

# 1

# The Study of
# Communication

The need to study communication, particularly interpersonal communication, may be so apparent to you that for us to treat it so early in our book may seem unnecessary. On the other hand, our students in the basic courses in communication have frequently raised the question, "Why study communication? I've been communicating all my life. . . ." We recognize that what we suggest as a focus in this section of our book may not be new to you. In fact, most of what is presented in this chapter is nothing completely different from what you've been doing all your life. You *have* been communicating as far back as you can remember; you may feel saturated with the noises aimed at attracting your attention throughout each day; and you do have the capability for sound, critical, and meaningful communication within yourself and with others.

Our purpose is to *stimulate* you to *think* seriously and *feel* deeply about the need for open, honest, meaningful, substantive, and often playful communication today in *your* life. So we study interpersonal communication in order to develop more humane and dialogic relationships which can have value for each of us.

The study of communication, in fact, is generally considered to be a humane study as well as one of the social and behavioral sciences.[1]

---

1. Keith Brooks, Jack E. Douglas, Carroll C. Arnold, and Robert S. Brubaker, "The Study of Speech Communication," 1972, distributed by the Speech Communication Association, reprinted in John J. Makay, ed., *Exploration in Speech Communication* (Columbus: Charles E. Merrill, 1973), pp. 4–18.

To introduce you to the study of interpersonal communication from a humanistic point of view, we will define communication and explain it as process and transaction.

## A Humanistic Approach

What is a humanistic approach to interpersonal communication? You will discover that "humanism" is a multidimensional term with quite a number of meanings assigned to it by scholars and laymen alike. Perhaps the quickest and most rewarding way to discover the meanings of humanism is to study *The Humanist Alternative,* a provocative collection of essays which will provide you with a mind-expanding awareness about humanism.[2] For the moment, however, let us make it clear that our humanistic approach to interpersonal communication is one which focuses on personal growth in developing and maintaining valuable human relationships. Furthermore, this approach seeks to guide you in humane ways to solve problems, to complete tasks, and to reach goals.

Our reliance on such an approach to interpersonal communication is based on the belief that through communication we can continually come to deal with ourselves and others in satisfying and meaningful ways. Courage, independence, openness, trust, and meaning are among the qualities upon which this approach is built, rather than fear, dependence, secrecy, mistrust and ambiguity. The theoretical basis for our approach is information found in communication and rhetorical theory, humanistic and social psychology, and in other appropriate disciplines which contributed to the concerns of this book.[3] A humanistic approach encourages us to express our feelings and ideas genuinely—those feelings and ideas which can improve our "selves" within our personal relationships, and our efforts within groups and organizations which are important to us.[4]

2. Paul Kurtz, ed., *The Humanist Alternative: Some Definitions of Humanism* (Buffalo: Prometheus Books, 1973).

3. Particularly good examples to review are: Frank Goble, *Third Force, The Psychology of Abraham Maslow* (New York: Pocket Book, 1971); Rollo May, *Man's Search for Himself* (New York: New American Library, 1953); Colin Wilson, *New Pathways in Psychology: Maslow and the Post-Freudian Revolution* (New York: Taplinger, 1972).

4. For further orientation at this point you can review "Humanism and Psychotherapy," in Albert Ellis, *Humanistic Psychotherapy, The Rational-Emotive Approach* (New York: Julian, 1973), pp. 1–16.

Recognizing the multidimensional nature of the term "humanism," Zen theologian Bernard Phillips states: "Humanism has signified many things, but most essentially, it is a concern with man and a faith in the adequacy of human resources—intellectually employed to actualize the promise and splendour of human life."[5] A professor of religion, Joseph Blair, shares this outlook in his view that humanism recognizes "human dignity and power in some of its important dimensions," so that humanism can be defined "as a perceptive caring for him. Its universal tendency is to stress human self-understanding and self-determination."[6] A statement by Edwin Wilson, former Director of the American Humanist Association, seems to sum up the views we've shared with you about humanism: "One thing can be said of all Humanists that are worthy of their name: their central concern is for man, his growth, fulfillment and creativity in the here and now."[7] It should be evident that philosophically humanism is a challenge to each of us to really be concerned with ourselves and our personal relationships in terms resulting in a genuine high quality of life. Interpersonal communication is essential to such living.

Although humanism traditionally has been associated with the humanities, especially ethics, in Western thought, in the field of psychology a new branch, humanistic psychology, has been developing as an alternative to psychoanalysis and behaviorism. Humanistic psychology is a major force which has been highly influential in the inspiration and subsequent writing of this book.

Humanistic psychology is relatively new in the philosophical, scientific, and psychological traditions. Although it tends to exist, organizationally, on its own and apart from other humanist organizations, humanistic psychology represents "a blending of psychological science and ethical humanism."[8]

Combining humanistic philosophies and psychology, and communication theories and principles, a humanistic approach to interpersonal communication can be studied and practiced. A realistic point of departure into the study of interpersonal communication is a discussion of the process and transactional nature of human communication.

---

5. Bernard Phillips, "Zen and Humanism," in *The Humanist Alternative,* p. 159.
6. Joseph Blair, "Toward a Definition of Humanism," in *The Humanist Alternative,* p. 42.
7. Edwin Wilson, "Humanism's Many Dimensions," in *The Humanist Alternative,* p. 15.
8. Ibid., p. 17.

## Communication: Process and Transaction

Before dealing with any precise definitions of communication we must consider its process nature. Although communication has been implicitly regarded as a process by theorists and practitioners for generations, one major treatise which zeroed in on the process nature is the work of communicologist David K. Berlo, *The Process of Communication.*[9] According to Berlo

> Communication theory reflects a process point of view. A communication theorist rejects the possibility that nature consists of events or ingredients that are separable from all other events. He argues that you cannot talk about *the* beginning or *the* end of communication or say that a particular idea came from one specific source, that communication occurs in only one way, and so on.[10]

Gerald Miller, a contemporary communication researcher, speaks of the term "process" in communication theory and operation in the broadest sense, and states that it "refers to a way of perceiving and responding to the world in which we live. . . . The notion of process implies a universe in constant flux," so that we cannot view communication as a static phenomenon which is fixed in time and space.[11] Instead, as communication theorist Kenneth Anderson points out:

> The way to understand communication is to appreciate the complexity of the process and to learn as much as we can about this complexity. . . . Understanding the nature of communication gives us a tool which helps us to understand one another more easily. Such knowledge enables us to become better communicators in our roles as both receivers and sources.[12]

Communication as a process could easily be the subject of a number of volumes. We intend initially to stimulate and generate awareness of this process. For now, remember that the term *process of communication* refers to a dynamic complexity in which a number of particular actions and variables are involved, and that communication operates

---

9. David K. Berlo, *The Process of Communication* (New York: Holt, Rinehart, and Winston, 1960).

10. Ibid., p. 24.

11. Gerald R. Miller, *An Introduction to Speech Communication,* 2d ed. (Indianapolis: Bobbs-Merrill, 1972), p. 33.

12. Kenneth E. Anderson, *Introduction to Communication Theory and Practice* (Menlo Park, California: Cummings, 1972), p. 5.

continually with energy and force. We are a part of this process, we are caught up in it, and our success, satisfaction, and growth depends to a great extent on how we live within it. Let's take a close look at the process of communication.

## Process

Research has provided us with an abundance of definitions of communication. In 1970, Frank Dance reviewed ninety-five of them.[13] His list was not exhaustive, and the definitions share what appear to be common meanings. We will work with a definition of communication which includes essential attributes of others.

In this study we can consider human communication as a process which is dependent upon the creation of meaning in symbolic interaction; we *construct reality* by assigning signals or symbols to what we perceive and communicate about. This "putting together" (construction or creation) of perceived reality suggests that each human engages in particular information processing when communicating. One can consider human communication as a process wherein a human being sorts, selects, and sends signals and/or symbols as messages which *evoke some meaning* in the self and/or another human being *who* in turn *creates* within herself or himself a response to the messages of the originator. Of course, communication takes place within a time, space, and cultural context. Clearly three important elements of the process stand out in this definition: the human being (originator), the messages, and the receiver (responding human). In communication the originator is usually labeled the source. "Originator" can range in meaning from one individual to a host of individuals who represent either themselves, a cause, a group or an organization of one kind or another. In interpersonal communication the source is a human being speaking generally for himself. The term "message" refers to the meanings, verbal and nonverbal, conscious and unconscious, in the *perceptions* of both speaker and listener; all communicators, in perceiving, structure meanings which are assigned to messages.

The sorting and selection of signals and symbols can be both conscious and unconscious. In the context of this study you can consider signals and symbols as providing the components of any message because meanings are in all communicators. Keep in mind that signals are messages which a communicator feels are beaming from a source,

13. Frank E. X. Dance, "The Concept of 'Communication'," *The Journal of Communication* 20 (June 1970): 201–10.

and they suggest very limited but concise meaning. Symbols suggest broader and more complex meanings assigned to the verbal and non-verbal language of the communicators.[14] Consider some examples to illustrate the concepts of signal and symbol.

When a person plays cards he knows the possibilities a player has of signaling a partner about what cards he is holding. A scratch on the side of the face could indicate what sort of play one wishes his partner to make. In playing bridge, a man may tip his wife off to a particular state his hand appears to be in with a short verbal cue— a signal. However, when a round of cards is completed players may discuss the play in terms of strategy and choices, and this complex expression involves abstraction at various levels of meaning which requires the use of symbols.

A second example can help to illustrate the distinction between signals and symbols. After a lecture on human values and communication an instructor was approached by a man and a woman who wanted to comment on the ideas expressed. One wore a cross and a white button with two words placed on it: "One Way." The friendly look on the faces of the students signaled warmth, interest, and ease to the instructor. The cross and the button beamed (signaled) at least one of the two was a Christian—the cross initially signaled a recognition of a martyred Jesus and the "One Way" button beamed the message that this was a member of the Campus Crusade for Christ ("One Way" is the CCC motto). Once the three began talking interpersonally, verbal as well as nonverbal symbols came into play, because language was used abstractly, flexibly, and in depth and detail to achieve mutual understanding as well as good feelings about one another. The perceptive communicator who seeks accurate meaning will recognize the limited information to be gained from signals and seek understanding through symbolic processes.

So symbols are the verbal and conceptual expressions which are far more precise and intentionally clear than signals. Both deal with units of meaning. Signals, as you can readily see, are less complex and more limited in meaning than are symbols. The language intentionally used by each can be considered a shared exchange of signals and symbols in the process of communication. Because meanings are most often in people and because one must respond one way or another, at least two claims about communication should become apparent: an individual cannot *not* communicate, and when people communicate there is the

---

14. For a detailed discussion of signs as signals see Wallace C. Fotheringham, *Perspectives on Persuasion* (Boston: Allyn & Bacon, 1966), pp. 54–61.

inevitability of some difference in meaning. Communication is a meaning-centered process.[15]

The statement you cannot not communicate means that observed behavior always generates some meaning in a communicator. Because one draws meanings from an observation of any behavior, one cannot behave without communicating in an intentional or unintentional way. Furthermore, because meanings are in people, and meanings in people are never identical, there is always the possibility of some difference in meaning. There can frequently be, of course, highly similar shared meanings among individuals when communication takes place. A humanistic view suggests communicators seek the lowest level of misunderstanding possible.

We should keep in mind that meanings are also shaped by such things as the time of day, the season of the year, the mental and emotional state of each communicator when he or she talks and responds to the others, the apparel of each, as well as a host of other factors which may have influenced behavior. Thus, we can see that signals or symbols are meassages *created in* human beings.

Both the originator of and responder to the communication may not be aware of some of the cues and concepts which seem to generate meaning, so we can easily admit that the levels of awareness in the communication process may be both conscious and unconscious.

Initially, in our definition of communication, the term transaction was used to refer to a human exchange of signals and symbols between communicators. The concept of transaction in communication needs explanation because it is a key to the humanistic approach.

## Transaction

When we talk of the process of communication in human activity we know we are not talking of a series of static entities. However, it would be easy enough for us to consider communication as human interaction, the dynamic interplay of forces which generate meaning. Communicologist John Stewart encourages us to become sharp in our focus, to view *interpersonal* communication as not simply an act of interaction but as human transaction:

> In contrast to an interaction a transaction is defined as a psychological event in which all parts or aspects of the concrete events derive

---

15. James R. Wilcox, "The Assessment of Meaning: A Communication Perspective," in John J. Makay, ed., *Exploration in Speech Communication* (Columbus: Charles E. Merrill, 1973), pp. 40–62.

their existence and nature from active participation in the event. This transactional perspective is important because if one sees human communication simply as an act or interaction he is likely to overlook the fact that we construct the persons with whom we communicate. . . . We construct the other with whom we communicate in the sense that we choose from the infinite number of cues (one) "gives off" and organize our chosen perceptions into a configuration that is him.[16]

Each communicator "puts together" what he thinks, imagines (exchanges/constructs), indeed, gives meaningful shape to the other and what the other's messages seemed to be. This is more than interaction, this is a transaction.

The event in which communication takes place gives rise to the transaction (exchange/construction) between communicators. In the example of the instructor and the religious students, the communicators were suggested to you and constructed by you. You have then engaged in a transaction in reading. Furthermore, the instructor and the students were constructed (in our minds) in reality by each other, and meanings, in reality, were created (constructed) in them about each other and each other's intent. And Stewart rightly advises: "Human communication is transactional because we construct the persons who are active participants in a communication event."[17] This construction, in trying to create accurate meaning between communicators, can be extremely complex because of the number and variety of impressions we conjure up.

Meaning is itself a concept we need to think about. We use the term literally in our thinking, writing, and speaking. What do we mean— "meaning"? We must recognize, as the writing of communicologist Dean Barnlund stipulates, that our approach to communication ought to be meaning-centered:

Meaning is not apparent in the ordinary flow of sensation. We are born into, and inhabit a world without meaning. That life becomes intelligible to us—full of beauty or ugliness, hope or despair—is because it is assigned that significance by the experiencing being. . . . Sensations do not come to us, sorted and labeled, as if we were visitors in a vast, but ordered, museum. Each of us, instead, is his

16. John Stewart, "An Interpersonal Approach to the Basic Course," *The Speech Teacher* 21 (January 1972):10.
17. Ibid., p. 12.

own curator. We learn to look with a selective eye, to classify, to assign significance.[18]

In short, we give meaning to experiences as we respond to and construct our world, and learn to know and value in our experiencing. We can respond psychologically in a way that is meaningful, we can signify one thing in relation to another in a way that is meaningful, we can refer to events, objects or others so as to create meaning, and we can convey words, gestures, or behavior patterns that are meaningful. Communication is centered in meaning, as our definition indicates, and because each person, in social intercourse, constructs perceptions of reality in human communication, this communication is transactional.

Now that we have studied the humanistic approach, communication as process, a definition of communication, and transaction in communication, we need to examine the process of communication as detailed in a relevant communication model. The model in figure 1 lays out the communication variables discussed to this point.

## Summary

We can easily see that, although we have been communicating since childhood, there is a need for us to learn a great deal more about the process and practice of interpersonal communication. This knowledge and skill can enhance the quality and productivity of life within ourselves and with others.

We also recognize the impact a humanistic approach can have for us. To be independent in interdependency, to solve problems as well as to find pleasure in a uniquely humane way is indeed a highly valuable approach to communication specifically, and life generally. Thus, we studied the multidimensional concepts of humanism as they relate to our study in interpersonal communication.

Within a humanistic framework, then, we sought to describe the process of communication and interpersonal communication as being transactional. As process, communication is dynamic and ever changing in signification and symbolization about reality. As a transaction, interpersonal communication recognizes the communicator's exchange of signs as signals and symbols according to what he perceives, and the resulting meanings of the receivers.

18. Barnlund's article originally appeared in *The Journal of Communication* 2 (1962). We refer to it as it appears in an abridged version in John Stewart, ed., *Bridges Not Walls, A Book About Interpersonal Communication* (Reading, Massachusetts: Addison-Wesley, 1973), pp. 45–46.

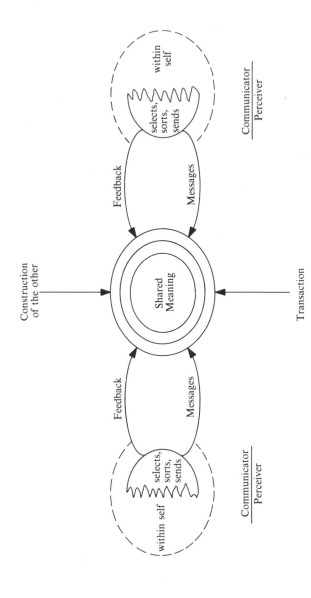

**FIGURE 1. Interpersonal Communication Model**

# 2

# Turning to You — Intrapersonal Communication

In chapter 1, we found that a universal tendency of the humanistic approach was to stress self-understanding and determination. We can best understand this concern by turning to self-communication. Initially there are a number of questions that arise. An example here should serve as an impetus to beginning a discussion of intrapersonal communication.

A student, let's call her Sarah, went to her instructor's office one day in tears. She *had* to move away from home, she explained. She just "couldn't take it any more." Because of one bad experience in which she had been involved Sarah's parents consistently maligned her. They refused to give her a key to her own home. They did not allow her to drive the family car any place but to school. They insisted she come home immediately after classes. They checked every person who called the house and kept tabs on her mail. Any accomplishment she attained, such as trophies for speaking and baton-twirling, they either ignored or derogated. They told Sarah that she had committed "a wrong" which could never be forgiven and that as soon as anyone found out what she had done, they would reject her as a friend. So she decided to run away from home and live with friends. She would work to pay her own way in life; she planned to leave without a note, at a time when her parents were not at home.

What took place *within* Sarah? How important was intrapersonal communication in determining her decision? How did she perceive the situation? What did she think and feel about it? How do you think she saw herself as a person? How was she evaluating herself? What choices and decisions was she making? What action was she going to take? How would she evaluate the success of that action? What did she hope to gain from it as a person?

# Definition

It is obvious that Sarah had talked within herself, and this is the simplest definition of intrapersonal communication—*talking within oneself.* Obviously, we talk within ourselves constantly throughout each day; we process communication within before we initiate communication with others. Within ourselves we contain all the necessary factors of communication.

How does this work? A person, object, or event stimulates thoughts and feelings. We become aware of this internal behavior by silently verbalizing our idea or emotion, by putting it into language—for ourselves. The thoughts and feelings are monitored, that is, checked for such things as personal logic, significance, and meaning. The thoughts and feelings are then either ignored, changed, reinforced, and/or acted upon. What all this means is that we have within us a network and the ability to both initiate (send) and monitor (receive) ideas/emotions (messages), which can be altered or reinforced (feedback).

Suppose a teacher receives a combined external/internal stimulus which leads to the thought, "It is a nice day. It would be fun to have my class meet outside." This thought is immediately monitored by such opposite thoughts as, "There's no chalk board," "The open space will make it difficult to hear," "The grass is probably wet," "The male and female students will direct their attention more readily toward each other." You can guess what conclusion she will reach intrapersonally—"The class will meet inside." The important consideration here is not the particular conclusion itself, but the fact that she came to a decision within herself. The process is activated, conceptualized, and monitored internally.

A basic model of intrapersonal communication is essentially the same as any other model of communication—whether interpersonal communication, or public communication—with one exception: *feed-*

*back occurs exclusively within the self,* rather than coming from another person or audience. (See figure 2.[1])

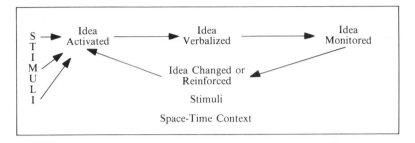

**FIGURE 2. Intrapersonal
Communication Model**

Perhaps you can now reflect on your intrapersonal communication while reading this chapter. If you have said things to yourself such as "I don't understand," and re-read a paragraph, or, "This example is dumb," and skipped four sentences, or "I know a situation just like this," and paused to review it or, "Will this chapter never end?" and checked to see how many pages remained—you have engaged in intrapersonal communication.

## Importance

At this point we might say, "So what? Why don't we get on to communication with other people—that's what it's all about." Well, this is exactly why an understanding of intrapersonal communication is important. It is not only the basis of all our individual decisions and actions, it is a basis of our communication with and actions toward other people.

Though it's difficult to separate purely individual communication and action from that communication and action which affects others, let's try to do so and linger with the importance of intrapersonal communication to us personally.

The way we monitor our thoughts and feelings is directly responsible for the quality of our decisions and actions. If we monitor intelligently, if we weigh advantages and disadvantages against personal

---

1. See Larry L. Barker and Gordon Wiseman, "A Model of Intrapersonal Communication," in John J. Makay, ed., *Exploration in Speech Communication* (Columbus, Ohio: Charles E. Merrill, 1973), pp. 62–71, for a more detailed model and explanation.

values and needs, our decisions will probably be self-rational and conducive to obtaining our goals. If we monitor unintelligently, if we allow wishful thinking or impulse to dictate choices, our decisions will probably be self-irrational and obstructive to obtaining our long-term goals. For example, assume a student's personal goal at this point in life is to carry a 3.5 cumulative average because she wants to go to graduate school. She has a sociology exam coming up which will determine the difference between a B or a C in the course. She considers the textbook and readings excruciatingly boring, so she hasn't begun to study for the exam. It's the evening before the exam. There's a rock concert on campus that sounds fantastic. She could miss the concert and study. She could go to the concert and stay up all night cramming. She could go to the concert and forget about the exam. She could go to the concert, give the professor an excuse, and ask for a make-up. Although there are many pertinent factors that cannot be included here (such as what her grade point average is *now*), we can ponder at this point how very important intrapersonal communication is even when it concerns essentially no one else. To a large extent it determines what a person gets out of life.

Second, we make intrapersonal decisions about what to say and what to do to other people. Communicologists Tony Clark, Doug Bock, and Mike Cornett state, "No matter how significant or insignificant our communication with others may be, it always involves intrapersonal communication."[2]

What determines what we say or do to others? The first determining factor is the goal we want to achieve in the transaction, whether acceptance of ourselves or a desired action from the other. The second factor is our estimate of the relationship and predictability of the other, whether it is an intimate relationship where we feel certain we know how the other will react or a more distant relationship where we have no idea how the other will respond. A third factor is our understanding of the space-time context, whether it is a public situation where others may be indirectly involved or a private one where consideration of others and their reactions is nonexistent.

This evaluation of the "I," "You," and "Us" takes place within, through intrapersonal communication. Our internal estimates and guesses about these factors will determine our communication and action toward the other. For example, let us say that John really enjoys his job as salesperson at a clothing store. One of his goals in

---

2. Tony Clark, Doug Bock, and Mike Cornett, *Is That You Out There? Exploring Authentic Communication* (Columbus: Charles E. Merrill, 1973), p. 102.

life is to express himself openly and honestly, especially where positive feelings exist. Now, one of the reasons John enjoys working at the store is that the owner is very informal and friendly and is inclined to treat his employees as equals. John figures that even though he is superior to the employees intellectually and financially, he appreciates compliments. However, some other employees, while secretly disparaging the owner, are all smiles, sunshine, and syrupy sentiments to his face, because they assume their salaries will benefit. John can tell that the owner is suspicious of this type of behavior. What intrapersonal decision will John make that will affect this interpersonal communication? Will he plunge in and communicate what he feels without worrying about the owner's reaction? Will he decide not to communicate because the owner might classify him with the other hypocritical employees? Will he offer a believable compliment after a disclaimer about "brown-nosing"?

Intrapersonal communication is vitally important. It takes place before any individual action and before any other type of communication. To the extent that we understand and therefore control it, we will be more or less effective in accomplishing individual, interpersonal and group goals.

The remainder of this chapter will go a long way in answering the questions we posed initially. Basically, there are four processes that we need to understand before we can exert better, more honest, and healthier control over our intrapersonal communication and subsequent behavior (which includes interpersonal communication). These four processes can be conveniently termed self-awareness, self-acceptance, self-assertion, and self-actualization. In this chapter we will be talking about what these processes are, how they operate and affect us. In a later chapter, we hope to gain some insight into what these processes can become—how we can control and change our intrapersonal communication through the understanding derived here.

## Self-Awareness

*Self-awareness is comprehension and understanding of self.* It is the ability to be cognizant of the existence and development of the five processes of sensation, perception, thought, emotion, and value.[3]

---

3. For an overview and model of these five subprocesses and their interaction see John J. Makay and William R. Brown, *The Rhetorical Dialogue: Contemporary Concepts and Cases* (Dubuque, Iowa: Wm. C. Brown, 1972), pp. 268–71.

### Sensation

We receive external information basically from five senses: sight, hearing, touch, taste, and smell. We gain information from situations around us from the senses and this sensation process has a direct bearing on subsequent behavior.

Sensing is receiving. Sensation is reception of *"energy change . . . differentiation of stimulation rather than the sheer amount of stimulation."*[4] We sense, focus on, and attend to that which is new to the situation. Sunshine is different from a study lamp. A bird's song is different from silence. If the birds were singing very loudly and there was a faint human scream, a person would sense the scream. The singing is greater in intensity, but the scream is different and new to the situation.

### Perception

Perception follows sensation. Perception is the process of (1) *identifying* the stimuli received by the senses and (2) *classifying* those stimuli into personally meaningful categories.

The point at which identification becomes classification is really arbitrary. We could say that by indentifying hair, face, body, clothes that we *classified* an image as a person. The arbitrary line is less important than the distinction between recognizing and identifying something *as* familiar (in whole or in part) and in organizing it into that category which *is* familiar. We might term that which is identified as a *percept* and that which is classified as a *concept,* the percept always being more concrete and immediate than the concept which is more abstract and delayed. "The process by which sensations are integrated into percepts is automatic; the integration of percepts into concepts is not . . . (percepts are) the given, the self-evident; (concepts) require a volitionally initiated process. . . ."[5]

The reservation that what we perceive is not necessarily what *is* must be acknowledged. There is, more often than not, some degree of difference between the perception and the reality, which, when translated into interpersonal communication, can cause confusion, distortion, and misunderstanding.

What causes this? Basically, there are two causes of misperception: physical and psychological. Physical misperception might occur because of personal physical limitations or optical illusions. If we have

---

4. Thomas M. Scheidel, *Speech Communication and Human Interaction* (Glenview, Illinois: Scott, Foresman, 1972), p. 160.

5. Nathaniel Branden, *The Psychology of Self-Esteem* (Los Angeles: Nash, 1969), p. 32.

a hearing problem, we may perceive deafening noise (a reality in decible measurement) as barely audible. If we are without our glasses and have a bad case of astigmatism, we may perceive a beautifully precise geometric drawing (a reality by tape measurement) as blurry and perhaps unexciting.

Illusions are manufactured to foil our senses, especially our sense of sight. In the Muller-Lyer illusion, one line appears to be shorter than another by the addition of four small lines. Various cubes, squares, geometric shapes and swirls appear to advance or recede, to be two-dimensional or three-dimensional, depending on how they are viewed. Have you ever sat in the dark with a lighted cigarette and swept it around and around rapidly in a circle? A lighted circle appears. You created an optical illusion.

Perception is also affected by psychological factors. Probably the most important factor is past experience. A person is likely to see what he has seen before. If a student walks into a class five minutes late and the professor isn't there, his perception of the situation might be that the class has been cancelled because he has always been there at least five minutes before class begins. The reality is that the professor's child was sick; he had to take him to the hospital and, consequently was late for class. The student's perception was based on past experience with the professor, but it was at variance with the reality of the situation.

Past experience has a way of affecting the physical aspect of perception, too. Because of our past experiences there are some sensations that seldom make it to our brain. The neurological processes involved are too difficult and as yet too indefinite to be detailed here.[6] Suffice it to say that because of past experiences we have trained our neurological pathways not to respond to certain information coming through our senses or to let only certain information come through and be sent on to the brain. Let us say that a person disciplines himself to study with great concentration. He could probably take his books to the student union, and sit down amidst the conversation and music and study effectively. He has trained himself not to perceive any external cues. His only reality is the textbook open before him. Past experience dictated what would be allowed to surface to consciousness.

Our present needs are also important in determining our perception of any situation. Present needs operate to control conscious informa-

6. George A. Borden, Richard D. Gregg, Theodore G. Grove, *Speech Behavior and Human Interaction* (Englewood Cliffs: Prentice-Hall, 1969), pp. 14–19.

tion as does past experience. On a long car trip a person will more readily perceive signs for gas stations than the majesty of the mountains if he has driven for three straight hours. If a person is waiting for a call from an intimate friend, she will more readily perceive the ring of the telephone than a call to dinner. What we perceive, then, is not necessarily, nor usually, what is, but what our physical and psychological filters make it seem to be.

We do, however, often attempt to check our perceptions for their accuracy. There are four methods of checking.[7] The first is *consensual validation*. If we think we perceive a woman walking down the street in a man's suit and tie we might ask a friend with us if he perceives the same phenomenon. The second is *repetition*. We might look again to see if we actually perceived what we thought we did. The third is *multisensation*. We might approach the person and ask a question, hoping that the voice will aid us in checking our initial perception. The fourth is *comparison*. We might check with our past experience to determine if we can recall any other time we have seen what appeared to be a woman in man's clothes and what the reality was at that time. Through these checks, we attempt to come as close to reality in our perceptions as we are able.

## Thought

Thought occurs concurrently with the classification stage of perception, but can also occur independently of it. Thought occurs because of some felt irritant or disturbance, something that doesn't fit into a normal pattern. When this disturbance occurs, we call up old information (stored from perceptions of past experience) and associate it with the new information. The combination of the old with the new changes to some degree the relevant mental construct which existed previously. The mental construct tends to change only in ways that will allow us to maintain consistence.[8]

To explain this process, consider an example. Bill looks out the window and notices a bright yellow Corvette parked in front of his apartment. This is the *disturbance*. He recalls that the woman in the next apartment has chattered nonstop about her new sports car. This is *old* information called up. He decides that this sports car must belong to her. This is *association* of old information with new. He decides that she was exaggerating as usual; the way she talked he

---

7. Gail Myers and Michele Myers, *The Dynamics of Human Communication: A Laboratory Approach* (New York: McGraw-Hill, 1973), pp. 25–26.
8. Borden, Gregg, Grove, *Speech Behavior,* pp. 42–43.

thought she had bought an XKE. This is *reinforcement* of the mental construct Bill holds about his neighbor and the *maintenance* of a consistent evaluation of her.

In the above example, Bill *thought* while he was *perceiving.* He had to in order to organize the *percept* (yellow Corvette) into a *concept* (a possession of his neighbor's). It is also possible to think independently of any immediate external stimulus. For example, Bill might be having difficulty deciding how to write the person he has been seeing exclusively a "Dear Joan" letter. He recalls that she has always desired honesty. So, Bill decides that he will tell her straight out that he wants to be free. He feels okay about the method he has chosen to communicate his decision.

When we think, we deal with beliefs. *A belief is a statement about reality that a person considers true* whether it actually is or not. A stated belief can be labelled true or false. For example, "That yellow Corvette belongs to my neighbor" is either true or false. "My friends want me to be honest with them" is either true or false. "Students will enjoy this book" is either true or false. The issue here is not the truth or falsity of the beliefs, but the fact that we act on them as if they *were* true or false.

We think with thoughts. We manipulate our beliefs in arriving at decisions.

## Emotion

An emotion is a psychological and physical response within a person to his environment. "Every emotion reflects the judgment 'for me' or 'against me' and . . . to what extent."[9] *An emotion, or feeling, therefore, is a response which stimulates us to approach or avoid a person, object, or event.* Let us say that one dark evening while you are walking from the library to your car, someone jumps from behind a building with a gun in his hand. Your heart begins to race, your hands turn cold, your knees tremble in physical reaction. You remember stories of rapists or perhaps a friend's graphic description of being attacked, and you now begin to visualize what could happen to you. Intrapersonally, a variety of appropriate images are activated, and you experience the emotion of fear.

Our beliefs and emotions cluster together to form attitudes. *An attitude is an inclination to respond in a certain way to a given person, object, or event* because of the beliefs/emotions (sometimes called cognitions and affects) we have about them. The more negative be-

---

9. Branden, *Psychology of Self-Esteem,* p. 71.

liefs/emotions we have about anything, the greater the predisposition to respond negatively. Conversely, the more positive the beliefs/emotions we have about anything, the greater the predisposition to respond positively. A person develops certain beliefs and emotions about a college education. He believes that a college education will enable him to get a better job and feels that a better job is something "*for* him." He believes that a college education will enable him to achieve more status among his peers and chalks that up as something "*for* him." Likewise, he considers that a college education will help him achieve independence and aid him in developing a more coherent philosophy of life. All of these beliefs/emotions together compose a favorable attitude toward a college education. He is predisposed to go to college.

### Values

*Values are deep-seated clusters of beliefs and attitudes which direct choices, decisions, and actions.* They command a person to take certain actions and not others. They determine "what we are and where we are going and what we do with our energy, time, and assets and how and with what and with whom we get involved."[10]

From the previous example, the person had a favorable attitude toward a college education. Let us also assume that because of beliefs/emotions that he holds he also has favorable attitudes toward the teaching profession, scholarly people, and libraries. These factors together interact to form a high valuation of the educational profession. Therefore, he might be motivated to continue to graduate school so that he can teach in college.

So, we can see that beliefs/emotions influence attitudes which in turn influence values. Once values begin forming, the process is circular, that is, values already established will influence attitudes and beliefs/emotions about new persons, objects, or events. If a person values the educational profession he will respond positively to someone introduced as a Ph.D. He will believe that this person is intelligent and that it would be beneficial for him to talk with him or her.

This circular process by which values affect incoming information might well be termed "imaging." Images constitute a person's total frame of reference at any given point in time for any given situation. The images we hold—the complex interacting set of beliefs/emotions,

10. Theodore I. Rubin, *The Winners Notebook* (New York: Collier Books, 1967), p. 161. See also John J. Makay and Thomas C. Sawyer, *Speech Communication Now!* (Columbus, Ohio: Charles E. Merrill, 1973), Chapter 3, and Makay and Brown, *Rhetorical Dialogue,* pp. 275–79 for how values affect communication specifically.

attitudes, and values—influence our "view and impression of life with each human encounter and experience."[11] Our images compose the framework for our intrapersonal and interpersonal communication. Charles T. Brown and Paul Keller sum up these ideas: "Our beliefs, values, and attitudes are formed out of our experience and they, in turn, determine how we shall listen, how we shall be formed."[12]

# Self-Acceptance

*Self-acceptance is awareness plus satisfaction with the self.* Whenever there is discussion about acceptance of self, we hear the terms self-concept and self-esteem mentioned. Again, since our purpose is not, at this point, to suggest what could or should be, let us merely explore these notions and see how they are related to self-acceptance.

For example, an instructor had a student who was tremendously talented. This young woman excelled in sports, wrote music and poetry, sang professionally, and accomplished a great deal of art and craft work. She earned her own money, maintained a B average in school, and was highly admired by her peers and those faculty who knew her. In spite of all this, she was terribly unhappy with herself. In attempting to help her determine the cause of this dissatisfaction, her instructor asked her what she thought she should be. She rapidly ticked off a list of "the best" in every activity in which she was presently engaged. When pressed further, she explained that this type of excellence was the only way that she would ever be able to gain her parents' approval and love, on which her self-concept was, at present, dependent.

What seems wrong here? What was preventing this young woman from satisfaction and happiness with herself when many others given her talents and successes would feel very much fulfilled? The answer is that she had low self-esteem, which led to a negative self-concept which prevented her from accepting herself.

## Self-Esteem

*Self-esteem is the evaluative component of the self-concept.* The young woman in the example above had low self-esteem which led to a negative self-concept. Had she had high self-esteem, she would have

---

11. Makay and Brown, *Rhetorical Dialogue,* p. 17.

12. Charles T. Brown and Paul W. Keller, *Monologue to Dialogue: An Exploration of Interpersonal Communication* (Englewood Cliffs: Prentice-Hall, 1973), p. 99.

possessed a positive self-concept and would have been generally happy and satisfied with herself.

Self-esteem itself is composed of two factors, the second being directly dependent on the first.[13] The first is *self-confidence,* which is the general impression that we are capable of thinking, judging, and knowing. It involves evaluation, not of specific skills and accomplishments, but rather evaluation of our unique way of facing and coping within the environment. The person in our example felt unsure about her general ability because she had difficulty in dealing with her thoughts and feelings about her parents.

The second factor is *self-respect,* which is a feeling of worthiness derived from self-confidence; that is, we know and feel that we are capable and therefore we feel that our existence is worthwhile. Since this person did not have self-confidence; it follows that she would not have self-respect. Missing a positive evaluation of these two important factors, it also follows that she would not have self-esteem.

It is important to note that self-respect does not follow naturally from self-confidence. Unless this general impression of our capability is exercised *in practice,* self-respect will not follow from self-confidence. For example, one can believe that he is capable of earning a 4.0 throughout a college career. However, if one does not strive to and actually achieve this in reality one's self-respect and, therefore, self-esteem may suffer.

Self-esteem can be viewed more clearly in another way. It can be considered the discrepancy between the "real self" (what we think we really are) and the "ideal self" (what we would like to be or think we should be). Theory has it that the greater the discrepancy, the lower the self-esteem; the smaller the discrepancy, the higher the self-esteem. (See figure 3.)

As you can see in the figure, the young woman was dissatisfied and unhappy because of a great gap between how she saw herself and what she thought she *should* be. In this case, no matter how numerous her accomplishments, she could make very little progress toward closing the gap between her real and ideal self, because the ideal self was so unrealistic.

The importance of self-esteem cannot be underestimated as Branden points out:

> The nature of his self-evaluation has profound effects on a man's thinking processes, emotions, desires, values and goals. It is the

---

13. Branden, *Psychology of Self-Esteem,* pp. 106–7.

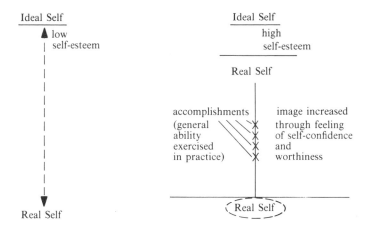

**FIGURE 3**

single most significant key to his behavior. To understand a man psychologically, one must understand the nature and degree of his self-esteem, and the standards by which he judges himself.[14]

## Self-Concept

Self-concept is composed of the beliefs we have about our characteristics, the way we feel about those characteristics, and our consequent predispositions to respond to any stimuli relevant to self. *Self-concept is, simply, an attitude toward self,* composed of beliefs about the self, emotions about those beliefs (self-esteem), and the resultant tendency to respond, positively or negatively.

Beliefs about the self generally fall into well-defined categories. At the beginning of a course in interpersonal communication we characteristically ask students to answer the question, "Who am I?" in ten words, phrases, or statements. Before reading further, try to answer this question yourself.

Here is a sample list:

1. I am   (name)      .
2. I am a black female, 24 years old.
3. I am a sophomore at Wright State University.
4. I am a single woman.
5. I am an intelligent member of the human race.
6. I am a fine arts major.

14. Ibid., p. 103.

7. I am a very inhibited person.
8. I am a person unaccessible to other human beings.
9. I am a professional artist.
10. I really don't know who I am.

These beliefs can be categorized as follows:

1. Physical attributes—what bodily characteristics the person possesses (#2).
2. Emotional attributes—what characteristic feelings the person possesses (#7).
3. Mental attributes—what intellectual characteristics the person possesses (#5).
4. Role—what function or functions the individual fulfills in relation to others (#3, #4, #6, #9).
5. Relationship with others—what characteristic stance, exclusive of role, one takes toward others (#8).

All of these beliefs are probably evaluated either positively or negatively, that is the person feels either good or bad about possessing these characteristics. So, if the list is weighted to the negative side (low self-esteem) the attitude toward self (self-concept) will be negative.

The beliefs about self exist not only along a continuum of positive to negative but also along a continuum of accurate to inaccurate. For example, a man may believe that at five feet eight inches, 175 pounds, he is obese and feel negative about it. The point is that his belief might be inaccurate by a doctor's weight chart, when his sex and frame is considered. The accuracy-inaccuracy continuum is extremely important, both in viewing the real self and the ideal self. Inaccurate beliefs and feelings can result in an inaccurate self-concept, be it negative or positive.

So how does all this occur? How does the self-concept develop? Probably the single most important causal factor in the development of the self-concept is one's relationship with *significant others.* Charles H. Cooley, Harry Stack Sullivan, and George Herbert Mead have contributed greatly to our understanding of this phenomenon.[15] Basically, this theory postulates that we become what others tell us we are. We look to others to tell us who we are, especially in early childhood. Obviously, the most significant "significant others" are our parents.

15. See Charles H. Cooley, *Human Nature and the Social Order* (New York: Scribner's, 1922); Harry Stack Sullivan, *The Interpersonal Theory of Psychiatry* (New York: W. W. Norton, 1953); George H. Mead, *Mind, Self, and Society* (Chicago: University of Chicago Press, 1934).

It is clear that self-concept is affected by such statements as "You're lazy," "You're a naughty child," "You're stupid," *or* "You're a good child," "You do such good work," especially if these statements are intensely, consistently, and frequently offered.

Recalling example at the beginning of this section, we can see that Sarah probably heard a number of statements from her parents which led her to believe that she was not achieving properly, that she was not a good daughter, that she did not produce as expected. Significant others had a tremendous impact on Sarah's self-concept.

Reinforcement from significant others, who later may be our teachers, ministers, and friends, tends to become "self-fulfilling" prophecies. In experiments where the teachers were falsely led to believe that students had high intellectual capability, they treated them as such, with the result that the students achieved beyond the established norm. They lived up to the teachers' expectations; they fulfilled the prophecy.[16]

Another factor in the development of self-concept is *social comparison.* Simply, this means that we compare ourselves to others. We develop a positive self-concept if we consistently come out favorably, a negative self-concept if the opposite is true. If we get better grades than three-fourths of the students in the class, we feel smart. If we get asked to join activities more than any other person, we feel popular. If we win at every sport we play, we feel physically competent.

A third factor in the development of self-concept is *role taking.* As you remember, much self-description involves the roles that we perform. Role taking affects self-concept according to the success or failure we experience in performing the role. If one performs the necessary functions of "student" by going to classes, taking notes, studying and getting good grades, his or her self-concept is strengthened. On the other hand, if one takes on the role of "husband" and cannot seem to perform the functions of provider, strength-giver, decision maker, and competitor, his self-concept suffers. You may have perceived that the role must be considered a *desirable* one for the self-concept to be affected. If we don't want to be a "student" or a "husband," then chances are that the self-concept will not be influenced. Also, the accuracy of the role description has little to do with the strengthening or weakening of the self-concept. The individual's definition and conception of the role is his reality.

---

16. See Robert Rosenthal, "Self-Fulfilling Prophecy," *Readings in Psychology Today* (Del Mar, California: CRM Books, 1967), pp. 466–71.

A fourth factor in the development of self-concept is *personal evaluation*. Unfortunately, this factor must be considered negligible, for by the time we evaluate ourselves "objectively," we have already been influenced by others. Others have helped to form our beliefs/emotions, attitudes, and values which we used as a *standard* of evaluation. For example, an athlete may look at five medals won in state track competition and feel very proud of that accomplishment, exclusive of praise from coaches, parents, and friends. But how did he or she arrive at that standard? What if the athlete's parents had always insisted that national championship was where the glory is? How would he or she feel then? It is very difficult to eliminate completely others' influence on the development of one's self-concept.

The self-concept is probably the single most important factor in intrapersonal communication. It is developed through our perceptions, beliefs/emotions, attitudes and values, and in turn affects how we see, think and feel about, and value ourselves or any person, object, or event. For these reasons the self-concept is extremely important in interpersonal communication. The better we feel about ourselves, the more we accept ourselves, and, as we shall see in later chapters, the more accepting we tend to be of others.

## Self-Assertion

*Self-assertion is the process of individual choice, decision, action, and accomplishment which has been motivated by values and/or needs.*

Tom was an intelligent young man who valued the control he exercised over his life. Over a period of time, however, he began to feel he was missing something by not allowing himself to feel deeply and express emotion openly. After a great deal of introspection, he made a *choice:* he would forego some control for more expression. Then, he made the *decision* to open up to his friends. He put this decision into *action* by consciously expressing his beliefs and emotions to those close to him. His goal became *accomplishment* when he began to enjoy his interpersonal relationships more. He became more intensely involved with others than he had ever thought possible.

### Choice

*Choice is simply a preference for one alternative over another or others in a given situation.* You might prefer a VW to either a Honda or a Toyota. You might prefer tennis to baseball or football. You might prefer double-fudge ice cream over cherry vanilla or mint chocolate chip.

The situation is, of course, important because it dictates what alternatives are available. A person may prefer double-fudge but if the ice cream parlor is out of that flavor then his preferences will be limited to the flavors on hand. Choice is limited as the number of alternatives are expanded.

Two interrelated questions arise at this point. What determines our choices? Do we, in fact, have the ability to choose?

Essentially, our preferences are dictated by our values and needs, as we discovered earlier. If through the processes of sensation, perception, and development of beliefs/emotions, and attitudes, we have come to *value* education, then it follows that we will prefer college to working in a factory. If we have lost a loved one, we will *need* consolation and understanding and will prefer being with family and close friends rather than going to a movie.

Psychologist Abraham Maslow's hierarchy of needs[17] provides further understanding of our preferences in any given situation. In simple terms, the theory states that there are five levels of needs. The lower level needs must be largely satisfied before we can progress to the higher level needs. Following are the five levels.

1. *Physiological*—these are the needs of human survival: food, water, shelter, sensory stimuli, and so on.
2. *Safety*—these are the needs of protection from external threat: a safe place to live, job security, etc.
3. *Love and belongingness*—these are the needs of inclusion and affection: parental love, romantic love, companionship, and dedication of friends, etc.
4. *Esteem*—these are the needs of self-respect and respect from others: liking yourself, being admired, having prestige, etc.
5. *Self-actualization*—these are the needs of personal growth: fulfilling capabilities, expanding one's interests, etc.

According to the theory, we wouldn't be concerned with external threat (2) if we were starving (1); we wouldn't be concerned with love (3) if our lives were in danger (2); we wouldn't be concerned with others' respect (4), if we didn't feel a part of a close and loving unit (3), and so on. The hierarchy of needs operates *specifically* in day-to-day situations. For example, we might drop from the level of self-

17. Abraham H. Maslow, *Motivation and Personality,* 2d ed. (New York: Harper and Row, 1970), Chapter 4.

actualization where we are motivated to absorb knowledge in class to the physiological level because we didn't have any breakfast and are starving. The hierarchy of needs also operates *generally,* that is, there is a characteristic level we have reached at this point in time. For example, we generally have enough to eat, a safe place to live, and some sort of loving relationship, so we may now be motivated to spend most of our time developing self-respect.

We won't spend much time on the question of the ability to choose. We happen to believe that man does possess free will.[18] The determinist, biological or environmental, would counter that we've been *programmed* to believe as we do. We really wish that we could prove that man is capable of making a truly free choice, but satisfactory proof is impossible. Suffice it to say that even the most dedicated determinist *acts* as if he has choice, that is, he weighs alternatives and gives reasons for preferring one alternative over another. An illusion it may be, but man treats it as a reality. So do we.

## Decision

*A decision is the exercise of choice.* While we may prefer rare steak over that which is well done, we must take some measure to exercise that choice. This is a fine line along the progression from choosing to acting, but it is nevertheless an important distinction. A person may prefer being president of a company to being a sales representative, but is he or she going to exercise that choice? Probably not. Why? Because deciding is generally a commitment to action, and when we decide we must look not only at the different alternatives available in relation to our values and needs, but also at the *possibility* of achieving each of them. That is, we must at this point face reality and determine which of the present alternatives are realistically viable and desirable. We may choose a Cadillac over a Chevy, VW or Ford, but we probably would not *decide* on a Cadillac unless we had the necessary money. We may *choose* champagne over scotch and water, but we would be better off to *decide* on the scotch and water if avoiding a hangover is desirable.

## Action

*An action is the realization of a decision.* (We are speaking here of truly human action, not conditioned-reflex responses.) It is the order-

18. Branden, *Psychology of Self-Esteem,* p. 49.

ing of the double-fudge cone or rare steak, the signing of a contract for a VW. What has heretofore been mental and emotional maneuvering becomes behavioral. Preferences are translated into talk and movement.

### Accomplishment

*Accomplishment is the result of action.* Perhaps a better word here would be feedback or effect. Accomplishment implies achievement of a goal or satisfaction of a need, and we all know it doesn't always work out that way. Expressing feelings openly may bring rejection, the chef may overcook the steak, the Cadillac may use too much gas. Regardless of whether the outcome is positive or negative, there is always some effect that can be evaluated in light of your values and needs. Evaluation of effect might be used to determine future choices, decisions, and actions, making them more realistic and more congruent with your unique values and needs.

## Self-Actualization

Self-actualization now needs definition. The concept includes choice, decision, action, and accomplishment, but differs qualitatively from self-assertion (and the first four steps of Maslow's hierarchy) in that it is never based on

> something *extrinsic* that the organism needs. . . . [Rather] self-actualization is *intrinsic* growth of what is already in the organism . . . development proceeds from within rather than without . . . self-actualization is growth motivated rather than deficiency-motivated. It is a "second naivete," a wise innocence, an "Easy State."[19] (italics mine)

We believe with Maslow that "human life will never be understood unless its highest aspirations are taken into account."[20] The study of the self-actualizing tendency in the human being focuses on understanding the heights man can achieve rather than the depths to which he sometimes falls. In a later chapter we will discuss self-actualization in detail, and we will explore in depth what we can "be" through improved intrapersonal communication. Let us close this chapter by

19. Maslow, *Motivation and Personality,* p. 134.
20. Ibid., p. xii.

describing briefly the directions that the choices, decisions, and actions of a self-actualized person take.[21]

Consider the case of Tom again, in this instance as a self-actualizing person. He avoids facades and masks; he attempts to be himself rather than to hide behind a role or play games. "Oughts" and "shoulds" are minimized in the self-actualizing person's life; he acts because the action feels right for him, not because it is something society dictates he should do. Along this same line he moves away from pleasing others and meeting others' expectations; he is self-directing, content with setting and maintaining his own personal standards rather than looking to social norms for guidance. Because he is open to all types of new experience, he constantly grows and changes, moving toward greater personal complexity; he continually adds new dimensions to his being. Finally, he tends toward total acceptance and trust of self; he feels secure, comfortable, and happy within.

To be more specific, picture the self-actualizing student. She doesn't "play the role" of student for either her professors or peers. She participates in those classes she enjoys regardless of whether her fellow students frown or her professor smiles. She joins a social group because she likes the people involved, not because it is "right" to "belong." She organizes her day so that she has sufficient time to maintain a satisfactory average, not because her parents expect it, but because she wants it. She seeks out new and different people on the campus; she tries new political, social, and sports activities; she searches for new and in-depth information on a variety of subjects. The self-actualizing student finds that the more she knows and feels, the more she desires to broaden and extend herself. Throughout this growing, she likes herself and trusts herself to take the best course for her and her future.

Self-actualization is often the result of effective intrapersonal communication. By focusing on the talk within that determines our ultimate development, we end at the same place we began—by *turning to our selves.*

With the concept of intrapersonal communication as our base, we now turn to others.

## Summary

In this chapter, we defined intrapersonal communication as talking within oneself, and discussed the intrapersonal process of initiating

21. Carl R. Rogers, *On Becoming a Person* (Boston: Houghton Mifflin, 1961), pp. 167–84.

and monitoring messages within. We noted that intrapersonal communication is important because it affects our personal decisions and behavior and our communication and actions toward others.

We focused on four processes involved in intrapersonal communication. In looking at *self-awareness,* we pointed out that sensation, perception, thought, emotion, and value are subprocesses that are essential to understanding of self. We analyzed *self-acceptance* by exploring the notions of self-esteem and self-concept, noting particularly the factors influencing their development. We traced the accomplishment of *self-assertion* through the steps of choosing, deciding, acting, and accomplishing. We briefly highlighted the essential characteristics of *self-actualization,* man's tendency to aspire, grow, and develop.

# 3

# Turning to Others — Interpersonal Communication

Extending the network of beliefs/emotions, attitudes, and values to others involves human transactions which we know as interpersonal communication. Our days and nights are filled with situations in which we turn to others for a variety of reasons. Generally, the reasons are familiar. Each of us daily speaks and listens in face-to-face situations to facilitate work with competence and creative tension. And we often turn to others for lubricating or cementing friendly relations, so that in many instances we engage in verbal play—communication simply for the fun of it.

Although many feel this sort of communication is natural enough in life not to warrant study, we hope to bring about new realizations about interpersonal communication. Indeed, interpersonal communication is our primary vehicle for creating meaning in human activity. Humans, in spite of all of their technological successes and scientific advances, still create, contribute to, or solve problems in ways which greatly depend upon interpersonal communication. Now, before we proceed, let's examine the definition of interpersonal communication by Robert Kibler and Larry Barker: "The exchange of messages between two or more persons. . . . Interpersonal communication involves all forms of two-person and small group interaction in social, business, and conversational settings. It includes dialog," which, according to experts, is a new revolution in terms of research, study, and implementation in the fields which deal significantly with communication.[1]

The major thrust of our treatment of intrapersonal communication came from information about self-awareness, experience, self-acceptance, self-asssertion, and self-actualization. The treatment of these concepts in exploring human communication does not cease with a discussion of intrapersonal communication. Instead, they must blend as we move into a study of interpersonal communication. After all, the humanistic view of interpersonal communication invites us to develop within ourselves full awareness, acceptance, assertion, and actualization and to share our growth with others as we continue the process of living.

We know that interpersonal communication is important. For example, we have been involved in interpersonal communication all our lives and we often seem saturated at day's end with ideas resulting from that communication. Yet, saturated or not, we must confess we often do not give a great deal of thought to the process and transaction descriptively, theoretically, and analytically. We can ask ourselves: "To what extent is interpersonal communication really important in my life?" "What seems to help or inhibit my capacity and ability to deal with others in an open, encouraging, and gratifying way?"

To declare that interpersonal communication involves one's life line in a society and the particular environments one operates in is a statement worth serious consideration. A core concern for this consideration is the relationship between perception and reality, for through perception, communicators structure reality.

## Perception and Reality

When we think about interpersonal transaction we ought to remember the nature of perception and the way in which it limits, modifies, and structures, reality as we speak and listen. A person does not respond to the real world but to his or her perception of it. Moreover, a thorough understanding of perception can give fresh and meaningful awareness to interpersonal communication by significantly increasing communicative skills.

---

1. Larry L. Barker and Robert J. Kibler, "A Conceptual Overview of Communication Dimensions," in Larry L. Barker and Robert J. Kibler, eds., *Speech Communication Behavior: Perspectives and Principles* (Englewood Cliffs, New Jersey: Prentice-Hall, 1971), p. 4.

An individual structuring reality through sensory perception looks, as philosopher Alan Watts has written, "at life bit by bit, using memory to string the bits together—as when examining a dark room with a flashlight having a very narrow beam. Perception thus narrowed has the advantage of being sharp and bright, but it has to focus on one area of the world after another, and one feature after another."[2] Remember: objects, individuals, things, and events of the world exist in reality, but what we know and understand of reality is *perceived* and *conceptualized* reality. We can only approximate this reality through perception. Because people seek to establish and maintain consistency within themselves and with others who are important to them, they perceive selectively at both conscious and unconscious levels.

When a communicator processes inwardly what he or she receives in perceiving outwardly, the information is processed through a sensory threshold and is filtered in the processing. Filtering occurs because the perceiver is limited as an individual in his or her capacity as an information channel. The peripheral nervous system in the human comprises a number of input channels each of which has many parallel input lines. At some point in the nervous system there is a bottleneck in the flow of information because a central channel in the nervous system has a lower capacity than the combined capacities of the peripheral receptors and neural input lines. Thus, through filtering, there is a loss of information. Figure 4 shows what happens when information is taken in and responded to by an individual. He filters information through his senses and interprets it according to what he knows and values. His response, of course, is feedback to perceived information.

A speech communication instructor brought into class a commercially produced advertisement which pictured a nude man and woman in a gentle embrace with their faces looking out at the viewer of the ad. They were pictured from the waist up. The ad indicated they were readers of a popular magazine and they invited others to read the magazine too. The instructor held up the ad so the students could see it and then asked for gut level immediate responses. The interpersonal communication in the class was affected greatly by the ways in which people in the class perceived the picture. Some, with an academic background in advertising and marketing, quickly tagged the

---

2. Alan Watts, *The Book: The Taboo Against Knowing Who You Are* (New York: Vintage, 1972), p. 28.

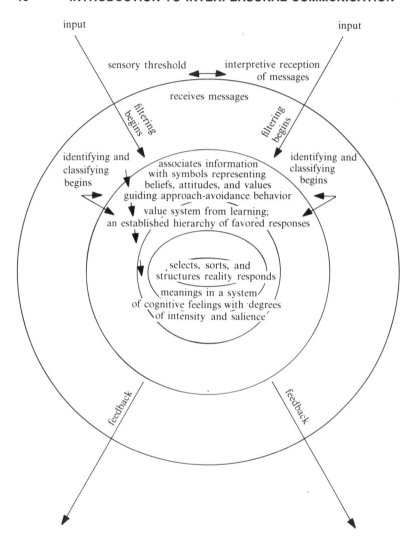

**FIGURE 4. A Basic Perception Model**

entire page as "slick" and well-produced. One man with a strong conservative religious background indicted the ad as "selling sex" rather than magazines, and he offered the class a mini-sermon about an "American preoccupation with sex and a loss of traditional moral values." One carefree soul in the room shouted out, "How sweet it is!" One woman indicated when she came to college from her small hometown she was not used to either the magazine or the sort of photograph in the ad; she indicated further that she now subscribed to the magazine and she thought the photograph, though certainly appealing to liberal sexual attitudes, was "ok." Several people paid little attention to the discussion at all because their attention was focused on the day's edition of the campus newspaper. What people saw (how they constructed and conceptualized) was a result of their ability and willingness to perceive and engage in interpersonal communication.

A second example can further illustrate the point. In a small graduate seminar dealing with the rhetoric of social protest a particularly interesting event took place. The class was made up of ten persons, six men and four women. One of the students, a black woman who was familiar with ghetto life and participation in the struggles of the Black Movement, became bored and angry with what she perceived to be "graduate student over-intellectualizing" with sole reliance of the professor and the other students (all white) on professional journal articles for source material. Her perception of the reality of social protest in the efforts of the Black Movement was considerably different from that of the others. Finally, one afternoon she stood up suddenly, walked to the board and wrote "fuck." Facing the class she stated loudly, "Now that's the rhetoric of social protest, sit around and analyze that for a while!" She then left the room.

What we have been examining about perception and reality can help to explain the angry graduate student's behavior, as well as the interpersonal communication behavior of everyone in the class. Her experience in the rhetoric of social protest was much different from the experience of the others. Because she filtered information from the seminar meetings and structured reality from her own experiences she was provoked to act the way she did. After she left the class the professor and students changed their direction and focus in their interpersonal communication to explore both the word, their reactions to her behavior, and how what they thought she meant related to their seminar.

Watts contributes to our thinking about perception with an example describing the behavior of a cat, and the perception of someone who has never seen a cat before.[3] He describes this "someone" looking through a narrow slit in a fence, while on the other side a cat walks by. In the words of Watts, "He sees the head, then the less distinctly shaped funny trunk, and then the tail. Extraordinary! The cat turns around and walks back, and again he sees the head, and a little later the tail. This sequence begins to look like something regular and

3. Ibid., p. 28.

reliable. Yet again the cat turns around, and he witnesses the same sequence. . . ." According to Watts the viewer reasons, by perception: the head is the invariable and necessary cause of the event, the tail. We know the parts all go together and make one cat![4] Often, in structuring perceived reality, we focus our attention, subsequent thoughts, and eventually interpersonal communication not unlike the individual who reasoned about the cat.

Remember *attention* is a process beginning with *noticing*, which involves the selection of bits of information or features of the world we view as being more noteworthy and significant than others. So we attend to some things while ignoring others. Perhaps physically we view, hear, taste, touch and smell more features than we actually choose to notice. *Our perception is indeed selective.* It's as if we have a scanning process in our psycho-physical make-up which observes the world, bit by bit. Watts raises an important question which demands our attention: "What governs what we choose to notice?" His initial response to this question is: "The first is whatever seems advantageous or disadvantageous for our survival, our social status, and the security of our egos. The second . . . working simultaneously with the first is the pattern of logic of all the notation symbols we have learned from others from our society, and our culture. . . ."[5] In a sense we structure reality through sensory perception. With our thoughts, feelings, and symbols we distinguish or make things. Without thoughts there are no things; there is, in the words of Watts, "just undefined reality."[6]

We need to understand that what a communicator perceives another person means depends upon what signals and symbols get through the filter and how they become symbolic interpretations, evaluations, and thus, personal constructions of reality.

When we speak and listen to another interpersonally, we do so through the perceptions we possess according to physical and psychological capacities, knowledge, experiences, interests, and values. Remember, however, that individual selectivity in perception serves to further filter the received information through the psychological processes of each perceiver. Modification operates in the filtering process because varieties of meanings and their associated emotions enter into a person's conscious awareness, the person interprets the symbols and messages and then measures these stimuli against his or her knowl-

---

4. Ibid., p. 28.
5. Ibid., p. 29.
6. Alan Watts, *The Wisdom of Insecurity: A Message for an Age of Anxiety* (New York: Vintage, 1951), p. 141.

edge, attitudes and values to experience comprehension and some sort of acceptability or rejection.

## One to Another Pattern:
## Image Maps

One way in which to focus the information which comprises our universe of experience and involves everything we have previously learned is to symbolize it as an image map[7] within ourselves. This map is continually being altered. It includes our emotions/ beliefs, values and attitudes, plus myriad mental pictures and recorded sensations. We structure this map and function in communication on the basis of the image map's changing in daily experience.

Behavior which is generated from this map is directed by following plans to create meaning with another, through the incorporation of feedback—perceived meaning from interpreting the cues of responsive behavior. Keep in mind that when a plan is viewed at a broad level of abstraction and perception it can be labeled communication design; this design is generated by the dynamic map within us. When this plan is viewed as *specific behaviors* stemming from the broad image map, we can label this specificity as design. Thus, each individual in the process of interpersonal communication possesses an inner world or universe which operates in terms of plans and design.

Communicator design operates from value-anchored positions which provide personal motives for behavior. When we find pleasure in communicating with another we may be satisfied with the process of communication. However, should problems or conflicts arise in interpersonal communications, plans for problem solving go into action and perhaps anxiety or its antithesis ultimately result. In any case, we then alter our plans (and subsequently the map) to reach a state of satisfaction with contained conflicts.

Consider yourself about to face an initial encounter with a roommate. What you bring to the communication setting is your personal and complex map with the means for expressing and processing ideas and feelings. Your views can be cued by the views which stem from the inner map of your roommate. Both of you possess a rich store of plans for maximizing pleasurable and/or satisfying outcomes and, hence, avoiding or minimizing the opposite.

7. Robert C. Carson, *Interaction Concepts of Personality* (Chicago: Aldine, 1969), pp. 82–83.

As interpersonal communication gets under way, you perceptually monitor yourself and the other and respond to the other's signals and symbols. Designs emerge according to dynamic mental and emotional outlooks in accord with points on your map, immediate motivation, and perhaps even long-range goals. As Carson suggests, each communicator may prompt behaviors for which no ready-made plan exists.[8] Each may engage in behavior which could involve withholding expectations of the other, or desired reciprocal responses. Each may communicate in such a way that emotionally loaded statements are generated and thus disruptive alterations in your images may result. Perhaps anxiety will permeate the atmosphere. But, in any event, each person can accrue information about himself or herself and the other which is inwardly processed and stored for future reference in the map.

If you and your roommate intend to agree upon a way of keeping the place clean and a place where you each can study, your communication will relate to *goals,* directly or indirectly. Interpersonal communication is usually goal-oriented, whether for immediate or long-range purpose. An immediate goal of yours may be to maintain a pleasurable relationship with your roommate. A long-range goal of yours may be to qualify for a place in a graduate or professional school. The success or failure of your interpersonal communication with each other can affect both goals.

## The Goals in Communication: Inevitable Aims

When we engage in interpersonal communication, our goals are implicit and/or explicit in the communicative situation. Therefore, we must give some basic consideration to communication goals. We know that the process of human communication involves both verbal and nonverbal behaviors. (Such behavior is examined in detail and depth in the next three chapters.) Communicators create within themselves some meaning for the behavior they are aware of in their perception. We can agree with communication specialists Paul Watzlawick, Janet Beavin, and Don Jackson, that inevitably in communication between individuals there are two levels of behavior: the

---

8. Ibid., pp. 85–87.

relationship level and the content level.[9] They suggest that the relationship level is expressed largely by our nonverbal behavior, while the content level is expressed by our verbal behavior. James Wilcox explains these levels with this illustration: "The phrase, 'Good to see you,' expresses both a content meaning (as expressed by the choice of words), and a relationship meaning (as expressed by the way in which the words are uttered)."[10]

In their work on rhetorical dialogue, John Makay and William Brown discuss rhetorical goals in terms of solving problems and achieving persuasive purposes through communication. They indicate that in general there are two sorts of goals for communicators: "the adjusting of human relations (the relationship side of any message) and the accomplishment of tasks (the 'content' side of any message)." Moreover, they state that in the relationship goals we can find two specific subtypes, "the intrapersonal and interpersonal."[11]

We have an intrapersonal goal in communicating with another when we seek to adjust ourselves to ourselves by using the other as a sort of mirror. In a sense, we can create messages to invite response from another which will tend to confirm or negate what we want to see and believe in our self-appraisals. A political leader may communicate messages that reveal him to be physically attractive and desirable, as well as intellectually appealing. He appears on radio and television programs, at forums and in the press. He seeks to have his message reflecting response in the perceptions of people which help him to adjust himself to himself; he may be working toward intrapersonal relationship goals through interpersonal communication. The words of psychiatrist R. D. Laing are appropriate to think about: "Other people become sort of an identity kit, whereby one can piece together a picture of oneself. One recognizes oneself in that old smile from that old friend."[12] Laing maintains personal identity is understood by individuals in part through interpersonal relations with others in terms of responses, perceived responses, and this, of course, is consistent with our recognition of intrapersonal relationship goals. Let's

9. Paul Watzlowick, Janet Beavin, and Donald D. Jackson, *The Pragmatics of Human Communication* (New York: W. W. Norton, 1967), p. 54.

10. James R. Wilcox, "The Assessment of Meaning: A Communication Perspective," in John J. Makay, ed., *Exploration in Speech Communication* (Columbus, Ohio: Charles E. Merrill, 1973), p. 48.

11. John J. Makay and William Brown, *The Rhetorical Dialogue* (Dubuque: Wm. C. Brown, 1972), p. 76.

12. R. D. Laing, *The Self and Others* (New York: Pantheon, 1969), p. 70.

consider now a second subset of relationship goals: interpersonal goals.

More dominant than intrapersonal are interpersonal relationship goals. As Makay and Brown cite: "When you want your honesty, intelligence, good will, or other traits not so much to be reflected *upon* you as to win *acceptance* for you, then your aim becomes an interpersonal one." They distinguish between these two related kinds of personal goals by talking less about the qualities of self that may be transmitted than about the responses from others that may be sought. Furthermore, they declare that a way to separate the goal emphases in these relationship goals is to realize: "in the intrapersonal emphasis, our aim is to be able to accept ourselves; in the interpersonal emphasis, our aim is to have others accept us." In reality, of course, such a separation is not possible.[13]

Sue moved from her parents home shortly after finishing high school into an apartment complex for "singles" only. The complex, "The Single Place," included apartments, tennis courts, a pool, a health spa, and a cocktail lounge. This move was a big step for Sue because she chose not to go to college but to take a position as a legal secretary and originally planned to live at home with her parents. Home life proved to be too restrictive for her and she decided to take the risk of a new life style. Her main goals for life in "The Single Place" were interpersonal ones. Once home from work each day she felt a strong need for friendships and to fill this need she continually sought the acceptance of others through interpersonal communication.

A second sort of goal is the content goal in interpersonal communication. When we speak of content goals we mean that communicators focus primarily on influencing each other for purposes of overt action. When a communicator's purpose becomes "content" it is task-centered: "He aims at approach or withdrawal behavior from the listener not in relation to himself, primarily, but in relation to some proposal of his or of another."[14] Thus, a communicator may seek to effect acceptance or rejection of concepts, proposals, or policies based upon facts or values. Communicators interact to make choices which will bring about specific action. Relationship goals may be sought by communicators who have their sights aimed ultimately on achieving content goals.

A member of a fraternity or sorority can recall the visits of salesper-

---

13. Makay and Brown, *Rhetorical Dialogue,* pp. 77–78.
14. Ibid., p. 85.

sons from jewelry companies who specialize in pins, mugs, and the like. The sales representative will engage in interpersonal communication with students to develop good human relationships and gain some responses leading to purchases. The salesperson's task is to sell products but sales are often determined in part by warm and positive relationships between persons.

# Responsibility

In the realization of both immediate and long-range goals, whether relationship or content, the matter of responsibility can be important in terms of the level or degree of satisfaction a communicator may achieve. People communicate because they have needs which can be felt at both the conscious and unconscious levels. Responsibility can be a *major* factor in an interpersonal relationship. It is at the center of a major approach to therapy initiated and developed to a considerable extent by William D. Glasser, a humanistic psychiatrist.[15]

Glasser explains that people who seek help through interpersonal communication with a psychotherapist suffer from one basic inadequacy—an inability to fulfill essential needs. Moreover, in an unsuccessful effort to fulfill needs, clients share a common characteristic: "They deny the reality of the world around them. . . . Therapy will be successful when they are able to give up denying the world and recognize that reality not only exists but they must fulfill their needs within it."[16]

Our needs are both physiological and psychological. We may describe our needs differently, but we can agree that we have certain basic ones. We can now take a personal inventory of our needs and/or we can review the needs as described by Maslow and presented in chapter 2. The assumption is offered that Glasser is correct when he maintains that those in his profession ought to be concerned with two basic psychological needs: (1) the need to love and be loved, and (2) the need to feel worthwhile to ourselves and with others.[17] *Responsibility* is a key factor in one's ability to satisfy these two needs, and accepting this responsibility can be a result of interpersonal communication—a careful effort, ability, and willingness to make a personal attempt to communicate. In fact, responsibility can be defined essen-

---

15. William D. Glasser, *Reality Therapy: A New Approach to Psychiatry* (New York: Harper and Row, 1965), p. 5.

16. Ibid., p. 6.

17. Ibid., p. 20.

tially as the ability to fulfill one's needs. A responsible person can give of herself or himself and can receive from others information which creates in transaction a personal feeling of worthiness, satisfaction, and the realization of a goal.

Glasser is chiefly concerned with those who have not learned or who have lost the ability to lead responsible lives, and he describes such persons as "irresponsible." We can be concerned in our work and be challenged daily in our lives with the fulfillment of basic needs through interpersonal communication, and thus act in responsible ways which are of benefit to us and those with whom we transact. Our gain, in this communicative behavior, is to be measured in self-respect, close relationships with others, and at times reaching content goals. In contrast, the more irresponsible we are in our interpersonal relations the more unrealistic we will be and the greater our essential needs will be also. It is through our transactions with others that we realize we can care for others and be cared for by others so that needs are met, and goals are reached, in the world as it actually is and appears to be in a realistic sense of perception.[18]

Moreover, interpersonal communication will affect the moral behavior of the communicators in terms of the actions of a person in ways that encourage worthwhile relationships. For example, when Jim arrived on campus he possessed negative attitudes and information about social fraternities. He vowed he would not become a member of any fraternity. One of the primary reasons for this vow was his belief that the general moral character of members of fraternities was low, that "Greeks" were interested chiefly in playful pleasure and did not possess much social consciousness. Jim had trouble making friends during his first quarter on campus and, though surrounded by people in class, dining halls, and his residence complex, he felt lonely much of the time. When the second quarter began he went through "rush" on campus and became a pledge in a large fraternity. Much to his surprise he found that the men he worked and studied with in his house had needs similar to his own, and the organization provided a wide array of activities and programs which encouraged responsible human relationships. What he enjoyed most in these relationships was the interpersonal communication.

Perhaps we ought to see communication behavior in terms of responsible behavior and irresponsible behavior because this view can be essential to the fulfillment of our needs and realistic interpersonal relations with individuals and the world in general. Furthermore,

18. Makay and Brown, *Rhetorical Dialogue,* p. 265.

partners in communication can more easily assume this kind of real responsibility if they can understand and improve their system of structuring ideas within themselves to transmit in a logic for interpersonal communication. The "responsible communicator" is willing to provide *reasons* for what he feels and believes, and accepts the *consequences* of his communication.

## Interpersonal Reasoning

To many people familiar with the study of speech communication the term reasoning may bring to mind argumentation, systems of logic, and public debate. To a student of interpersonal communication, especially one taking a humanistic approach, reasoning can be quite important too. One who studies humanist literature will find that reasoned communication which allows and encourages people to sense how they feel in concert with what they really think, based upon the information they have, is prevalent. Humanistic philosophers and scientists seem to develop and communicate emotions/beliefs, attitudes, and values carefully according to systems of reasoning. Humanistic psychologists who practice therapy seek to help their counselees to explore and restructure their thinking in reasonable ways which bring feelings and ideas out into the open, allowing them to gain insight as well as sound ways to change their troubled lives. Reasoning is a way in which persons communicate interpersonally to arrive at some idea or notion, or claim which seems accurate, probable, and truthful to themselves and others in an interpersonal setting. We can say that reasoning is the process of using the known or believed information to explain or prove other statements less understood or accepted.

Consider the case of Bill, a young attorney, to illustrate the importance of reasoning in interpersonal communication. One afternoon, he suddenly felt his head swimming and his breath getting short as he was charging down the hallway of the court house on his way to a hearing. He stopped at a desk and asked a clerk to call a doctor. Then he sat down on the floor. An emergency squad appeared shortly and a team of paramedics took Bill to a hospital emergency room. A doctor's examination could not reveal a medical explanation, so Bill returned home to rest for a day until he could see his personal physician. His doctor could not find a reasonable explanation and so, mystified, he advised Bill to consult a psychiatrist. Reluctantly, Bill began counseling and together he and the psychiatrist *began reasoning* to discover and treat what Bill perceived to be unreasonable symptoms. They engaged in intimate interpersonal communication over a necessary period of time, for the psychiatrist wanted Bill to gain not just insight into his problem, but a knowledge of how to deal with tensions which caused him to become dizzy and to hyperventilate. Both therapist and client sought to help the client heal from what appeared to be nervous exhaustion and deep-seated frustration (they established content goals), and in this process they sought to build a warm and strong relationship (relationship goals) which would help facilitate the client's healthy growth through therapy. The meaning-centered communication between the two could not be built upon myths nor unfounded assertions, obviously, but upon a logic in concert with feelings, which both could claim was a responsible way to behave.

Reasonable expressions which follow some pattern in structuring meaning possess at least five major elements: (1) information possessed by a communicator, (2) a claim or conclusion to be drawn from the information, (3) a premise which allows movement from the information to the claim or conclusion, (4) reservations which can be certain conditions under which a claim may not be accurate, sound, or highly probable, and (5) a qualifier, which registers the degree of probability about a claim in terms of accuracy, soundness, or truthfulness. These elements exist in interpersonal reasoning to the extent they are implied or explicit in human transactions.

For example, a white southern politician, who favored segregation even in the 1970s, and a newspaper reporter were engaged in intense communication about race relations. In spite of the rapid social, political, and economic gains by blacks in the country in the past two decades the politician still held an "Old South" belief that ideally segregation was desirable in his society and that southern blacks were genetically and culturally inferior to whites. His claim to the reporter that blacks are inferior to whites was gleaned from the views communicated to him by unnamed authorities he respected who told him southern blacks with very dark skin were not as intelligent as northern blacks, whose skin tended to be lighter. This was, he said, "Because southern blacks generally did not have white blood in them while northern blacks did." The premise of his reasoning was his belief that the view of unnamed authorities was sufficient evidence to serve as a premise for the conclusion he held. The newsman denied the validity of the information, the premise, and the claim of the politician's line of reasoning and was quick to provide additional information from educators and social scientists, whose research supported a claim opposing the politician's. So the politician believed his reasoning was highly probable and the reporter did not.

Our task is to see the five major *elements* in reasoning so that we can understand more fully the nature of human transactions. When we respond, we move from information to claim (or conclusion) and we operate from a premise. If humanistic goals are to be sought, communicators who construct their image maps, their plans, and design statements in responsible ways must be aware of the validity or weakness in reasoning which takes place in their interpersonal settings. The process of human communication inherently involves reasoning. We ought to challenge our perceptions continually and explore the reasons of others by attempting to get in touch with ourselves in light of what seems highly probable. We can view reasoning as diagrammed in figure 5.[19]

Determining the accuracy or validity of reasoned statements is dependent upon the ways in which we communicate in order to discover and use beliefs/emotions, attitudes, and values based upon facts and essential human rights rather than unfounded myths and distorted human biases. The entire process of gaining advanced degrees in higher education, for example, is centered in the dissemination of information aimed at making persons deeply humane, highly informed, and able to think independently and reason interpersonally.

When communicating interpersonally we need to demonstrate *care, concern,* and *accuracy* in reasoning and structuring our perceptions of reality with others. This will provide growth in our human potential and satisfaction in dealing with others, even when controversy is unresolved. Being able to identify the elements in reasoning and to criticize them objectively can lead to reasoning which is far more effective than one would experience in the careless, clumsy, or un-

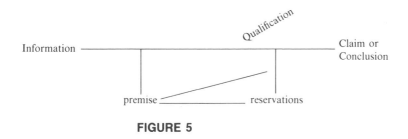

**FIGURE 5**

19. Stephen Toulmin, *The Uses of Argument.* (Cambridge: The University Press, 1958). Our diagram is only inspired by Toulmin, we certainly do not detail his approach in our study.

founded stringing together of generalizations which may have only a passing relationship to truth.

Objective criticism of reasoning can be simple or complex, depending upon the nature of the transactions and the needs of the communicators. If we are engaged in verbal play, our reasoning is for fun and pleasure and critical response is unnecessary. On the other hand, if we are engaged in an in-depth conversation concerning matters we feel strongly about, we ought to be cognizant of the probable or apparent strengths and weaknesses of the information, premises, and claims in the interpersonal transaction. Often the application of criterional questions during the reasoning process can sufficiently appraise and create sound transactions. Consider the following for examples of some critical questions:

1. Is the information sufficient, relevant, and significant enough to be accepted as highly probable? Accurate? Truthful?
2. What kinds of premises are we operating from and are they sound?
3. Do the claims of our transactions seem most clear, reasonable, and probable in terms of our information and premises?
4. What reservations seem to affect our reasoning?
5. Do we need to explore additional ideas and feelings (information) in order to gain satisfaction in our interpersonal reasoning?

In dealing with each other in meaningful communication, perception, image maps, goals, responsibility, and reasoning are basic to success and satisfaction. We ought to explore ourselves and reality as fully as possible and respond to each other in reasonable ways. The reasoning process involves effort and judgment, but is worthwhile in meeting the challenges of meaningful communication.

## Summary

We have taken a step in moving from the study of intrapersonal communication to interpersonal communication, for the purpose of enriching our human relationships. A logical point of departure for taking this step is a focus on perception and reality. A thorough understanding of perception can give fresh and meaningful awareness for improving skill in interpersonal communication. Essentially, when we respond to others in human transactions we do so in accordance with physical and psychological capacity and willingness to create meaning which we think is approximately accurate and serves our needs.

At the base of this process of creating perceptual meaning for each of us is an image map, comprised of emotions, and values/attitudes plus myriad mental pictures and recorded sensations. The map is always in a state of change, whether slight or radical. When we engage in transaction we often rely on a plan or design, the use of specific behaviors which stem from the image map. The plan is designed for the attainment of interpersonal goals, both relationship and content. Relationship goals help to adjust oneself to oneself or to adjust oneself to another while content goals focus primarily upon purposes of overt action and task achievement.

People set and pursue relationship and content goals in order to meet essential needs, so the matter of responsibility becomes important. Responsibility is the recognition and pursuit of healthy needs such as love and self-worth. The responsible communicator is willing to provide reasons for what he or she feels and to accept the consequences of his or her communication. So interpersonal reasoning becomes important in the enrichment of communication.

Reasoning is a way in which persons communicate interpersonally to arrive at some idea, notion, or claim which seems accurate, probable, and truthful to themselves and often the other as well. Although we operate a great deal on the basis of our feelings, we express ourselves, in structuring reality, by speaking through the use of information, premises, and claims or conclusions which seem logical. Our claims are usually probable, for there are reservations to most statements we make. A knowledge of the reasoning process can significantly help us to express what we really feel and know and to respond honestly and intelligently to the views of others.

# PART TWO

# Meaning in Interpersonal Communication

# 4

# Nonverbal Communication

Now that we have some basic understanding of intrapersonal and interpersonal processes, we will examine in more detail the two basic subprocesses in communication—nonverbal and verbal. Here is an incident experienced by an eighth-grade student which made such an impression that the person, now an adult, can still recall it clearly today:

> I was riding on the bus. I sat on the long seat at the very front, next to the driver. Across from me sat an old man in work clothes. He was a "lumber jack" type character: big, gnarled, but with wrinkles that made me picture him as a person who had been happy with his life. Next to him sat a "peaches 'n' cream" little girl, with curly blond hair and that look of wonderment and curiosity so often found in the very young. Next to the child sat her mother.
>
> The little girl was bouncing up and down and looking around in awe at her surroundings. She began to pat the old man's knee. Her mother laid a calm but firm restraining hand on her arm and shook her head "no." The old man, over the child's head, smiled slightly at the mother. Then he looked down at the child, opened his big gnarled, work-worn hand and placed it palm up on his knee. The child looked at his hand, then at him, and with no hesitation placed her pink chubby hand in his. As he enveloped her tiny hand, the two looked at each other and his face broke into a genuine smile of almost youthful happiness.

In this exchange not a word was spoken. Somehow words would have ruined the message not only for participants but for the observer. This act of communication was very close to poetry in its beauty, and that's why it is remembered.

The type of communication we are concerned with in this chapter is nonverbal communication, which is everything we experience in an act of communication other than the specific words being used. And, of course, as in the example above, sometimes words don't even have to be a part of the communication. We will suggest examples throughout the chapter, but the following should suffice to indicate what kinds of things are included in nonverbal communication.[1]

> An instructor glances at her watch while a student confers with her.
>
> A mother catches her breath in the midst of a telephone conversation.
>
> A friend touches your arm as he tells you that there is a telegram for you.
>
> A man smells his fiancée's new cologne.

Something is being communicated in all these instances and people are perceiving what is being communicated through the basic senses of sight, hearing, touch, and smell (taste could also be included, but this sense is used to a minor degree in perceiving nonverbal communication). In a communicative act nonverbal communication encompasses all that is taken in by senses *except* any words being spoken.

The most important characteristic of nonverbal communication is that it is, unlike verbal communication, generally continuous and multidimensional. It is going on all the time during communication and coming from many different places at once. While we are engaged in conversation with another, we are being continuously bombarded with messages from the other's face or hands or posture, the sound of his or her voice, the distance that separates us, the amount of time we spend together and spend looking at each other, and so on. We can't escape from nonverbal communication. As stated earlier, this fact has led communicologists to assert: "You cannot NOT communicate."[2]

---

1. Abne M. Eisenberg and Ralph R. Smith, Jr., *Nonverbal Communication* (Indianapolis: Bobbs-Merrill, 1971), p. 20 suggest that the term nonverbal indicates what is *not* included under the rubric, but fails to suggest what is included.

2. Paul Watzlowick, Janet Beavin, and Donald D. Jackson, *The Pragmatics of Human Communication* (New York: W. W. Norton, 1967).

Anything that pervades the act of communication to the extent that nonverbal elements do is obviously important to the further understanding of interpersonal communication. As we become capable of sending clearer and more meaningful nonverbal messages and interpreting and evaluating them more accurately, we will become more effective communicators and be able to establish better interpersonal relationships.

## Importance

We have already mentioned one of the three main reasons why nonverbal communication is important to interpersonal relationship—its *omnipresence.*[3] To elaborate, let's once more refer to a classroom situation. What are the various things that communicate some message to the student about his environment? He walks into a classroom with nondescript beige walls and windows with white blinds pulled to half-mast. The desks are in even rows and bolted to the floor. He sits down with the other students in alphabetical order, facing the instructor's lectern which is set on a small platform. The instructor walks briskly into the room at the sound of the bell, and without looking around, moves to the lectern. He opens his briefcase, takes out his notes and arranges them, puts on his glasses and then looks at the class. After a brief pause, while he scrutinizes the room, he begins lecturing in a tight monotone, clearing his throat often. He refers regularly to his notes, does not pause for questions, and does not move from the platform.

Let's go to another classroom and see how it, though serving the same educational function, may communicate something different. In this classroom the walls are sun yellow and draperies, some pulled, some open, hang at the windows. Chair-desks are scattered about the carpeted room. Some students are seated and others are moving about or standing and talking, while still others are sitting on the floor. The instructor is sitting on his desk, drinking a cup of coffee and talking with a student about an assignment. No bell rings, but the instructor begins talking in an animated voice. Moving from the board to his desk and then moving among the students, the instructor pauses a

---

3. Richard Crable, "A Situational Approach to Purposeful Nonverbal Communication," in John J. Makay, ed., *Exploration in Speech Communication* (Columbus, Ohio: Charles E. Merrill, 1973), p. 302. Crable mentions "function" as a fourth justification for the study of nonverbal communication; this will be treated separately in another part of the chapter..

great deal for feedback and maintains constant eye contact with his students.

So no matter where we are or what we are doing, nonverbal communication is present, too, from the broadest perspective of the architectural layout of the building and rooms to the smallest focus on the movement of the instructor's eyes. In fact, it is suggested that only thirty-five percent of any perceived message is verbal; the remaining is nonverbal.[4] Not only is nonverbal communication continuous, but it also carries much more of the message when there *is* a verbal element.

A second reason that nonverbal communication is important is that it is a part of our *human-ness.* There is much controversy over whether nonverbal communication is cross-cultural (for example, widened eyes and raised eyebrows mean the same wherever you go) or culturally specific (for example, Americans and Europeans point with their forefingers, while Indians, Mongoloids and Africans point with their lips).[5] Though there is some evidence that nonverbal communication is pancultural,[6] in that there is an innate capacity for nonverbal skills and a similarity in the expression of some states of emotion, such as happiness and fear, more authoritative opinion suggests that it is determined by the society in which we live and that cultures differ distinctly and widely in their nonverbal communication.[7] So, while it is a part of our general human-ness that we all have the potential to develop skills in sending and receiving nonverbal communication, it is also a part of our unique human-ness that we develop nonverbal communication which is consonant with our particular culture and congruent with our own individual personalities. For example, if we attempted to stand as close to a stranger as a Latin American would when speaking, we would notice that there is a distinct cultural difference.[8] The Latin American style of standing within inches of one another would be much too close for our American comfort. Because of this cultural difference the stranger would increase the distance between us in order to establish a greater distance in his own individual style. He might frown and step deliber-

---

4. Albert Mehrabian, "Communication without Words," *Psychology Today,* September 1968, p. 53.

5. Eisenberg and Smith, *Nonverbal Communication,* p. 76.

6. Ibid., p. 40.

7. The best regarded and one of the earliest books delineating cultural differences in nonverbal communication is Edward T. Hall, *The Silent Language* (Greenwich, Conn.: Fawcett, 1959).

8. Ibid., p. 164.

ately backward, or smile shyly and inch backward hesitantly, or he might even push *us* backward to establish the required distance. Whatever a person's own particular style, a comfortable cultural space will be maintained. Nonverbal communication is a part of human nature in general, people within their cultures, and the individual within himself.

Nonverbal communication is also important because of its *richness.* The slightest sound or movement can be fraught with meaning, and when we put together all the things we do with various parts of our bodies and their extensions, the nonverbal context is rich indeed. As you know, sometimes not doing anything, remaining perfectly still, is the most meaningful communication of all. For example, consider the following which show how the smallest instance of nonverbal communication is rich with meaning.

> An instructor focuses carefully on a student as she asks a question.
>
> Someone you love slides closer to you on the sofa.
>
> A friend's voice cracks as she tells another she really didn't want to be invited to the party the other was about to attend.
>
> A doctor frowns as he is taking the blood pressure of a middle-aged man.

Because it is always within us and around us and because the slightest bit of it is meaningful, nonverbal communication in terms of interpersonal relationships must be part of our attention.

## Sending and Perceiving
## Nonverbal Messages

We communicate nonverbally and we interpret others' nonverbal communication. Information about nonverbal communication definitely overlaps in these two areas, because obviously what we send can be read by the other and what the other sends can be read by us. In this section, we will concentrate on the nonverbal messages we send to ourselves and the individual styles we exhibit to others along three general dimensions of feeling, and then proceed to what goes into the accurate perception of nonverbal communication.

Our *intrapersonal* nonverbal communication manifests itself in many ways. The phrase, "Your body is trying to tell you something," is one that we often use with our students when they are tired or ill or nervous. Here are a few examples of intrapersonal nonverbal communication:

Bruce gets headaches regularly every Friday night. They are accompanied by tense shoulder muscles which are sore to the touch.

Cathy is constantly tired. She has trouble getting up in the morning and going to school and difficulty in making it through work.

Gary's stomach is upset after every meal. He eats Tums like candy and takes antacids for dessert.

Joe's hands become sweaty and his heart begins to pound before he has to speak to a group of people.

Ann has trouble breathing when she is about to express anger.

It is possible, of course, that these problems are mainly physiological, caused by lack of sleep, overwork, or improper eating. However, there is evidence to indicate that the person's body is trying to tell him something such as, "I don't want to be doing this—I'd rather be doing something else," or "I don't think I'm capable of this—I'm afraid I'll look stupid," or "I've got myself into too many things—I don't have any time for myself."

We don't presume to be certain about others, but we are sure about ourselves. Right now, to be honest, there are several things we would rather be doing than working on this chapter (as much as we wish to share with you, it *is* work to put pen to paper), so what do our bodies do to make this clear? For one thing squirming—we get up and down and change positions many times. For another, feeling sleepy—we want to rest. However, if a friend were to ring the doorbell right now, would we be tired any longer? Of course not. Our bodies are saying, nonverbally, "You don't really want to be doing this right now and if you insist on trying, I'm going to make it uncomfortable for you." And it is.

William Schutz, one of the proponents of "encounter culture," holds very firmly to this idea. He relates:

> One day I was sitting in a friend's room talking with two people. Suddenly my throat began feeling tight. ... I started wondering whether or not I wanted to be somewhere else. Of course, I became aware that I wasn't enjoying the conversation; I wanted to do some shopping, but felt obligated to my friend to remain and talk. As long as I wasn't dealing with the conflict consciously, my body had to deal with it. Part of my body was stationary, complying with what

I thought was my friend's wish, while another part, my throat, was straining to get away, responding to my personal desire. Once I became aware of the conflict, I could make a conscious decision to stay or go, I decided that my feeling for my friend was greater than my desire to go shopping, so I stayed. My throat tension disappeared. I had changed the level of conflict from my body to my consciousness and resolved it there. My body therefore did not have to absorb the conflict; it did not have to prepare itself to move in two conflicting directions.[9]

As we talk to ourselves verbally, we also talk to ourselves nonverbally, and, as we have our own individual verbal style that we display to others, we also have our own unique nonverbal style.

Psychologist Albert Mehrabian suggests that there are three primary dimensions of feeling exhibited in interactional nonverbal communication: liking, power, and responsiveness.[10] These dimensions can be found in any interaction, and the frequency and intensity with which they are found will characterize not only that interaction but, over time, an individual's characteristic style of nonverbal communication. As psychiatrists Jurgen Ruesch and Weldon Kees, pioneers in the study of nonverbal communication, explain, "Everyone has a certain *identity*, known to himself and to others that for all practical purposes remains stable regardless of the social situation in which he participates. This identity expresses itself in physical appearance, movements, and speech patterns."[11]

The *liking* dimension involves approach-avoidance nonverbal communication. In any particular situation one might sit close to a person he likes, turn his chair so that he sees him better, look at him a lot, and touch him. If, conversely, he finds himself in a situation with a person he dislikes, he might avoid sitting near him, turn his back on him, avoid looking at him, and if in physical contact with him, tense up. This is how it would operate in a specific situation with a specific person, but one will also have a unique style that is congruent with his personality and which he will transmit to others if they are observant. One may be characteristically outgoing, that is, she may exhibit much more frequent and intense approach behavior than many people. If this is her style, she might engage in a great deal of eye contact,

9. William C. Schutz, *Here Comes Everybody* (New York: Harper and Row, 1971), p. 2.

10. Albert Mehrabian, *Silent Messages* (Belmont, California: Wadsworth, 1971), pp. 113–18.

11. Jurgen Ruesch and Weldon Kees, *Nonverbal Communication* (Berkeley: University of California Press, 1972), p. 57.

try to close the physical distance between herself and others, and touch people frequently.

The *power* dimension involves dominant and confident, or submissive and insecure nonverbal communication. In a situation in which we find ourselves with someone subordinate to us, we might assume a relaxed posture, gesture broadly, and move without hesitation. On the other hand, if we find ourselves with someone we feel is superior in position to us, such as our boss or instructor, we may stand or sit rigidly and tensely, avoid eye contact, and make small gestures and movements with hesitation. Again, we probably exhibit personality characteristics nonverbally toward either submissiveness or dominance. Consider Bob, a man who consistently exhibits a dominant type of nonverbal communication. He walks firmly, rapidly, and purposefully, and yet, when he is seated he is nearly always relaxed, reclining slightly with his legs crossed and his arms resting on the back of the sofa or chair. He gestures expansively and engages in a great deal of direct and prolonged eye contact when he is speaking to someone.

The *responsiveness* dimension involves the amount of reaction toward the environment. We may find ourselves more or less nonverbally responsive to our surroundings in a situation. For example, we may exhibit much more movement, more gesturing, and more facial expression at a party than we would in English lit class. Or we may find ourselves responding differently to our environment depending on our mood at the moment. If we are irritable, we may jump when someone touches us. If we are sleepy or very comfortable, we may not even notice or react to another's touch. Personalitywise we are either basically nonverbally responsive or unresponsive. Sally is characteristically and uniquely unresponsive to her environment. She sits without moving, her only gestures involved with lighting and smoking cigarettes, and she stares a lot, not seeming to notice what is occurring around her.

As Mehrabian sums up, "Any behavior that is observable can serve as an outlet for feelings and is thus, in principle, communicative. Behaviors as diverse as the eye blink, crossing of legs while seated, postures, gestures, head nods, facial and vocal expressions, tension in the muscles, and twitches are all potentially significant in communication."[12]

We've discussed how you transmit messages nonverbally both to yourself and others, now let's turn to the other side of the coin and look at the reading of nonverbal messages that others transmit.

---

12. Mehrabian, *Silent Messages*, p. 119.

Fritz Perls, founder of the Gestalt school of psychotherapy, gives a concise, if blunt introduction to the reading of nonverbal communication. He says:

> So don't listen to the words, just listen to what the voice tells you, what the movements tell you, what the posture tells you, what the image tells you. . . . Everything a person wants to express is all there —not in words. What we say is mostly either lies or bullshit. But the voice is there, the gesture, the posture, the facial expression, the psychosomatic language. It's all there is you learn to more or less let the content of the sentences play the second violin only. And if you don't make the mistake of mixing up sentences and reality, and if you use your eyes and ears, then you see that everyone expresses himself in one way or another. If you have eyes and ears, the world is open. Nobody can have any secrets because the neurotic only fools himself, nobody else.
>
> . . . the total personality . . . expresses itself with movements, with posture, with sound, with pictures—there is so much invaluable material here, that we don't have to do anything else except get to the obvious.[13]

Interestingly, Dr. Perls was quite a bit more perceptive than most of us. Not only was he more alert to and aware of others' nonverbal signals, he was also more adept at reading them. Perhaps, however, we can increase our ability to read and interpret nonverbal communication.

The key term here is obviously *awareness.* One needs to be alert to much more than the words that the other is speaking. As a counselor often suggests to his counselees, you must attend to, listen to, and look for, the "something else." For example, one Saturday one close friend said to the other, "I hope you have a good day." Saturday was the day the two usually spent a few pleasant hours together talking over the week's activities and thoughts and feelings. They couldn't be together this particular day. The other person noticed the "something else"—her friend's voice was shaky, her lip was quivering, and she wasn't maintaining eye contact but looking at the napkin she was folding and unfolding. This gave her the clue that her friend was disappointed that the two could not see each other, and prevented her from reacting insensitively to the situation.

It isn't too difficult to increase awareness of nonverbal cues. Often it's a simple matter of concentrating more and focusing more sharply, but what do we do with this additional information? How do we interpret it more accurately?

---

13. Fritz Perls, *Gestalt Therapy Verbatim* (Toronto: Bantam, 1969), pp. 57–58.

Some studies have found that people who can express themselves accurately and clearly to others and who can identify their own feelings precisely are generally more sensitive to others' nonverbal cues.[14] Perhaps one answer to better interpretation is to begin by getting in touch with our own emotions and seeing how they manifest themselves in nonverbal form. We could also ask for feedback from others about how we are coming across nonverbally. To someone with whom we feel secure, we might say, "I'm depressed. Am I communicating that nonverbally to you and if so, how?"

Another way to improve interpretation of nonverbal cues is through "empathic assessment."[15] When we attend to another's nonverbal cues we can ask ourselves how we would feel if we were doing the same thing he is. For example, if we notice that a woman is drumming her fingers on the desk, we ask, "What type of feeling would make me do that?" Or, a man is sitting back in a chair with his arms crossed tightly across his chest. What would we be feeling if we did that? *Awareness* plus *empathy* should equal more accurate interpretation of nonverbal cues.

A final suggestion is based on experimental studies. If we want to find out accurately what the other is feeling, attend to the movement of the feet and legs, then the hands, and finally the face. In following this order, we should find what are called "leakage and deception clues."[16] These areas of nonverbal communication supposedly tell us what we really want to know about what the other is feeling. The theory is that people are accustomed to exerting more control over what is usually attended to, and we usually attend to the face and eyes when interacting with another more than to any other part of the body. Of course, it becomes easier to read the other the longer we know him and the closer we are to him. We obviously can read our immediate family and close friends more accurately then we can someone we are meeting for the first time.

Communicologist Dean Barnlund sums up the idea of nonverbal transmission and reception:

> From the moment of recognition until the moment of separation,
> people observe each other with all their senses, hearing pauses and

---

14. J. R. Davitz, *The Communication of Emotional Meaning* (New York: McGraw-Hill, 1964). This speaks mainly to reading emotions in the voice, but we believe the senstivity and skill transfers to nonverbal cues.

15. Ruesch and Kees, *Nonverbal Communication,* p. 57.

16. P. Ekman and W. V. Friesen, "Nonverbal Leakage and Clues to Deception," *Psychiatry* 32 (1969): 88–106.

intonation, attending to dress and carriage, observing glance and facial tension. . . . Every harmony or disharmony of signals guides the interpretation of passing mood or occurring attribute. Out of the evaluations of kinetic, vocal and verbal cues, decisions are made to argue or agree, to laugh or blush, to relax or resist, to continue or cut off conversation.[17]

# Types

We have chosen two ways to view types of nonverbal communication. The first is along the continua of conscious to unconscious and intentional to unintentional. We transmit nonverbal messages all the time. We are conscious of some and intend to transmit them; for example, we may know that we are smiling in greeting and intend to do so. We are conscious of some that we do not intend to communicate; for example, we may know that our hands are shaking but wish that they weren't and that we could stop them. We are unconscious of some that we really intend to communicate; for example, we may unknowingly lean forward to talk with someone when we want her to know that we are interested. Finally, we may be unconsious of some that are also unintentional; for example, we may not know that our voices are showing fear and if we did, we wouldn't want it to be known.

Some of us (though nonverbal communication is supposedly more spontaneous, natural, and indicative of what we really feel) have learned to control our nonverbal cues almost as much as we have our verbal ones. When this happens, people do not get an accurate reading on us, which may be exactly what we want. Still, alert and perceptive people can pick up the unconscious cues. Fritz Perls zeroed in on this unconscious nonverbal communication in his therapy sessions. Here are two short examples of his technique:

*Fritz:* What's your right hand doing?

*Sam:* Playing with my left hand.

*Fritz:* Can you invent a dialogue between your right hand and your left hand? Have them talk to each other?[18]

*Fritz:* Now I'm interested, what is your left foot doing to your right?

---

17. Dean C. Barnlund, *Interpersonal Communication: Survey and Studies* (Boston: Houghton Mifflin, 1968), pp. 535–36.
18. Perls, *Gestalt Therapy Verbatim*, p. 83.

*Carl:*    Sort of exercising my knee.

*Fritz:*    You're exercising your knee.[19]

The second way that we can look at the types of nonverbal communication is to focus on the voice, different parts of the body, and bodily extensions that serve to transmit the message. We find that these forms can be indicative both of personality characteristics and emotional states.

### Voice

There has been one main approach to this classification. Frazer divides what he terms paralanguage (nonverbal vocal communication) into vocal qualities such as pitch, rate, and articulation; vocal characterizers such as laughing, crying, or clearing the throat; vocal qualifiers such as loudness; and vocal segregates such as pauses and "uh."[20] We can use these notions in speaking about vocal quality, pitch, rate, volume, and characterizers.

When we talk about quality, we're talking about whether a person has a pleasant or unpleasant voice. If a person's voice is characteristically harsh or husky or tight, this is at least a small indication of his personality.[21] For some reason this person has chronically tightened his throat and neck muscles, and this has resulted in a harsh vocal quality. A particular vocal quality can also be a clue to the emotional state of the person at any given moment. For example, a person might have a voice which tends to become tight and rather nasal when she is under pressure.

Pitch is a person's normal vocal range on a scale from high to low. While women tend to have higher voices than men because of anatomic makeup, a characteristically high pitch could be indicative of a tense, excitable person for the same reasons as mentioned above. High pitch and a wide variety of pitch may indicate intense emotion such as joy or anger; whereas low pitch and lack of variety may indicate depression.[22] When we talk to a friend on the telephone we may not have to ask how things are—the pitch of his voice might tell us whether it is a good or rotten day.

19. Ibid., p. 98.
20. G. L. Trager, "Paralanguage: A First Approximation," *Studies in Linguistics* 13 (1958): 1–12.
21. Barnlund, *Interpersonal Communication*, p. 528, from Paul Mases, *The Voice of Neurosis* (New York: Grune and Stratton, 1954).
22. Davitz, *Emotional Meaning*, p. 63.

Rate is a person's characteristic rhythm on a scale of fast to slow. Perhaps a person who speaks rapidly all the time is more excitable than the person who speaks slowly and deliberately. Fast rates tend to indicate intense emotion, whereas slow rates are often found with depressed emotion.[23] In discussing rate, we also have to look at phenomena such as vocal pauses, those fillers like "and uh" and "you know" that pre-empt what should be silence between thoughts. There is some indication that vocal pauses are associated with emotional arousal and the need to reduce anxiety.[24] Some of our students seem to use "you know" as a filled pause three or four times in one sentence. Does that mean that they are consistently aroused and trying to reduce anxiety?

Volume is a person's characteristic vocal intensity on a scale from soft to loud. We are not certain what a characteristically soft or loud voice would indicate about a person's personality. A number of people with loud voices tend to be dominant. On the other hand, many people maintain control by speaking softly, so that one has to strain to hear them. Some attract attention by not saying anything—by remaining silent when everyone is talking. It seems that, generally speaking, loudness is associated with the more extreme emotional states such as anger, whereas softness is associated with the more depressed emotional states such as boredom.[25]

Vocal characterizers are such things as sniffing, crying, laughing, and coughing. Certainly you know people who seem to have a chronic nervous giggle that pops out at the most incongruous times. It is easy to see how some of these characterizers are directly related to momentary emotional states. For example, if a person is crying while he is trying to talk that usually tells you that he is upset unless he tends to cry when very happy.

To conclude this discussion of vocal nonverbal communication, here is a familiar example. Tom calls his friend on the phone. He says, "Hello, how are things going?" His friend responds, "Fine." Tom says, "What's the matter?" Now what you've read and reacted to, probably accurately, is vocal nonverbal communication. Perhaps Tom's friend didn't respond as quickly as usual, or the "fine" was

---

23. Ibid.
24. F. Goldman-Eisler, "A Comparative Study of Two Hesitation Phenomena," *Language and Speech* 4 (1961): 18–26; and W. P. Levant, "Antagonistic Functions of Verbal Pauses: Filled and Unfilled Pauses in the Solution of Additions," *Language and Speech* 6 (1963): 1–4.
25. Mark L. Knapp, *Nonverbal Communication* (New York: Holt, Rinehart, and Winston, 1972), p. 163.

dragged out in a low monotonous pitch, or there was a catch in his voice, or all of these. Putting all the various vocal cues together gave Tom an accurate picture of how his friend was feeling, especially since he knew him well.[26]

## Body

There are a great number of subcategories under bodily nonverbal communication. We communicate with our build, our face, our eyes, our posture, movement, and gestures, our touch, the distance we establish between others, and the way we transport our bodies through time.

It seems that there are a number of stereotypes associated with body build. This may be hard to believe in this day and age when we are all trying hard not to be prejudiced and to accept people as they are. Apparently, a heavy person is regarded as older, shorter, less good looking, warmer, more agreeable, and more trusting as opposed to a thin person who is regarded as more ambitious, more tense, more suspicious, and quieter. In contrast to these two the athletically built person is regarded as stronger, better-looking, more self-reliant, and more adventuresome.[27] In addition to this type of stereotype, it seems that physically attractive people have it made (all talk about personality aside). They are considered to be more desirable as dates and to have more character as speakers.[28] When you look at your friends, you may find that they are all generally attractive, or good looking, or on the thin or athletic side. Perhaps this says no more about you than you like thin, athletic, attractive people. Perhaps the theory might be that one's physical appearance nonverbally communicates certain personality traits to others that others think they would like, and that's why they are attracted to this type of person.

Facial expression, as much as any other form of bodily nonverbal communication, seems to mirror both emotion and personality. The research findings on facial expression suggest that certain basic emo-

26. Ibid., p. 173, reminds us "obviously, we should consistently remind ourselves that any given individual may vocally express the same emotion differently on different days, in different situations, with different provoking stimuli."

27. W. Wells and B. Siegel, "Stereotyped Somatypes," *Psychological Reports* 8 (1961): 77–78.

28. E. Walster, V. Aronson, D. Abrahams, and L. Rohmann, "Importance of Physical Attractiveness in Dating Behavior," *Journal of Personality and Social Psychology* 4 (1966): 508–16; R. N. Widzery and B. Webster, "The Effects of Physical Attractiveness Upon Perceived Initial Credibility," *Michigan Speech Journal* 4 (1969): 9–14.

tions such as happiness, anger, surprise, sadness, disgust, and fear are different enough that they can be identified; that the face can exhibit more than one emotion at the same time such as pleasantness and anger; that some areas of the face are better predictors for some emotions than others, for example, sadness is best seen in the eyes; and that knowing the person and the situational context helps a great deal in accurate perception of a given emotion.[29]

When talking with a friend we may say something that hits a sore spot. Her face may not change expression, but we can sense hurt in her eyes. Some people believe that the eyes are the most expressive part of the face. They look at a person's eyes first when making contact. They may look for clearness and sparkle and depth—vague descriptive terms to be sure, but many believe these qualities can be identified. In addition, much attention is often given a person's eye contact. There is an old cliché, "If a person doesn't look you in the eye, somehow they aren't quite honest." The cliché seems to be supported by research; it has been found that the person who has something to hide does, in fact, engage in less eye contact. Knapp summarizes the research:

> Eye contact is influenced by a number of different conditions: whether we are seeking feedback, need for certain markers in the conversation, whether we wish to open or close the communication channels, whether the other party is too near or too far, whether we wish to induce anxiety, whether we are rewarded by what we see, whether we are in competition with another or wishing to hide something from him, and whether we are with members of a different sex or status. Personality characteristics such as introversion-/extroversion may also influence eye behavior.[30]

Postures, movement, and gestures are other forms of bodily nonverbal communication. Like voice, posture is often interpreted as indicative of personality or attitude toward life. A person who is chronically round-shouldered and hunched over and looks at the ground telegraphs different characteristics than does one who is straight and keeps his eyes ahead of him. This is the reason that many how-to-succeed formulas suggest that you "stand tall." For better or worse, others draw conclusions about us from our habitual posture, gestures, and movement. Some experimental studies on the posture/ movement/gesture complex have concluded that:

---

29. Knapp, *Nonverbal Communication,* pp. 119–29.
30. Ibid., p. 138.

1. The degree of relaxation exhibited with another is indicative of liking for another, with moderate relaxation indicating the most liking.
2. In a power relationship, higher status persons tend to be more relaxed, hold their heads up more and use the arms-akimbo position more than lower status persons.
3. While the face may portray a specific emotion, body posture, movement, and gesture tend to indicate more the intensity of that emotion.
4. People who seek approval not only smile more but tend to engage more in head nodding and gesticulation.
5. Posture/gesture/movement can reveal "quasi-courtship behavior," i.e., there are certain movements and gestures that are indicative of desiring further, closer, and exclusive contact with a person.
6. Movements and gestures in a conversation can indicate the end of a thought, a theme, or the interaction.[31]

Generally, Americans tend to avoid touch as a primary form of bodily nonverbal communication. We communicate with touch less than many other cultures.[32] John Stewart finds it distressing that we tend to perceive touch as legitimate only in handshaking, sexual intercourse, or aggression.[33] Although some segments of the humanistic movement are attempting to break down the barriers to touching,[34] many people still react with distaste to this form of nonverbal communication. Perhaps one might transmit something negative about his own personality if he touches people a lot—to some it would have a consistently sexual connotation, to others it might indicate that he sought approval or was aggressive. To us, it is a manifestation of wanting to establish contact with others and to exhibit warmth and caring. We all know people who draw away when they are touched. It seems sad that something so basic to human emotional and cognitive development should be so much avoided later on in life.[35] Whether we shy away from touching or are comfortable with it,[36] it

31. Ibid., pp. 97–107.
32. S. M. Jourard, "An Exploratory Study of Body-Accessibility," *British Journal of Social and Clinical Psychology* 5 (1966): 221–31.
33. John Stewart, ed., *Bridges Not Walls* (Reading, Mass.: Addison-Wesley, 1973).
34. William C. Schutz, *Joy* (New York: Ballentine, 1973).
35. C. David Mortensen, *Communication: The Study of Human Interaction* (New York: McGraw-Hill, 1972), p. 226.
36. Jourard, "Exploratory Study."

does appear to be a desirable form of communication and preferable to both verbal only and visual only communication.[37]

Closely related to touch as a form of nonverbal communication is the distance we establish between ourselves and others. Anthropologist Edward T. Hall has defined four increasingly wide spheres that surround us.[38] The first is the intimate sphere which extends about eighteen inches and is often called our personal space or bubble, into which we let only our closest friends; the second is the private sphere which extends to about two feet, into which we admit our friends; the third is the social sphere which extends to about four feet and in which we converse; and the last is the public sphere reserved for everyone else.

A professor who was very interested in nonverbal communication tried the following experiment:

> Herb stood at one end of the room and I at the other, facing each other. He motioned for me to walk toward him. I did and then stepped about four feet from him. He motioned for me to move closer and I shook my head "no." Then he began moving toward me. As he got about two feet away from me, I took a step backward. For every step he took forward thereafter, I took one backward. He kept walking and so did I. Finally, I ended up against the wall with no place to go. The funny thing is that I *knew* what he was doing, but because he was moving into my intimate sphere, I seemed to have no choice other than to keep moving backward. It was almost compulsive.

The discrepancy between what people say about space and the ways they use it is often amusing. Many instructors and students claim that they don't want distance between teacher and student, that there should be more closeness between them in the educational enterprise. Yet it never fails, when an instructor walks into a classroom the first day, what does she see? Invariably the first two rows are empty, the students are sitting in the back of the room, and the instructor is planted firmly behind a lectern. This speaks more loudly than any words about wanting to break down barriers.

The way we use space communicates a great deal about the interaction occurring in a group. The following conclusions about the use of space in small groups seem to hold true:

37. J. P. Bordeen, "Interpersonal Perception Through the Tactile, Verbal and Visual Modes" (Paper presented at the Convention of the International Communication Association, Phoenix, 1971).

38. Edward T. Hall, *Hidden Dimension* (New York: Doubleday, 1966).

1. Men sitting at the head of the table are more often chosen as leaders.
2. Task oriented men tend to sit at the head of a table while socially oriented men tend to sit in the middle.
3. The positions people chose vis á vis one another depend on the task, varying according to whether it is conversation, cooperation, co-action or competition.
4. The higher the motivation to affiliate, the more frequent the choice to sit close.
5. Extroverts choose to sit closer to others than introverts.[39]

The final form of bodily nonverbal communication is the way we move our bodies through time. There is a great difference here among cultures, for while we would consider over fifteen minutes "late" for an appointment, other cultures do not consider an hour unreasonable.[40] But even in the United States, we can use arrival and departure times to communicate something. For example, consider the wife who had been trying for years to tell her husband that when they received an invitation for 8 P.M., that did not always mean that they were supposed to *be* there at eight. In social situations an early or on-time arrival can nonverbally communicate a certain lack of social intelligence. The use of time in business situations is even more important. Being late can be interpreted as immaturity or lack of respect for the other person.

We've looked at myriad forms of bodily nonverbal communication. More than any other form this is the complex of factors we attend to in interpersonal relationships.

### Extensions of the Body

The extensions of the body include such things as clothes, make-up, jewelry, the cars one drives, and the way one decorates one's rooms. Often these extensions communicate both mood and personality. For example, there are days when a person might feel like wearing jeans and a sweatshirt; it seems to fit his mood. Then again, sometimes *what* a person wears will affect his mood; if he dresses in a formal and flashy way he may feel sophisticated. Many people have a characteristic style of dress; for example, wearing tailored clothes rather than frilly ones.

---

39. Knapp, *Nonverbal Communication,* pp. 47–54.
40. Hall, *Silent Language,* pp. 136–37.

According to one study, that means those people are responsible, conscientious, alert, efficient, and intelligent.[41] If the tailored clothes are deep shades of brown or blue, according to another study, that means that those people are high in sociability.[42] People tend to stereotype according to clothing styles. We all have favorable or unfavorable impressions, depending on our attitudes toward baggy jeans or grey flannel suits or halter tops.

Jewelry can be very symbolic and nonverbally transmit something about the wearer. The most obvious example of this is an engagement ring or wedding band. Of course, crosses, peace signs, ankhs, and so on also may be interpreted as saying something about the wearer, whether it is intended or not.

Cars are supposedly sex symbols for men, but they are also sometimes interpreted as being indicative of personality traits. For example, suppose you drive a VW bug and others think it "fits" you. You probably know people you think "look like" they ought to be driving a Porsche or a Lincoln Continental or a Ford station wagon. There are even people who "fit" motorcycles and racing bikes.

Finally, our dwellings indicate something about us nonverbally, and perhaps whether we are decorating for others or for ourselves. As Ruesch and Kees explain:

> Every interior betrays the *nonverbal skills* of its inhabitants. The choice of materials, the distribution of space, the kind of objects that command attention or demand to be touched . . . have much to say about the preferred sensory modalities of their owners. Their sense of organization, the degree of freedom left to imagination, their coerciveness or esthetic rigidity, their sensitivity and fields of awareness are all revealed in their homes.[43]

You probably surround yourselves with things that make you feel happy and comfortable and secure, whether it be posters or snapshots or trophies or stuffed animals or beer mugs. Posters are used frequently to indicate the inhabitants' personality. What would you surmise about another if you saw, among pictures of friends and family, an ink drawing, some plants, a stop sign, and a huge furry pillow, this poster in the room?

---

41. L. Aiken, "Relationships of Dress to Selected Measures of Personality in Undergraduate Women," *Journal of Social Psychology* 59 (1963): 119–28.

42. N. Compton, "Personal Attributes of Color and Design Preferences in Clothing Fabrics," *Journal of Psychology* 54 (1962): 191–95.

43. Ruesch and Kees, *Nonverbal Communication,* p. 135.

I do my thing, and you do your thing.
I am not in this world to live up to your
expectations.
And you are not in this world to live up to mine.
You are you and I am I.
And if by chance we find each other, it's beautiful.
If not, it can't be helped.[44]

We have now covered basically what is known and presently being explored in nonverbal communication. The main thing to remember about the forms of nonverbal communication is that they cannot be viewed in isolation. They must be observed as they interact with each other and the situation. We can tell a lot from nonverbal communication, but our inferences should be tentative rather than definite. Individuals *are* unique and they will again and again defy the most apparently valid generalizations.

## Summary

In this chapter we have tried to stress the importance of nonverbal communication to the total communicative act. We have found that nonverbal communication is significant because of its omnipresence, human-ness, and richness. We have seen that we communicate nonverbally to ourselves intrapersonally as well as interpersonally.

In the interpersonal realm, we nonverbally communicate on the feeling dimensions of liking, power, and responsiveness, not only in a specific situation but in a characteristic individual style. One means of reading nonverbal communication more accurately is to exercise more awareness and empathy.

We looked at the types of nonverbal communication on the continua of conscious to unconscious and intentional to unintentional and in the broad categories of voice including quality, pitch, rate, loudness, and characterizers; body, including build, facial expression, eye contact, posture/movement/gesture, touch, and use of space and time; extensions of the body, including clothes, jewelry, cars, and furnishings.

We agree with Mehrabian that the "contribution of our actions rather than our speech is especially important, since it is inseparable

---

44. Perls, *Gestalt Therapy Verbatim,* p. 4.

from the feelings that we knowingly or inadvertently project in our everyday social interaction and determines the effectiveness and well-being of our intimate, social, and working relationships."[45]

45. Mehrabian, *Silent Messages,* p. iii.

# 5

# Words and Meanings

The verbal process in communication is considered to be *the* truly human process. This chapter is concerned with the seemingly unique human ability to conceive and use language and in so doing, to transform our worlds symbolically.

Before we continue, analyze the following exchange. Try to determine from this simple example some of the reasons that language is important in enabling us to be fully functioning human beings.

*Pete:*   Did you decide to take that survey course in philosophy?

*Cathy:*  No, Sherry told me it was really a bear last quarter when she took it and I figured I didn't need that hassle. I'm too uptight about grades as it is.

*Pete:*   Well, what are you going to do to fulfill your humanities requirement?

*Cathy:*  I think I'll wait for that new course, "The Images of Man," that's being advertised for next quarter. It's supposed to be relevant and the prof isn't too hard.

*Pete:*   Sounds like a decent idea. I'll check it out.

## Definition of Verbal Communication

One of the ways to isolate and define verbal communication is to differentiate it from nonverbal communication, the concept we explored in our last chapter.

While nonverbal communication is continuous, verbal communication is *discrete* and *intermittent.* Even if we are just staring off into space with blank looks on our faces, we are communicating something to those who observe us. Usually we are in constant motion and therefore communicating nonverbally: we are tapping our fingers, playing with the cuffs on our pants, crossing one leg over the other, jiggling our feet. Verbal communication, on the other hand, is characterized by stops and starts. Even people who seem to talk incessantly have beginnings and endings to their utterances. Parts of our bodies are always in motion, our mouths (or our hands for writing) are not always engaged.

Language is also discrete in that a word standing alone generally does not have meaning, and if it does, it is usually the nonverbal vocal component that has given it meaning. For example, "dog" means little by itself, but with the nonverbal added, it might mean: "There is a dog," "Watch out! You'll hit the dog!", "There's a dog chasing us." We must hear an utterance through to the end to gain meaning; we must put together all those separate symbols to transmit or perceive a complete thought. We do not have the same problem with completion in nonverbal communication because it is never-ending. It can be observed and assessed at any time we are in the presence of another, and, if we are perceptive, we can derive immediate meaning from nonverbal behavior.

Nonverbal communication is generally more *natural* and *spontaneous,* while verbal communication is *arbitrary, conventional,* and *learned* (there are, of course, nonverbal signals, such as a handshake which are also conventional and learned). The infant does not have to be taught to smile and laugh when he is happy to see his mother, nor to reach out for the new toy he wants, nor to cry when he is uncomfortable in a dirty diaper. Even though anthropologists like Edward T. Hall have found a number of cross-cultural differences in nonverbal communication,[1] there are, nevertheless, certain cultural similarities, such as raising the eyebrows as a sign of recognition.

---

1. See Edward T. Hall, *The Silent Language* (Greenwich, Conn.: Fawcett, 1959); and *Hidden Dimensions* (New York: Doubleday, 1966).

Language, on the other hand, because it means only what we choose it to mean, and because we agree that "friend," for example, will refer to "a person we regard with affection," must be learned and acquired.

Because nonverbal communication appears to arise spontaneously, it is less subject to control than verbal communication and is therefore best for expressing *emotion* clearly and honestly. We do learn, of course, to exert partial control over our nonverbal communication— we learn not to touch or not to react with a frown or smile, but we never achieve complete control over our vocal and bodily reactions. Language, however, is under our control. We learn to pick the precise word to convey an idea. For this reason, language is best suited for expressing mental concepts; we can abstract, generalize, and create; we can talk about love, Irishmen, and unicorns—activities that are not possible in nonverbal communication. We have the opportunity to think before we speak, and we can control what we say. It is much easier to disguise true feelings by verbal communication than it is by nonverbal communication. We can avoid saying, "My feelings are hurt"; we may not be able to avoid crying.

What then, exactly, is verbal communication? It can be considered as so much a part of us that we assume it doesn't need analysis and explanation. "Why, it's words. Words put together to form ideas. Everybody knows what language is." But language has definite characteristics, so let's explore the concept further and move beyond common sense notions of language. From our reading, we can identify four basic characteristics on which nearly all linguists agree:[2] (1) Language has sound. (2) Language has structure. (3) Language has rules. (4) Language has meaning.

*Language has sound.* Even written language or sign language is based on spoken language; i.e., all human languages are based primarily on a system of oral transmission and aural reception. We form sounds with our vocal mechanisms and receive them through our hearing mechanisms. Sound is such an integral part of language that we can almost "hear" words as we read. Though phonetics, the branch of linguistics which studies the production and combination of speech sounds, is important to a thorough understanding of lan-

---

2. See, for example, Archibald A. Hill, *Introduction to Linguistic Structures* (New York: Harcourt, Brace, and World, 1958), pp. 1–12; Robert A. Hall, Jr., *Leave Your Language Alone* (New York: Linguistica, 1950), pp. 53–119; Suzanne K. Langer, "The Origins of Speech and Its Communicative Function," in James W. Gibson, ed., *A Reader in Speech Communication* (New York: McGraw-Hill, 1971), pp. 87–93; Mario Pei, *The Story of Language* (Philadelphia: J. B. Lippincott, 1949), pp. 95–148.

guage, it is not the characteristic which most interests us in dealing
with language in interpersonal communication.

*Language has structure.* Language in any culture is systematic. It
has, in the proper terminology, syntax. In other words, in each culture, there are certain correct ways to combine sounds, words, and
phrases. For example, you would know immediately that there is
something wrong with the utterance, "Gary Ann to the birthday card
gave." In our language, the correct combination would be: "Gary
gave the birthday card to Ann," where (if we remember our English
grammar correctly) with these words given, the "natural" way to
structure them is subject-verb-object-indirect object. When we grow
up with a language, we seem to sense the proper combination intuitively. Of course, because that language which pervades our environment is the one whose sounds and structures we adopt, we often find
it difficult to learn another language whose sounds and structures
differ from our own.

*Language has rules.* It follows from the above two characteristics
that once the sounds and structure of a language are identified and
described, the system will become codified and rules will be formed.
All of us have had experiences when we have been "ungrammatical,"
i.e., we didn't follow language rules properly and we were chastised
for it. Children's first attempts to talk are often laughable because they
are ungrammatical, such as "The mices runs into the hole." Though
language instructors try to be broadminded, they are sometimes ap-
palled at violations of the most elementary rules of grammar, such as
"I have went to the ad building and I see the registrar." Though what
is said may be perfectly understandable, there is something that
doesn't quite "sit right" about a statement phrased that way.

For the sake of how persons come across interpersonally, perhaps
it is best to master those rules of grammar which may have not been
absorbed naturally from our environment. Likewise, there are certain
standards or rules of pronunciation. Regardless of talk about as-long-
as-it-has-meaning-it-is-acceptable, others will react if you pronounce
a word differently from them, regardless of whether they understand
the word or not. In "educated" circles, one says "re*search*" not "*re*-
search." The point here is not that there is any inherently correct way
to sound a word or to structure a sentence. It is merely that if we wish
to communicate effectively on an interpersonal level, we will try to
direct attention to the *meaning* of what we are saying. We are most
successful in focusing on meaning when we do not attract attention
to our utterances by violating the norms of pronunciation and grammar of the people we are talking to. (If the last sentence bothered you,

you have as a standard that one should never end a sentence with a preposition. And if you were thinking "How can they talk about grammar and then structure a sentence that way?" the point is made. Attention was drawn to something other than meaning, and the meaning, which is most important, was lost.)

*Language has meaning.* Obviously, to many, this is the most important characteristic of language. The fact that language has sound, structure, and rules is subordinate to the fact that it has meaning and useful only to the degree that it aids us in making our interpersonal communication more meaningful and clear. Because the transmission of meaning is so important to our personal, social and cultural existence, language is often characterized as an *instrument,* i.e., its main use is to help us achieve some other end, whether it be personal or social, practical or aesthetic.

We can see the importance of meaning in such questions as: "Do you mean that . . . ?", "How do you mean . . . ?", "Am I correct in assuming that your meaning is . . . ?", where the person interrogating is trying to determine what we think or feel or want him to think or feel or do.

As we indicated in our beginning chapters, language has meaning because it is symbolic. It represents or refers to something other than itself. It is by this symbolizing, representation, and reference that the words which compose a language come to *mean.* Likewise, a word is a symbol of something. The something to which a word points or generates thought about is called a referent. It is important to note here that we are not just concerned with two notions—those of symbol and referent—but also of thought. Consider the semantic triangle shown in figure 6.[3]

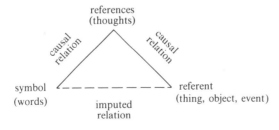

**FIGURE 6**

3. I. A. Richards and C. K. Ogden, *The Meaning of Meaning* (New York: Harcourt, Brace, Jovanovich, 19). Ogden and Richards exclude attitude and emotion from the "reference" wishing to consider only those symbols which are subject to verification in external reality.

As you can see from the diagram there is no direct or inherent relation between the symbol and the referent. The only relation the symbol has to the referent is that which *we* give it, in thinking about

it. For example, "cat" refers to       only because in our mind

such an image is created. If we so thought, "cat" could refer to

for us. We must remember that the only reason certain

words seem "proper" in referring to certain things is that we have agreed to use them in that way. This is what we meant by saying that language is conventional and arbitrary. At one time, someone chose the word "house" and established the convention that it should refer

to structures suitable for habitation similar to    . There is no

inherent reason for "house" to be the symbol for      .

As commonsensical as this sounds, we know many people who believe that a word can mean only one thing, that it has a "proper" or "correct" definition, or that because a word exists, the thing or concept does also. People will argue interminably over the symbols "democracy," "religion," "love," or even "interpersonal communication," believing that there is only one true meaning of each term. Or people will say, "You don't look like a 'Mary,' " and proceed to use another name for the person who doesn't fit their proper concept of a "Mary." Or people will persist in believing that things such as heaven, mermaids, and democracy exist because there happens to be a word for these concepts. In other words, because a symbol exists, there is no guarantee that something "out there" to which it refers exists. In addition, there is only the slightest possibility that everyone thinks about the same referent when a particular symbol is used.

This discussion is not meant to imply that we should be frivolous with words, that on whim or impulse we should call what is conventionally symbolized as "friend," "enemy," or call what is conventionally symbolized as "baby," "chimpanzee." There is good reason for the use of convention. It enables us to communicate more swiftly and efficiently than we could if we had to stop and decide on a symbol for everything we wished to discuss. For that reason, if we want to communicate effectively, we should abide by convention and not just use symbols "as the spirit moves us." On the other hand, we want to be aware of this distinction between symbol and referent, and the mediating influence of our minds in using words. In this way, we will be more open to the possibility that thoughts about referents other than our own do exist, and can be just as valid as ours, and that others' language is always influenced by their own experiences; it has its own "to-me-ness" quality about it. It is only through understanding this distinction that we will be able to communicate effectively on an interpersonal level—that we will really get to the *meaning* of what another is saying to us.

At this point we would like to share with you some relevant contributions that noted general semanticists (people who are concerned with the scientific study of symbols and how people respond to them) have made to our understanding of meaning in language.[4]

The three basic premises of general semantics are non-identity, non-allness and self-reflexiveness. The principle of *non-identity* states that the word is not the thing it refers to, or to use the semanticists favorite analogy, "the map is not the territory." A map may be a very accurate representation of a particular territory or it may be a very inaccurate representation with streets misnamed and buildings misplaced—whichever it is, it is not the *same thing* as the territory. The map is only a *symbol* of the territory.

The principle of *non-allness* states that a word can never express all there is to know about anything. The term "interpersonal communication" does not tell us who is involved, what their relationship is, how they feel about each other, how their beliefs coincide or differ, etc. The reason that a word can't tell us all there is to know about anything is that a word or symbol is an abstraction from the person, object, or event as it exists and as we perceive it on a physical level in reality. Of course, our direct perception of anything is in itself an abstraction. Let's say that we look at a friend. We see that he has blond hair and blue eyes, that he is six feet tall, about 190 pounds, that he has on plaid slacks and a blue pullover, that he sits slumped in his chair while listening to us talk. There is much more that we can perceive, of course, but it would take a chapter to detail everything. But what about those things we can't perceive on the direct level? A stomach ache, ambitions to be a ball player, fond thoughts of a certain woman. So we take all those things we can't perceive, all those many things we can, and abstract all of that into a name. And we can

---

4. See Wendell Johnson, *People in Quandaries: The Semantics of Personal Adjustment* (New York: Harper, 1946); S. I. Hayakawa, *Language in Thought and Action,* 3d ed. (New York: Harcourt, Brace, Jovanovich, 1972); Irving J. Lee, *Language Habits in Human Affairs: An Introduction to General Semantics* (New York: Harper, 1941).

abstract that much further. The observable person is abstracted into "male friend," which is abstracted into "human being," etc. This process of abstraction, of each symbol being more general and encompassing more than the one that went before it, can be characterized clearly by semanticist S. I. Hayakawa's "ladder of abstraction"[5] shown in figure 7.

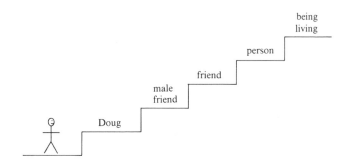

**FIGURE 7**

The farther we move up the ladder the more general, abstract, and to use the semanticists' term, "intensional" we get. That is, we get away from the specific, the concrete, and the "extensional." What the semanticist wishes to stress by this diagram is that we cannot know *all* unique individual differences in the first place; and second, the more we abstract, the less we can acknowledge the person's idiosyncracies we *do* know. This is the reason that semanticists use the indexing system, quotation marks, and etc.[6]

The indexing system, using subscript numbers, reminds us that $friend_1$ is not $friend_2$, that each of our friends has his or her own unique characteristics which in combination make him or her unlike any other friend. The quotation marks remind us that when we talk about a "friend," we are working from our own particular conception of and generalizations about friends or that we are using a term that can be conceived of in many different ways, such as "love." The abbreviation "etc.," which means "and so forth," reminds us that there is always much more that can be said about anything.

Another notion included in the principle of non-allness holds that one reason that we can't say everything about anything is that reality is dynamic, ongoing, changing, and fluctuating. You are not the per-

5. Hayakawa, *Language in Thought and Action,* p. 153.
6. Johnson, *People in Quandaries.*

son today that you were ten years ago, five years ago, a month ago, or even a day ago. You, because of exposure to experience, are constantly changing. Therefore, for us to regard friend "Doug" as the same type of friend he was last year is in violation of a semantic principle. An unreliable friend *can* turn into a dependable friend, a lazy student can turn into a dynamo. The semantic device used to remind us of change is called "dating," so that we would speak of Doug$_{1973}$ and Doug$_{1974}$. In 1973 perhaps Doug was just an acquaintance. In 1974 Doug may have become a close friend with whom we can communicate on a much deeper, more personal level.

The principle of *self-reflexiveness* states that words can be used at different levels, that statements can be made about statements. One can understand this principle more clearly by the analogy of taking a picture of oneself in a mirror taking a picture of oneself in a mirror, and so on. The process can go on indefinitely. For example, we can use the word "interpersonal communication" to refer to a unique relationship we have or to all face-to-face interaction involving two or more people. A symbol is not in itself abstract or concrete and the semanticist cautions us to indicate how we are using it.

Words can also be made about words and statements made about statements. Definitions do this. Look up the word "friend" and you will find initially "an intimate and trustworthy companion." You can then proceed to find other statements about the symbols "intimate" and "trustworthy," and so on indefinitely.

Language, then, is a symbolic system instrumental in the transmission of meaning. By its nature it is abstract and discrete and exists in a particular form only because we agree that it shall. When we use language, we always tell something about ourselves, for it is our thoughts that mediate between the word and the thing it represents.

We have implicitly indicated some of the reasons why an understanding of language is important to us. Now, let's discuss these reasons in more detail.

## The Importance of Language

Using language is a very human activity. It has often been said that the ability to use language is one of the main characteristics that separates man from the animal. Although communicologists have discussed with students the possibility that porpoises and chimpanzees have a language similar to humans, there is not adequate proof as yet that animal language can approach the sophistication and depth of meaning of human language.

There are two main characteristics generally thought to separate human language from animal language. The first is that human language is *time-binding*. We are not restricted to talking only about the present, about the here and now. We can re-create the past and create the future. Even in the simplest conversation, as the example at the beginning of the chapter shows, we can move ourselves through time by our language. Because of language, we can "stand on the shoulders" of the men of the past; we are not condemned to learn everything anew nor to solve present-day problems by trial and error. Though some would argue that we don't do a very good job of learning from history, our language has preserved our past and we can take advantage of it if we so desire. Take a simple activity like conversation at a party. Aside from the fact that we need language to converse, think about how time consuming it would be if no rules for the etiquette of conversation had been preserved. Each of us would have to work out his own system. Without language, we should be doing everything for the first time as if it had never been done before. Language, by giving us access to the past, helps us live more efficiently in the present.

We can also create our future through language. At one time putting a person on the moon was just talk, but our talk can materialize into a new reality. If you say simply, "I'm going to marry that girl," you might be creating your future. Now, of course, some language never materializes into reality and it is often well that it doesn't. The point is that language gives us the *potential* for dreaming of, conceiving and building new worlds. Every day there are millions of people envisioning a new and better life through language. We do not know that porpoises talk about different oceans with friendlier fish; we do know that man talks about a world free from war and poverty and disease. Wendell Johnson sums up this notion of time-binding: "To be human is to speak. . . . To be more human is to speak and listen too. And to be most human of all is to communicate cooperatively over the widest possible range of space and into the farthest reaches of the past and future."[7]

Another characteristic that separates our language from animal language is that human language can reflect *self-awareness*. Though

---

7. Wendell Johnson and Dorothy Moeller, *Living with Change: The Semantics of Coping* (New York: Harper & Row, 1972), p. 14.

animals do communicate by sound (such things as danger or where to get food) they cannot communicate in detail what is going on in their heads. We, as human beings, can. We can describe our thought processes. For example, you can tell another that you decided to go to college because you thought you would get a more satisfying job with more prestige and better pay. You can verbalize a problem such as trouble communicating with your parents and tell another how you reached the decision to stop trying to explain your life style to them. You can also describe your emotions. You can tell another that you feel frustrated at home or happy at school or angry with your lover. As far as we know at this point, only humans can describe what they are thinking, feeling, and doing and why.

Our brains appear to be what really separate us from the animal. We seem to have the mental capacity for conceptualization that far surpasses any other living being. We form concepts, categories, or images, i.e., we impose a human construction on a multitude of persons, objects, and events to bring order to our world. These categories, based on perceived similarities, are given names and the names become a part of our language. In order to make sense out of your university world, you may have formed the categories of administrator, staff, faculty, students, sorority and fraternity people, freaks, etc. Although one person's set of similarities may differ from everyone else's—for example, he or she may perceive a "freak" as anyone who has long hair and wears beads—there will be a method to the categorization and "naming." Therefore, language and our use of it is one evidence of this ability to abstract. So, if we are interested in understanding what makes us human, we will study our language. We will want to discover how we use language in an attempt to control, not only ourselves and our interpersonal relations, but also our world.

## Uses of Language

As we communicate on different levels, we of necessity use language on different levels. We have seen that one can communicate on an intrapersonal, interpersonal, public, or cultural level. As the situation and goal change, so must our communication and, therefore, our language. We will now turn to the various uses of language and discuss each one in turn: thinking, expressing, informing, persuading.

*Thinking*

It seems safe to say that we make use of language when we think. There are some who hold that language is a prerequisite to thought,[8] that when we see a newborn infant reach for a jingling key chain, he is not thinking, but simply reacting to the noise in a reflexive way.

It does seem impossible to conceive of thinking without the use of language. Now, you might say, "Well, when a car pulls in front of me and I swerve to avoid a collision, I thought what to do and didn't use any language." We could explain incidents like this as conditioned reflex action, as habits so well ingrained that thought is not necessary and action is automatic. At the time you were learning to drive, it was necessary *then* to think, to use language. You probably silently verbalized to yourself something like, "Foot off accelerator. Foot on brake."

When we think, we use the language categories or concepts available to us. Our concepts are on varying levels of abstraction from the category of one, the woman-in-the-room-across-the-hall, to a more abstract concept, women-who-live-in-my-apartment-building, to an even more abstract concept, "women." The concepts with which we think, then, can be very specific and concrete or abstract and general.

For example, suppose a person is thinking about changing jobs. "It'll be a good move. I'll be supervisor and able to make my own decisions without a 'boss' on my back telling me what to do. On the other hand, I'll be making less money at first, so I won't be able to buy a car. Well, it's worth it to be free." In this example many concepts occur at various levels of abstraction. "Boss" is very specific and refers to a category of one; "car" is more general since it is not specified what car. "Free" is probably the most general concept in the thought because it is the most intangible.

Now, the fact that we use concepts when we think really doesn't mean too much by itself. What is of importance is the quality and accuracy of those concepts, i.e., how well they correspond to reality, their "veridicality." The concepts we form affect our use of language, our use of language affects our thinking, and our thinking affects our actions.

The concepts that we form and the way that we use them are affected by our beliefs, attitudes, and values as discussed in chapter 2, and might be considered synonomous with images discussed in that and the following chapter. Our concepts, categories, or the names that we attach to things shape our world in no uncertain terms.[9] If your

---

8. Roger Brown, *Words and Things* (Glencoe, Ill.: Free Press, 1958), p. 8.
9. Ibid., p. 7.

concept of instructors is that they can't do anything in the real world and that is why they teach, and that they are all insecure, lazy, and really hate students, that concept will shape your world. If you categorize every football player as a dumb jock who doesn't know anything and is having it easy with a scholarship and lenient instructors, that categorization will shape your world. If you name as evil every magazine that prints obscenities, then that naming will shape your world. The point is: Are we shaping our worlds accurately?

The semanticists gently remind us that the more we attend to the principles of semantics, the more accurately our language reflects the real world and therefore the more accurate our thinking is.

> As he becomes conscious of abstracting he becomes conscious of perception and projection and of language as a self-stimulating mechanism that affects ... our *thinking*. ... He sees that if he is going to think differently ... he must talk a different language. Because language is basic. And so he develops a language with much to-me-ness in it. ... When he fails to do this he can live a life of constant combat in the shadows. He does this linguistically. How else? Not bothering to observe very much, he talks himself into more problems than he has. ... But once he begins to look around and to talk about what he can observe, once he begins to describe what he sees and does ... then he knows what he is talking about as he never knew before and he is talking about something he can do something about.[10]

The main result of the semantic approach to language in thinking is that, being aware of uniqueness, difference, change, and process, we develop a multivalued orientation toward life rather than a two-valued orientation. For example, rather than seeing another as either honest or dishonest, warm or distant, smart or dumb, we recognize that the other can be partially honest, warm with a select number of people, and smart in math. The semanticist holds that a two-valued, black or white approach to language is not only inaccurate but dreadfully unhealthy. The multivalued orientation, on the other hand, preserves sanity because it is a truly scientific approach to language and life.

Previously we have suggested examples of two-valued orientation. All instructors are lazy, insecure, and hate students. All football players are dumb. All pictures of nude people are evil. There is no middle ground here, no room for the possibility of a confident instructor, intelligent football player, or aesthetically pleasing picture of a

10. Johnson and Moeller, pp. 115, 116.

nude person. If we form our concepts with a multivalued orientation we will still generalize, because that is necessary to the order and structure in our world. But we will generalize with a view to individual differences and the fact that things change. Multivalued orientation allows us to form concepts more flexibly, to use language more flexibly, to communicate intepersonally more flexibly, and therefore to live more flexibly. If our use of language can do that for us in our daily decisions and control of our world, the semanticist says we are approaching life sanely.

## Expressing

We use language to express ourselves for ourselves and for others. The main characteristic of expressive language is that it is consummatory, it is an end in itself, rather than instrumental or a means to some other end.

Psychologist Abraham Maslow helps us in making the following distinctions between coping (instrumental) and expressive (consummatory) behavior which can be applied to the use of language.

1. Coping is purposeful; expression is not.
2. Coping is determined by the external environment; expression is determined by the internal state of the organism.
3. Coping is learned; expression is unlearned or released.
4. Coping is more easily controlled; expression is uncontrolled or uncontrollable.
5. Coping is designed to cause changes in the environment; expression is not designed to do anything.
6. Coping usually means behavior directed toward some end; expression is an end in itself.
7. Coping is effortful; expression is effortless.[11]

In expressing ourselves for ourselves we use language in different forms to express different emotions. We tend to use language as we have described it in oral or written form. Although much self-expression can be realized through the various art forms of painting, sculpture, dance, and music and each can be rightly considered to have its own language, we are not concerned here with symbol systems other than the verbal.

We express ourselves for ourselves orally by speaking out loud. The range of emotions that we can express seems to be unlimited. In the

11. Abraham Maslow, *Motivation and Personality,* 2d ed. (New York: Harper and Row, 1970), p. 132.

following examples, we are sure that you will find some that apply to you, to thoughts and emotions you have experienced, and to the ways that you chose to deal with them.

Probably the main use of expression for ourselves is release of tension or catharsis, and probably more often than not the tension that needs to be released is anger. Consider Vic who jogs every morning and, if he is angry, swears in cadence to release the tension. But for Bev things are not so well planned. Her tension is released in explosive spurts when the bread burns, the dryer breaks, the battery dies, or someone calls an unscheduled meeting. Perhaps the example most familiar to all of us is driving a car. Other motorists seem to exist to create tension and anger in us which needs to be released vociferously. We doubt that you have not exploded in anger at a motorist cutting in front of you, or turning from a wrong lane, or stopping at a yield sign on the entrance to a freeway. Being a student also seems to create tension that needs to be released. Many instructors have their own amusing memories of obscenities being shouted down empty halls or echoing behind closed doors. And we witness this self-expression in our own students. One of them, after taking a test on which he felt he performed poorly, handed his paper in, walked down the hall, opened the door to the stairwell, yelled a number of words, then returned to the classroom with a peaceful smile.

Another emotion released in expression for ourselves is disgust. There have been days when both of us have sat at our desks as all absent-minded instructors allegedly do, talking to ourselves in recriminating tones: "I shouldn't have put off that report until the last minute. Now I have all these essay tests to grade and I'll never get it done. Why didn't I give an objective test, so the secretary could grade it. Because my students hate objective tests. My students hate *any* kind of test. I shouldn't listen to them so much. . . ." And most of us have expressed ourselves in the typical, "Now why did I say_____? I should've known he would react that way. Now it'll take me ages to set things right again."

We also express ourselves for joy. We may express joy vocally over a beautiful day, a new found love, a hard-won accomplishment. Though not commonly thought of as a tension, we have all had moments where happiness fills and overwhelms us so much that we must let it out; we must emote and express.

Sorrow is also an emotion that needs to be expressed. If we have just lost someone or something that is very dear or important to us, we often express our grief by talking, though no one else is there.

There are, of course, many other emotions that we could catalog, such as fear, surprise, despair, etc., but we believe that the point has been made that at times we engage in talk only for the sake of itself and for ourselves and the release of emotion.

Though occurring less often, we also talk through new ideas and problems that we need to clarify for ourselves. Our language for this purpose will utilize full and more sophisticated sentences rather than the short phrases and exclamations of the expression of emotion. Some people try to figure out budgets in their heads. Since this seems to be a very difficult task it helps to verbalize the thinking process when there is not pen and paper available.

When we do have pen and paper available, there is often the urge to "put it down in writing," to get it out there instead of inside our heads. When we feel depressed and the reason is not immediately apparent, we may write down the day's events to enable us to locate the cause of the problem, what exactly has disturbed us. Writing, then, is the second form that expression for ouselves takes.

We often write thoughts and feelings down and tear them up, as if doing that destroys the original thought or feeling. On the other hand, sometimes it makes the thought or feeling more real to us. People may share with others thoughts and feelings that were initially written only for themselves, and among them may be fine and beautiful poetry and literature, because they were written not to *impress,* but only to *express.*

We also use language to express ourselves for others. It is much more difficult to be sure that this is really always expression, however, because often it is really persuasion. We are saying what we are saying to influence the other person in some way and our language is being used instrumentally rather than consummatorily. For example, if we say to someone, "Now I'm just expressing myself, but I really like it when you wear brown instead of blue," are we just expressing ourselves or do we want the other to act on what we are saying and wear brown instead of blue? Or we write to a loved one and say, "Now I don't want a response to this, I just want to tell you that it really irritates me that you don't write more often." This may be persuasion in the guise of expression and what we really desire is to change the other person's behavior. We want more letters. So the line is a difficult one to draw. There are many communicologists[12] who say that there is no such thing as pure expression, that all communication directed to another person is persuasion because it is designed to be instrumen-

12. Hayakawa, *Language in Thought and Action,* pp. 192–217.

tal in reinforcing and/or changing behavior. Though the distinction is difficult to make, we believe it can be made.

We believe with others who have been fortunate enough to find true dialogic friendships that it is possible to express ourselves in the presence of another empathic and accepting person without thinking of persuasion. Most of us have devoted friends who will just sit with us and listen to us rant and rave about the latest blow the world has dealt us. Or, on a different day, they may listen to us talk like teenagers about how lucky we are to have such wonderful friends or fortunate circumstances. Perhaps the key here is that the talk is about something other than the relationship between the person doing the expressing and the person listening. For if language is used positively, as in, "I sure appreciate it when you listen to me like that," perhaps subconsciously we want to reinforce the listening behavior. If language is used negatively as in, "I wish you would look at me when I'm talking," perhaps subconsciously we are attempting to change the listening behavior. It may be that when we communicate to another *about the other or the relationship,* we are always directly or indirectly attempting to get them to see things the way we do, to get them to accept our concepts, names, and images.

Be that as it may, we have isolated the use of language for expression—talking or writing when there is no purpose other than to let it all hang out. In expressing ourselves for ourselves or others we seem to be fulfilling a need to release stored up emotion, to clarify our thoughts and ideas, and to let others know a bit more about us.

## Informing

We also use language to inform, to transmit new facts and ideas, or to increase understanding of familiar facts and ideas. Informing is different from expressing in that it tends to deal with the objective world more than the individual's subjective world and always involves at least one other person. Informing is often contrasted with persuading or influencing in the same way that expressing is. Informing is said to be consummatory communication; we are communicating only to transmit information, not to influence beliefs, attitudes, values, or behavior. Rhetorician Karl Wallace provides a very convincing argument that informative communication has two persuasive assumptions at its base: (1) that this knowledge is important to you; and (2) that what I am going to tell you is true.[13] Usually, we try to escape

13. Karl Wallace, "The Substance of Rhetoric: Good Reasons," in J. Jeffrey Auer, ed., *The Rhetoric of Our Times* (New York: Appleton-Century Crofts, 1969).

this dilemma by suggesting that all communication takes place on a continuum, with the extremes being consummatory and instrumental. In this way we can see that informative communication will have a certain amount of persuasion and vice versa.

You are undoubtedly familiar with examples of primarily informative communication: directions to the administration building, instructions for hanging a picture, most college class lectures. Again, informative communication is a language use that we're sure we know-it-when-we-hear-it.

Two cautions about informative communication are in order here if we are to better recognize, understand, and utilize this type of language. First, we must remember that when some people appear to be informing they are really persuading, as we found to be the case in expressing. This appearance can be maintained consciously or unconsciously. It is to our benefit to be aware that the concepts, names, and images people possess direct the selection of the information they will transmit to us. This selection process and focus on certain aspects of a subject rather than others is a natural and necessary human use of language. The purpose in focusing awareness on this is not to accuse others of distorting, but to make us more alert to the possibility that we probably are not getting the "whole story" from anyone.

In some classes the instructor's biases may lead him to portray capitalism or religion as an evil. Or transcendental meditation or astrology may be revealed through the instructor's language to be the answer to everything. Or an instructor might indicate by what she chooses to relate that there is only one approach to reading or math in education. Our own humanistic biases have led us to stress and include certain information and only touch upon or omit other information, which should make you aware of how our concepts are directing our use of language.

The second caution is that we need to know the difference between reports, inferences, and evaluations.[14] These are all used in informative communication, and the first two legitimately so, but the distinction between them is often muddled and needs to be clarified. Read the following three statements:

1. Cindy's book hit the table with a loud noise.
2. Cindy slammed her book on the table in anger.
3. Cindy certainly is a temperamental person.

14. Hayakawa, *Language in Thought and Action,* pp. 34–48.

The first statement is a report. It uses the language of description and the concepts are specific and concrete observable events. This is factual information because it can be verified by another observer. We can see the book hit and hear the noise.

The second statement is an inference. It uses the language of induction, and the concepts become more general and abstract. This is conclusion-drawing because the person making the statement is going beyond what can be observed and described. "Slammed in anger" is inferring a purpose and emotion that can be verified only by asking the person if she did, in fact, slam the book (it could have fallen) and if so, was it because she was angry (she could be playfully attempting to get attention). The point is not that we should *not* draw inferences —we have to live and the verified facts will never all be apparent for us to make a completely accurate inference. Rather, we should note the difference between the two types of statements and be careful not to pass off a conclusion derived *from* facts as a fact itself.

The third statement is an evaluation. It uses the language of judgment and the concepts are the most general and abstract. This is the level of valuing because the person making the statement is not only going beyond what he can observe, he is expressing a subjective opinion. An evaluation can never really be true or false as reports and inferences can be, it can only be agreed or disagreed with. You think Cindy is temperamental and if your friend says, "Boy are you right," he is agreeing with your subjective judgment because his is similar. Mutual agreement does not, however, make the statement true. The language of evaluation must also be used in communication because it is with the help of evaluation that we make our choices; however, it does not find its proper place in informative communication. Because it is subjective it is rightly used in expressing, and when it is used to seek agreement it is rightly used in persuasion.

With the understanding that much communication that appears to be informative and consummatory is not, we can discuss the final use of language.

### Persuading

The final way that language is used is to persuade or influence. When we persuade, we use language to effect some sort of change in belief, attitude, value, or behavior. Persuasion occurs on all levels, from the very simple to the very sophisticated, from the very trivial to the very crucial. Such diverse communications as, "Please pass the salt," "I really think that Bergman's 'The Lie' is superior to anything else that he's ever done," "I'd like you to pick up a *Time* from the drugstore," and "We believe that intercultural communication is the only key to world peace" are all persuasive; they are instrumental in accomplishing some goal of the person initiating the communication. As in all interpersonal communication, the initiator selects his words based on his own particular concepts and his communication is therefore personally biased. We are usually more aware of this process and more analytical of it when we recognize that the communication is persuasive.

There are any number of ways to classify the persuasive use of language and we will use a combination of two different approaches. The first is the use of language to achieve a certain goal (task or relationship goals are the basic ones suggested in chapter 3), that of influencing beliefs, attitudes, values and/or behavior. The second is the means by which these goals are accomplished, specifically the use of language to polarize or identify.

The first approach to persuasive communication is a traditional one, and focuses on the task or relationship *goal* our use of language is to effect. The goal may be to reinforce or change a belief. We may want to change another's belief that "no one can be trusted." The goal may be to reinforce or change an attitude. We may want to reinforce an already positive attitude toward "openness in communication." The goal may be to reinforce or change a value. We may want to increase the importance that the generalized value of "honesty" holds for another. Finally, the goal may be change or reinforcement of behavior. Though you will have to attend to beliefs, attitudes, and values to influence behavior, a change or reinforcement of a particular action, say, influencing another to tell you what is bothering him, is the ultimate goal.

The second approach to persuasive communication is more contemporary and focuses on the *means* to the goal, the language strategies that can be employed to achieve one of the objectives mentioned above. Though many have been identified, two appear to be superordinate to the rest: polarization and identification. When we use the language of polarization to achieve a communication goal, we force the other to stand in opposition to us, we antagonize him in the hopes that this strategy will effect change. For example, to change the belief that no one can be trusted we tell the other, "Only people who can't trust themselves can't trust others." By using this particular strategy, we are creating two mutually exclusive concepts: those who trust themselves and therefore others and those who do not trust themselves and therefore do not trust others. In this way we force the other to choose between the two, to be either with us or against us. When we use the language of identification we try to bring the other together with us, as rhetorician Kenneth Burke, originator of the concept, explained:

> Identification is compensatory to division. If men were not apart from one another, there would be no need . . . to proclaim their unity. If men were wholly and truly of one substance, absolute communication would be of man's very essence.[15]

Identification is an attempt to put you and the other in the same place. You want him to be with you rather than against you. For example, if your goal is to persuade the other to open up to you and tell you his problems, you might use the language strategy of identification by saying, "I know that sometimes it's difficult to talk about what's bothering you. I often feel that way, too. But I always feel better after I talk with someone I can trust who listens to me with sensitive understanding." Here you are using empathy, trying to "put yourself in the other's shoes" so that you can achieve your goal.

In passing we might note the difference in the length of the two approaches. It seems that polarization can be achieved much more quickly than identification. Identification takes time and effort and patience. We can push someone away rapidly, but to get another to follow where we lead is more difficult. Use of the language strategy of identification seems to be the most humanistic approach to persuasion.

It should be clear by now that through language we try to achieve structure and order in our world and control over it. So important is language that sociologist Hugh Duncan maintains that it is impossible to talk about human relationships without recognizing the force that language plays in shaping them. We live in a symbolic as well as a physical environment, says Duncan, and we must realize that "social structure . . . is created and sustained in symbolic action."[16]

We create our language to help us control our world, but our language can begin to control us. There are even some linguistic theorists, such as Benjamin Whorf, who maintain that our language shapes our way of perceiving and thinking, our philosophy of life, and

---

15. Kenneth Burke, "A Grammar of Motives and a Rhetoric of Motives," in Richard L. Johannesen, ed., *Contemporary Theories of Rhetoric: Selected Readings* (New York: Harper and Row, 1971), p. 84.

16. Hugh Dalzel Duncan, *Symbols in Society* (New York: Oxford University Press, 1968), p. 5.

ultimately our world. Because we have a number of different words for "automobile" and only one for "snow" we will have a different philosophy of life than the Eskimo who has various terms for snow. A professor once said, "We will march to our death for the symbols we have created." Another, reinforcing this point, added, "Man is on one hand blessed with the capacity to use symbols and on the other hand cursed by it. We are constantly trying to adapt to the symbols we have created. Man will be the first creature to die because he changed and created the environment that killed him." This unfortunately becomes apparent when we view the killing that has taken place in the name of "democracy" or "Christianity," or the evils that have been committed in the name of "progress" and "power," and the hurt that can be inflicted in the name of "honesty." This is what the semanticists have been saying all along. We must understand our language and keep it flexible so that we maintain control of it rather than allowing our symbols to control us.

# Summary

In this chapter we have tried to define and characterize language. Verbal communication differs from nonverbal communication because it is discrete, arbitrary, learned and controlled rather than continuous, natural, and spontaneous. We identified the four basic characteristics of language: sound, structure, rules, and meaning. Our greatest emphasis was on the characteristic of meaning and we explained in some depth exactly what meaning is. To do this we used the approach of the semanticist. We distinguished a symbol or word from its referent or what the word refers to. The only relation that the symbol has to the referent is an indirect one which takes place through our thought and conceptualizing processes. There are three basic principles of semantics: non-identity, non-allness, and self-reflexiveness. These principles emphasize uniqueness, difference, process, and change and our language use must be flexible rather than rigid in order to acknowledge these characteristics of human experience.

Having thus characterized language we pointed to its importance by suggesting that language is what makes man man. The ability to use language allows man to recreate the past and create the future, and in the present allows him to engage in the description and reporting of his own thought and emotional processes.

The last section of this chapter was devoted to exploring the different uses of language. We talked about the necessity of language in thinking and differentiated between expressive, informative, and persuasive uses of language. Expression is consummatory and attempts to relate the objective world to another; information transmits new thoughts and ideas; persuasion is instrumental as a means of changing or reinforcing beliefs, attitudes, values and/or behavior through the language strategies of polarization and identification.

Finally, we stressed the fact that not only do we shape our language but our language shapes us, and the symbols we create may even harm us.

# 6

# Minimizing
# Misunderstanding

Communication at its best achieves the lowest level of misunderstanding.[1] We should continually realize the importance of communication in achieving satisfaction and progress. The recognition that communication is a meaning-centered process in which language is crucial is essential to clear communication. We can minimize misunderstanding in our lives if we have a sound and thorough *understanding* of the ways in which nonverbal and verbal language operate and if we arm ourselves with some useful principles to apply in our interpersonal communication.

This chapter is a further exploration of the ideas and principles reviewed in chapters 4 and 5.

## Clarity or Ambiguity

"I WANT YOUR BODY!" What do you think and feel as you look at these four words? Is this statement clear? Imagine a metal button three inches in diameter with I WANT YOUR BODY printed in

---

1. John J. Makay and William R. Brown, *The Rhetorical Dialogue* (Dubuque: Wm. C. Brown, 1972), pp. 78–79.

large white letters on a black background. A class of students was asked to react to a hypothetical situation: What if you were crossing the campus and passed a professor who was wearing that button? What would you feel and think? From the 300 students in attendance in the lecture-discussion meeting, a wide range of reactions was heard. Some of them included the following statements: "You're not my type," a young man stated jokingly. "He must be a professor in anatomy, either looking for subjects or recruiting majors," a young woman volunteered. "He's sexually inhibited," offered one student. "No, just the opposite!" cried another.

Finally, the students were asked: "Is there anybody here who is clear about what these words are intended to mean by the originators of the message?" A lone hand went up and the young woman replied, "I saw some TV ad for a health club. I think the message is part of the commercial." This student was correct. A national health spa with local facilities was conducting another membership drive and the core statement for the messages was "I WANT YOUR BODY." As part of their campaign, members and employees were given buttons to draw attention to the organization's campaign. Both out of context and in context the phrase suggests a variety of meanings. Essentially, the intention was to attract people, especially young adults, to develop their physical appearance and thus become healthier and more attractive. The campaign involved both nonverbal and verbal messages. When the purpose becomes clear, the specific intention of the statement was to be persuasive in building membership.

Meanings are often not clear in interpersonal communication because communicators either intentionally or unintentionally confuse the forms and functions of language.

## Language: Forms and Functions

Makay and Brown indicate confusion in communication results when the intended function of a message is not identical with that suggested by the form. They point to five forms and five functions of languages and indicate how the intent, in terms of *form* and *function* of task-oriented messages, can invite approach and/or withdrawal responses in human behavior. This principle is not the exclusive principle for task-centered or content messages, but relational ones as well. The five types of form and function are: expressive, designative, interrogative, evaluative, and directive. The intended function of an expression may be *directive* while the form is *interrogative*. For example, suppose you and a friend are about to buy cokes from a vending machine and you discover you have no change. You would probably ask, "Do you have a quarter?" (interrogative form). You hope your friend will provide you with one (directive function). The form may be evaluative, "That book in our communication course is quite good, for a text," while the function may be expressive, "In making this statement I am showing you I am concerned about texts for my studies." Study table 1 to grasp this concept. Using simple statements about food, Makay and Brown reveal ways in which people may not say what they mean, or mean what they say, which can result in verbal games and misunderstanding.

### TABLE 1

| Message | Explicit Purpose (Form) | Potential Implicit Purpose (Function) |
|---|---|---|
| Expressive: report a state of being in self | I am hungry. | I am hungry.<br>Is food available?<br>Food is available.<br>Food is desirable.<br>Give me food. |
| Designative: report of external condition | Food is available. | Food is available.<br>I am hungry.<br>Food is desirable.<br>Give me food.<br>Is food available? |
| Interrogative: request for designative or expressive report | Is food available? | Is food available?<br>I am hungry.<br>Food is desirable.<br>Give me food.<br>Food is available. |
| Evaluative: value appraisal | Food is desirable. | Food is desirable.<br>I am hungry.<br>Food is available.<br>Is food available?<br>Give me food. |
| Directive: recommended or ordered action | Give me food. | Give me food<br>I am hungry.<br>Food is available.<br>Is food available?<br>Food is desirable. |

Reprinted from John J. Makay and William Brown, *The Rhetorical Dialogue: Contemporary Concepts and Cases* (Dubuque: Wm. C. Brown, 1972), p. 79, with permission of the publisher.

A communicator may give information with what appears to be an explicit purpose, while the implication, in a functional way, is quite different. The five message types can be useful in making form and function analyses for trying to understand ourselves and others in interpersonal communication settings. Consider, for example, that message form may be *designative*.

You: An X-rated film is now at the flick.

The intended function may be *evaluative*.

X-rated films are good films.

The intended function may be *interrogative*.

Should we attend the movie because it is X-rated?

The intended function may be *directive*.

We will see the X-rated film.

When we study the tabular information and the examples above we can easily conclude, "Why don't people say what they mean?" "Why aren't we clear in our speaking?" "Why not say what we mean in the first place?" "Be more specific." "What is it that we're getting at?"

The implied function, which is different from the form used, often involves relational messages as well as task-centered ones. For instance, consider Judy, a student undertaking an in-depth study of a nationally known figure who speaks frequently in public. In her effort to gain access to the man, she came to know his secretary reasonably well and his wife to a minimal extent. Both possessed positional power by virtue of their control of routes of access to him: they brought some things to his attention, and others they steered away. Both liked Judy, especially the secretary. Eventually, they were instrumental in setting up an important interview between the student and the famous spokesperson. Initially misunderstanding had to be eliminated. Some of the conversation between Judy and the secretary (p. 107) illustrates mixing forms and functions.

When we probe deeper into the uses of language and problems of misunderstanding two principles are most helpful: (1) words are not things and (2) maps are not territories. The first principle is a rule of semantics while the second is a primary one of general semantics.

| FORM | FUNCTION |
|------|----------|
| *Interrogative* | *Expressive* |
| Student: I realize Mr. X is very busy, but he isn't all tied up for the next two weeks. | I want to see and talk with Mr. X. |
| *Expressive/Interrogative* | *Directive* |
| Secretary: Well, he's awfully busy with legal matters; what sort of study are you doing, did you say? | I am not going to let just anybody get to my boss. |
| *Evaluative* | *Interrogative* |
| Student: I think Mr. X is one of the country's finest speakers, and as a graduate student, I plan to undertake a worthwhile analysis of Mr. X. | Won't you please let me see him? |
| *Expressive* | *Directive* |
| Secretary: I am the one who schedules appointments for Mr. X with persons whose requests are in the nature of yours, and you seem like such a sincere and nice person anyway. | You will be able to see Mr. X because I have made a decision to arrange your meeting. Be the kind of person I like so I can reward you. |

## Words Are Not Things

The semantic triangle in the chapter on verbal communication was used to describe the thought-word-thing relationship. Things (objects, events, and experiences) can be symbolized by the use of language. Symbols represent things, but words or symbols are not things.[2] When people fail to realize this principle communication misunderstandings result. Experience and research studies show that persons often act as if the word they are using is an actual object, or as if it has but *one* meaning—theirs. To the contrary, we have already realized that the

2. C. K. Ogden and I. A. Richards, *The Meaning of Meaning* (New York: Harcourt, Brace & World, 1923), pp. 1–23.

relationship between words and things is only implied. During the 1960s, for example, a word often used by student political and social activists was "revolution." The word frequently appeared in campus rhetoric as a part of incidents of campus unrest, which attracted the attention of thousands of citizens, many of whom listened and watched the activity broadcast by the news media. Is the *word* revolution a thing? Certainly not. It is a symbol which can represent wide varieties of things associated with change.

To further illustrate this principle let's examine the behavior of a young woman, Sandy, who is a college freshman. Sandy comes from a small rural village and has spent only several days on the campus, which has a student population of 40,000. Her family background is very conservative in social, political, religious, and economic matters and behavior. She has been feeling lonely and almost overwhelmed by the enormous campus and student population and has pressured herself into conforming to new behaviors to gain friendship with the women in her dorm. One moral rule she has lived by is that smoking is both unhealthy and immoral. Most of the women seem to smoke so she feels she may be able to diminish or remove social distance between her and them by learning to smoke. Late one night she creeps out of her room while her roommate is sleeping. She goes to the student lounge and buys a pack of cigarettes. Quickly, she walks back to her room and silently goes into the bathroom. She takes the matches her roommate left on the table. She lights up, sucks in hard on the cigarette, pulling the smoke back into her lungs, and then she begins to cough and choke. She becomes sick and feels guilt. The next morning a new acquaintance joins Sandy for breakfast in the dining hall. Jane is a smoker who loves her habit and every puff she takes on a cigarette. In a routine way after they are finished eating, she asks Sandy, "Do you want a cigarette?" and holds her open pack out. Sandy, remembering her dreadful experience the night before, turns pale and says, "No!"

The word *cigarette* is a key symbol verbally and in this case visually. On the one hand it means negative things and experiences to one communicator and on the other some things quite the opposite. Words are symbols often centered in thoughts, which have only an implied relationship with things. For the sake of interpersonal clarity and mutual understanding in communication we need to remember this principle and, thus, how words can work in the use of language.

## Maps and Territories

We may think that language is like a map and what it is used to discuss and describe can be regarded as a territory. Thus, the principle we need to understand is "the map is not the territory."

A crucial point to be considered is the relationship between language and reality, especially in the interpersonal context. General semanticists hold the view "except as we understand this relationship we run the grave risk of straining the delicate connection between words and facts, of permitting our words to go wild, and so creating for ourselves fabrications of fantasy and delusion."[3] A simple question to help us avoid running such a risk is: "Does the map fit the territory?"

Suppose you decide with a friend to travel by automobile throughout the western states. Certainly you would not plan your route with a map prepared in 1954. The travelers' facilities and the state and national highway systems have changed remarkably since then. If you spent several vacation months years ago in a tourist spot you would be naive to expect it to be today exactly like it was when you were last there. In a similar way when you use language to represent reality (in this sense you deal in symbolic realities), to be accurate and avoid misunderstanding your symbolic reality must correspond with that part of the real world with which you are dealing. Remember we spoke about the fact that a statement about reality does not represent *all* of anything because it is, on the verbal level, an abstraction about part of something, and it may or may not be an accurate and descriptive abstraction. One who, in interpersonal communication, speaks vaguely and is out of touch with reality will operate with a map that does not fit the territory. Furthermore, to minimize misunderstanding we need to be aware, as general semanticists point out, that what we see is only part of the real whole. Our language is thus part of the real whole.[4] (See figure 8.)

Language represents an abstracted part of the whole of an event, object, or experience, as maps depict selected aspects of territories. Perception was discussed specifically in chapters 2 and 3, and we recall that perceptive channel capacities, along with our selective

---

3. S. I. Hayakawa, *Language in Thought and Action,* 3d ed. (New York: Harcourt, Brace, Jovanovich, 1972), pp. 30–32.

4. John J. Makay and Thomas C. Sawyer, *Speech Communication Now!* (Columbus, O.: Charles E. Merrill, 1973), p. 183.

LANGUAGE

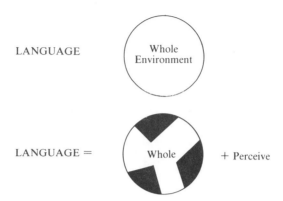

LANGUAGE =         + Perceive

**FIGURE 8**

perception behavior, govern how we symbolically represent parts of the whole in reality. When one's verbal map does not carefully represent the territory which is reality, confusion, misunderstanding, and a host of communication problems can result. Overall, a word which summarizes maximum meaning and understanding is clarity. In interpersonal communication, a sound way to validate whether your verbal map is realistic is to "check it out." Here we raise a highly pertinent question, "Do you want to check that out?"

## Do You Want to Check That Out?

Rather than take the responsibility for determining how others might react or respond toward us and what they mean by their words, we can check it out by asking them. Perhaps this sounds simple. Yet far too often in our lives misunderstandings develop basically because communicators do not check matters out through direct interpersonal communication.

In a small group setting a psychologist who was the group facilitator would contribute when he wanted to by facing another participant directly and saying, "I want to give you some information." Then very descriptively, as close to the object level as possible, he would give information which seemed very clear. Shortly after the group was underway others would do likewise. When someone, however, made a vague inference about the probable feelings and responses of others, the facilitator would say, "Do you want to check that out?" This was a reminder for the communicator to ask *everyone* in the group to tell how they felt and would respond. This can be illustrated by considering the behavior of Marilyn. She was an aggressive young woman who believed she figuratively suffocated her former husband by showering him with attention and making most social and economic decisions for him. She decided a number of her problems related to the fact that she did not have a strong and loving father, and this had been the case in her family life with father and mother since she was a child. At the suggestion of a member of the group she considered having an older male member of the group "parent her," in other words, act as her father might have acted toward her as a little girl, had he been a stronger and loving person. She, of course, would have to go back to age six (her current age was around twenty-four). She retreated from the suggestion because she was afraid she would look foolish. "Do you want to check that out?" She did, and asked each member of the group how they felt about the suggestion. To her amazement everyone affirmed it. Thus, for about an hour everyone experienced a warm father and daughter relationship in interpersonal communication.

As a result of this experience and other similar experiences, any time members of the group began to wonder how another felt about them during or after an interpersonal exchange of information, they tried to "check it out." They wanted to see if the verbal maps fit the perceived territory. In instances where another may not have the courage, trust, or desire to be open and unguarded, "checking" this person out may not produce a genuine response, and a confusing transaction could result. An intimate dyad or group experience is far more open and trusting than many day-to-day settings. Yet, *if we are not clear* about someone's feelings or meanings, expressed or implied, here's one practical question to guide us: "Do you want to check that out?" The best response is, "yes."

At this point you may wonder about clarity in relationship to nonverbal cues and language. From the onset of this chapter we have dealt solely with verbal clarification. At this point, then, we can turn to nonverbal communication.

## Checking Out
## Nonverbal Communication

In chapter 4 we suggest that the number and variety of nonverbal cues and clues can be long and wide as well as explicitly clear or implicitly vague. One way to achieve clarity is to think of nonverbal elements in terms of five subsystems in a message display system. The five subsystems are: illustrative, affective, regulatory, adaptive, and emblematic.[5] They are explained and differentiated in figure 9. Before examining the table remember several important principles. The display system is interpretive in analysis according to how communicators perceive intentions (theirs or the other's) in human transactions. The same nonverbal cue or clue may be related to more than one subsystem. A primary reason for considering the display system is to help us increase our sensitivity to nonverbal communication and how it helps to make meanings clear or foggy.

Suppose, as the information in figure 9 suggests, a communicator intends for behavior in one instance to convey his primary intention in concert with a verbal message. Perhaps, however, knowingly or unknowingly, he behaves simultaneously in a way which brings other subsystems into communicative play. Is it not probable, depending upon circumstances and relational/content goals, that implied intentions perceived by the other may significantly blur the primary intention? A listener who suddenly responds to a speaker's description of a personal tragedy may want to display affective signs, but by maintaining a frozen face, a sign of ambivalence, he may actually serve functionally in an emblematic way. These sorts of behaviors and meanings are active in interpersonal communication. Thus, we must learn to analyze and deal with them. What you display can seem to serve an explicit purpose, and at the same time other functions which serve the same or other implied purposes may be operating.

A problem in meaning becomes obvious when we try to make accurate judgments about whether nonverbal cues are intended to be illustrative, affective, regulatory, adaptive, or emblematic (perhaps the emblematic is not quite as bothersome as the first four). A communicator seeking to stress a shape by outstretched hands may be frowning, knowingly or unknowingly, so that the other reads *affective* or *adaptive* meaning, which may or may not be consciously implied by the speaker.

Nonverbal communication plays a vital role in interpersonal communication, and of course, in healthy or unhealthy human growth or productive or unproductive interpersonal relationships. We must be cautious about reading wrong meanings from the observation of nonverbal communication. Social psychologists tell us if eye contact serves both to communicate love and to communicate threat, for

---

5. *Social Psychology: Explorations in Understanding* (Del Mar, California: CRM Books, 1974), p. 91.

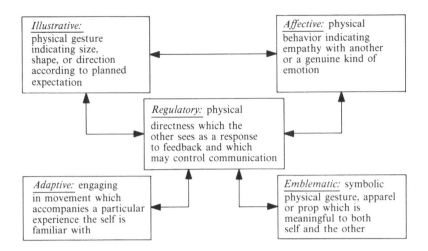

**FIGURE 9. Display System**

example, how is the receiver to know which message the sender is trying to convey? Perhaps because messages sent nonverbally are open to ambiguity, people use verbal channels more often than nonverbal channels for sending complex information.

We know that nonverbal communication is often planned by a communicator. For example, news commentator Paul Harvey uses nonverbal cues and symbols in numerous ways to enhance his verbal message. His facial expressions, dramatic pauses, careful manipulation of hands, and his lively and energetic voice seem planned and yet help him to communicate with clarity. What about the effect of nonverbal communication in an interpersonal setting where clarity is essential? To answer this, we can use five major questions to guide us in the examination of nonverbal communication for purposes of minimizing misunderstanding:

1. How does nonverbal communication affect my perception, inner map, and response when I am constructing the other in interpersonal communication?
2. What body language is operating and what does it seem to mean? What elements in the context, including the environment, seem designed or planned to enhance meaning?
3. What vocal features are being used and how do they affect perception in the communication setting?
4. What am I wearing and/or doing which sends nonverbal messages which are consistent and/or inconsistent with the meanings I intend to create?

We must remember to be cautious about meanings in nonverbal communication and, if we are experiencing difficulty because of nonverbal cues which seem to be distracting, we can ask ourselves, "Why don't I check that out?" An instructor in communications was lecturing a group of nurses one afternoon on the subject of nonverbal communication. Suddenly, in the middle of the period a young woman with a puzzled look on her face raised her hand and said, "You're talking to us about maximizing meaning in terms of nonverbal communication, and I am continually distracted by the thing you're wearing around your neck!" As she finished her statement about half the audience nodded in agreement. "The thing" the nurse referred to was an ankh in shining silver, set against a dark blue turtleneck sweater. "I didn't intend to confuse and distract you," he responded. He then digressed for several moments and explained what the emblem meant to him.

We can see that ambiguity results when communicators draw faulty inferences from decoding nonverbal communication or if words and nonverbal elements are not checked out.

## Summary

As an extension of ideas explored in chapters 4 and 5 we focused on minimizing misunderstanding by dealing with the alternatives of clarity or ambiguity. One significant way to minimize unnecessary ambiguity (or unfortunate calculated ambiguity) is to avoid confusion when the intended function of a message is not identical with the suggested form: the five types of form and functions are expressive, designative, interrogative, evaluative, and directive.

In addition, three major principles for minimizing misunderstanding are: words are not things, maps are not territories, and communicators can check each other out. Confusion and misunderstanding can easily result when communicators act as if words are things instead of symbols, and as if language (maps) is reality (territory). However, when we are making faulty assumptions in interpersonal communication we can create mutual understanding by checking each other out.

# PART THREE

# Dialogic
# Interpersonal
# Communication

# 7

# Dialogue and Monologue

## Dialogue

We will now move *deeper* into interpersonal communication by discussing being an authentic person, which is impossible without the inclusion of *dialogue* in our concept of communication. Through genuine dialogue we can move closer to becoming authentic persons in interpersonal communication.

Essentially, to be *authentic* as an individual is to be primarily self-directed in an effort to get along with yourself by yourself, with yourself with others, and with others but not at the expense of compromising who you know you are and what you value. Being autonomous is essential to authenticity. In the words of psychologist David Johnson, the *autonomous* person is "liberated from rigid pressures and expectancies. He flexibly applies his values and principles in order to behave in ways appropriate to the situation he is in."[1]

Authenticity in interpersonal communication results from engaging in dialogue. Although dialogue has been identified as an emerging concept, it is really a *quality* of communication which is thousands

---

1. David W. Johnson, *Reaching Out: Interpersonal Effectiveness and Self-Actualization* (Englewood Cliffs: Prentice-Hall, 1972), p. 3.

of years old.[2] But, as rhetorician Richard Johannesen reminds us, the term dialogue has been used in such a wide variety of communicative contexts that it can be a label as multidimensional as "communication" or "rhetoric" which often need focused operational descriptions for realistic study and subsequent practice.[3] Although dialogue can occur in political arenas, religious meetings, college or university classrooms, family rooms in suburban houses and the like, we can examine it as a kind of interpersonal communication.

## Definition

Dialogue is a term used in a seemingly infinite number of contexts. The first connotation which may come to mind is from the field of dramatics. We often hear people in the entertainment media speak of the dialogue in a particular film or play. In contrast, comedians who stand alone and talk to make people laugh speak of themselves as monologists. These and other popular connotations have no relevance to our definition of dialogue and monologue in interpersonal communication.

To sharpen our focus we must turn to the work of Martin Buber, a great thinker, teacher, and writer who has been best described as a philosophical anthropologist. Buber wrote a book, first published in 1921, which pervasively and profoundly treated the concept of dialogue as we consider it in interpersonal communication. The book, *I and Thou,*[4] is a treatise about relationships and is used in a variety of disciplines such as theology, philosophy, psychology, and communication. We recognize Buber as an initiator of the dialogic concept as our study views it and we recognize his work as a major influence in most of the work on dialogue.

Referring to Buber's work, Johannesen explains that essentially "dialogue seems to represent more of a communication attitude, principle, or orientation than a specific method, technique, or format. One may speak of the 'spirit of dialogue' in the human communication process."[5] Here dialogue transcends the boundaries of a particular situation where two or more people are speaking and listening to each

2. Floyd W. Matson and Ashley Montague, eds., *The Human Dialogue: Perspectives on Communication* (New York: Free Press, 1967), p. 3.

3. Richard L. Johannesen, "The Emerging Concept of Communication as Dialogue," *The Quarterly Journal of Speech* 57 (December 1971):373.

4. Martin Buber, *I and Thou,* 2d ed. (New York: Charles Scribners, 1958). We use the second edition in all our references to this work.

5. Johannesen, "Emerging Concept," p. 374.

other. Dialogue is given a particular dimension that may or may not exist in an interchange of ideas.

This approach is not inconsistent with a definition of dialogue offered by others. Makay and Brown treat dialogue as a "process of communication in which all parties in the communicative situation identify the rhetorical purpose and work together honestly, carefully, and dynamically to be meaningful in achieving mutual understanding and solution to a rhetorical problem."[6] We note that the quality of this dialogue stems from honesty, care, and dynamic communication. Though the definition suggests any number of communicators might be involved, we can consider this view in terms of interpersonal communication.

A third explanation is offered by theologian Reuel L. Howe. According to Howe:

> Dialogue is interaction between two or more people in response to the truth; it is also the process of assimilation by which perceived truth becomes embodied in the person, becomes a part of him. As we see it, dialogue provides the give and take, check and balance, test correction, that human beings need both to understand and communicate accurately.[7]

Howe limits his notion of dialogue to two or more people. Dialogue can take place within one person and be extended to others in interpersonal communication. Howe's explanation is valid. Especially unique in his explanation is the idea of dialogue as interaction about something thought, believed, or perceived to be the truth.[8] In such an instance or situation the communicators are reaching out for more than what can be gained in small talk, gossip, order giving, and enactment of predictable routines (e.g., "How are you this morning?" "Oh, I'm fine. How about you?") The thing sought is something which the communicators can accept, at least for some period of time —that often nebulous, but always satisfying element in perceived and/or validated reality which is labeled truth. This, along with honesty, care, and dynamic interplay of substantive ideas, is essential if dialogue is to take place. Howe emphasizes "that human beings need both to understand rightly and communicate accurately."[9]

---

6. John J. Makay and William R. Brown, *The Rhetorical Dialogue: Contemporary Concepts and Cases* (Dubuque: Wm. C. Brown, 1972), p. 3.

7. Reuel L. Howe, *Partners in Preaching: Clergy, and Laity in Dialogue* (New York: Seabury, 1967), p. 46.

8. Ibid.

9. Ibid.

Buber initially identified dialogue as a relationship which is developed between what he refers to as the "I" and "Thou," rather than the "I" and "It."[10] A key word to underscore is *relationship*. Buber's terms can be confusing and vague in an initial study of interpersonal communication. The I-Thou and I-It relationships are primary attitudes and human orientations of one person toward another. The I-Thou relationship is dialogic while the I-It relationship is monologic.

The I-Thou relationship is an extremely human and nonmanipulative relationship established by persons involved in interpersonal communication. "I" is the beginning, obviously, and "Thou" is a genuine and emphathic concern for another to the extent that communicators establish a sense of communion, one with the other. When an I-Thou relationship exists, each communicator *accepts* the other for what that person is, and the relationship is open, intimate, and caring in its deepest sense. "Dialogue is not merely the interchange of words . . . it is rather the response of one's whole being to the otherness of the other,"[11] and that otherness can only be comprehended when one person opens himself or herself in a present and concrete situation. Each communicator fully attempts through speaking and listening to respond to the other's need for communication.

The I-Thou relationship Buber develops is clearly explained by Johannesen when he attributes the relationship with qualities of "mutuality, open-heartedness, directness, honesty, spontaneity, frankness, lack of pretense, nonmanipulative intent, communion, intensity, and love in the sense of one human being for another."[12] These qualities are essential for dialogic interpersonal communication. Humanistic psychologist Sidney Jourard expresses his view by disclosing that a communicator experiences another as a person, as the origin and source of his intentional acts.[13] Those engaged in dialogic interpersonal communication *reveal* themselves as "it really is" with them in the context of the communication. Perhaps this is what Reuel L. Howe means about this sort of relationship when he writes, "Indeed, this is the miracle of dialogue: it can bring relationship into being, and it can bring into being once again a relationship that has died."[14] Clark, Bock, and Cornett pull together what we have been describing

10. Buber, *I and Thou.*

11. Martin Buber, *Between Man and Man* (New York: Macmillan, 1971), p. xvii.

12. Johannessen, "Emerging Concept," p. 375.

13. Sidney Jourard, *Disclosing Man to Himself* (New York: Van Nostrand Reinhold, 1968), p. 21.

14. Reuel L. Howe, *The Miracle of Dialogue* (New York: Seabury, 1963), p. 3.

in their view: "Genuine dialogue produces a relationship in which two people become a part of each other."[15]

What sort of a definition of dialogue can we now embody in our study of interpersonal communication? Dialogue is a process of communication which initially takes place within you and is eventually extended to another person. The communication is purposeful and truth-seeking, open and honest, but nonmanipulative and not imposing. The person with whom you are communicating shares in this view of communication so that both reach out to join each other in a communion of meaning to bring about mutual understanding or a solution to a problem. In the dialogic experience of interpersonal communication a relationship is brought into existence which seems to the communicators to have a unique spirit and is realistic and genuine.

### Essential Characteristics

Early in the chapter we defined dialogue with special emphasis on Martin Buber's concept of the I-Thou relationship. This kind of relationship is essential to dialogue in interpersonal communication. The characteristics of dialogue we are about to discuss cannot exist outside of an I-Thou interpersonal relationship. Moreover, the basic need for dialogue as we see it can be eliminated or significantly minimized through use of these characteristics in interpersonal communication.

The essential characteristics are drawn from the literature of communicology, rhetoric, philosophy, theology, psychology and other fields of study within the social and behavioral sciences as well as the humanities. The list could become lengthy but basically can be reduced to seven: courage in communication, genuineness in self and image projection, accurate empathic response, unconditional positive regard, realistic communicative equality, presentness, and love.

*Courage in Communication.*    When we speak of courage we refer to the courage that it initially takes for one to be as he really is, in self-acceptance and in extending oneself to another in interpersonal communication. Theologian Paul Tillich tells us courage *to be* is an ethical act in which we affirm ourselves within ourselves in spite of elements in our experience which conflict with self-affirmation.[16]

---

15. Tony Clark, Doug Bock, and Mike Cornett, *Is That You Out There? Exploring Authentic Communication* (Columbus: Charles E. Merrill, 1973), p. 108.

16. Paul Tillich, *The Courage to Be* (New Haven & London: Yale University Press, 1952).

Surely anyone reaching the learning level for higher education has an inner store of experiences which, if reflected on, can result in periods of insecurity. The courage to be requires a person to rise above conflicting elements within himself and to speak out without a significant hindrance to self-awareness and realization as well as letting another know who one is and where one stands. In essence, the essential part of us prevail over the less essential and be evident in our interpersonal communication with others. Much of the anxiety we face, in one degree or another, stems from an inability or unwillingness to find courage within and extend it through interpersonal communication with others. Courage can help open communicators to reality as it is before them in the lives they face. Meaningful dialogue cannot take place in interpersonal communication without courage. To be "existential" in the use of courage in dialogic interpersonal communication is to know ourselves as we exist and participate with this knowing in the existence of another we communicate with in a positive and affirmative way. At the same time we can encourage the other to share courage as we accept the other in an effort to achieve *communion* both with ourselves and with the other person.

*Genuineness in Self and Image Projection.*    Commonly, communicators wear masks to suit the roles they play with others. Rhetoricians Rod Hart and Don Burks recognize the reality of role-taking, and while not completely dismissing the humanistic notion of discovering and being the real or authentic self consistently, they seem to advise their readers to abandon a unitary view of the self in an advocacy of each one developing a repertoire of roles.[17] The vulnerability of this position is that it could, if taken lightly or misunderstood, encourage one to move toward being phony rather than genuine, or continually being an actor who assumes a role judged to be appropriate for some means to an end. Plato indicted ancient rhetoricians for this kind of activity since it encourages "masking" rather than"unveiling"; it does not encourage genuineness in self and image projection congruent with the authentic self.

Self-image is realistically discussed by John Makay and Thomas Sawyer when they admit "central to any individual's participation in a speech communication course requiring formal or informal participation is self-image or self-concept."[18] They detail the variety of

17. Roderick P. Hart and Don M. Burks, "Rhetorical Sensitivity and Social Interaction," *Speech Monographs* 39 (June 1972):78–79.

18. John J. Makay and Thomas C. Sawyer, *Speech Communication Now! An Introduction to Rhetorical Influences* (Columbus: Charles E. Merrill, 1973), p. 31.

images one person can project with variance depending upon each unique communication setting. They stress that a unity of self and a genuine self-image congruent with a communicator's *genuine* self-perception and the perception of communicatees is desirable. This genuineness is essential to dialogue in interpersonal communication.

> You readily recognize . . . that "life-style" for your friends—no matter how well they know you—is largely a matter of taking on roles on your part. In some circles are you the joker? In others are you the swinger? If you are a normal person . . . there is a consistent organization of traits running through all such roles; but the emphases vary with the social context, and you therefore are amplifying or projecting differing versions of your self.[19]

We contend that the consistent organization of traits can be an expression of the genuine and unified self in response to your appraisal of your partner in information, problem-solving, or tension-releasing needs. Essentially this requires honesty, directness, and being straightforward, gaining the impetus from the courage to be.

*Accurate Empathic Response.*    The title of a popular song states, "Walk a Mile in My Shoes." The title, like the rest of the lyric, is an invitation to empathize. Empathy is placing oneself in the shoes of another. Picture a championship basketball game with a few seconds remaining, the score tied, and a player at the foul line about to shoot the ball. The gymnasium is stilled with silence. Why? Because consciously and unconsciously the spectators are in the act of shooting the ball—in other words, empathizing with the young players and the pressure of the moment.

In a human experience involving interpersonal communication empathy is essential to dialogue. Psychotherapist Carl Rogers testifies about the importance of empathy and explains the term by saying that a deep empathic understanding allows him to see the private world of another through the other's eyes.[20] This idea is clearly detailed by communicologists Charles T. Brown and Paul W. Keller. At one point in their work they declare, "Empathy is the act of imagining the universe of thoughts and feelings from which a statement emerges. In short, it is the ability to perceive from the standpoint of the speaker, and it is probably the most sophisticated and the most imaginative

19. Makay and Brown, *Rhetorical Dialogue,* p. 167.
20. Carl R. Rogers, *On Becoming a Person* (Boston: Houghton Mifflin, 1961), p. 34.

skill a person performs."[21] One *feels* as well as sees an event from the other side as well as from one's own side. This, of course, requires careful, sensitive, and accurate listening by communicators in an interpersonal experience; each must strive for *accuracy* in information processing. A major contribution to dialogue in interpersonal communication, then, is accurate, empathic response—meaningful listening.[22]

A principal was sitting in her office and a teacher came in to plan the next faculty meeting. Suddenly this teacher began to shake and cry. Both entered into a discussion which lasted an hour. Each responded to the other with a great deal of empathy. The principal seemed strongly in touch with the teacher's feelings and much of her past experience was similar to the teacher's. The teacher found in their relationship feelings within herself she believed to be highly similar to the principal's. Their dialogue revealed each of their selves in meaningful ways. At the end of the hour both persons had grown from the experience and a major problem for the teacher was minimized.

*Unconditional Positive Regard.*    We can gain insight into this component of dialogue by considering an idea expressed by Johannesen and initiated by Rogers. According to Johannesen, in unconditional positive regard in dialogue,

> One expresses nonpossessive warmth for the other. The other is valued for his worth and integrity as a person. A partner in dialogue is affirmed, not merely tolerated, even though one opposes him. The other is confirmed in his right to his individuality. And confirmation, or unconditional positive regard, implies a desire to assist the other to maximize his potential, to help him become what he can become. The spirit of mutual trust is promoted.[23]

In unconditional positive regard in dialogue, we can affirm another as a unique individual whether or not we approve of the other's behavior.

This component is a basic attitude used by many psychotherapists today. As they listen to their clients, especially in cases where individuals have low self-esteem and perceive their own behavior as varying considerably from the norm, they "judge not" but rather seek to affirm the troubled communicator as a unique and worthwhile person,

---

21. Charles T. Brown and Paul W. Keller, *Monologue to Dialogue: An Exploration of Interpersonal Communication* (Englewood Cliffs: Prentice-Hall, 1973), p. 23.

22. Carl Rogers, *On Becoming a Person,* p. 66.

23. Johannesen, "Emerging Concept," p. 376.

one who actually possesses a great deal of potential for growth as a person and creating a meaningful life. Rogers tells us, "The more a client perceives the therapist . . . as having an unconditional regard for him, the more the client will move away from a static, fixed, unfeeling, impersonal type of functioning, and the more he will move toward a way of functioning marked by a fluid, changing, acceptance, experiencing of differentiated personal feelings."[24] Consequently, unconditional positive regard in the dialogue of interpersonal communication moves communicators toward increased realistic relationships to self, others, and environment. Admittedly, for many of us this is a difficult component to internalize, embrace, and practice, but as in the cases of the first three components discussed and the three to follow, unconditional positive regard is essential to dialogue in interpersonal communication.

*Realistic Communicative Equality.* Essentially what this feature means is that, regardless of the societal status of communicators, the partners in dialogue view each other primarily as unique and distinct persons, and certainly not as things or objects for manipulation or exploitation.[25] A general controversy about this component took place in a class discussion, when a flushed-looking student challenged the instructor, "How can you speak about this? It's unreal. You're the teacher (image? stereotype?) and we're just students (image? stereotype?). We can't say what we think! You have the power of the gradebook." The instructor's response was that she tried to practice what she preached. Certainly status and responsibilities go along with "being teacher" and "being student." Still, in interpersonal communication with any student she regarded persons as *persons* to be dialogic with, of equal worth as persons, not as simply "full time equivalents" to be processed and used to serve institutional ends. Admittedly this component is not an easy one to engage in when statuses are different or unequal between communicators.

Several years ago a professor was teaching a basic speech course at the Pentagon. Seventy-five percent of the class were men in military service and the remaining twenty-five percent were employees of the federal government. One civilian was a woman and one Army officer was black. The rank among the military ranged from private first class to full-bird colonel, a rank short of being a general. The students were told by the instructor to set aside "rank" and "civilian job status" as

24. Rogers, *On Becoming a Person,* p. 66.
25. Johannesen, p. 376.

well as discriminating feelings. In short, the spirit of mutual equality was to prevail in the interaction among students, the instructor included. What an extremely difficult task this was for people trained to respond to each other in designative communication shaped by strict adherence to rank and status! Eventually most students in the class were able to use realistic communicative equality; they could view and communicate with each other as persons and not just as titled militiamen and government officials.

*Presentness.*    In our views of interpersonal communication in the segments of society in which we live, we can raise the question, "Are most people actually getting involved in meaningful dialogue, with a full and genuine commitment to meaning, tension reduction, problem solving, or other aims for speaking and listening?" Presentness essentially means that partners in dialogue provide full concentration of their authentic and real selves to the interpersonal communication experience.[26]

Presentness means full involvement, one with the other, which includes taking time, avoiding distraction, being accessible. Unfortunately today this sort of dialogue seems limited to counseling sessions with those in "healing or helping" professions, where persons seek happiness and growth through interpersonal communication. A good psychotherapist will listen to and talk with a client without taking phone calls or allowing outside interruptions, providing total involvement in interpersonal communication in an established time period. One essential component of counseling is presentness.

How often this dialogic component seems missing from interpersonal communication as communicators are preoccupied with other things instead of each other! Picture a husband with his face buried in a newspaper while his wife is trying to communicate something to him which she feels is of importance to both of them. Think of a man and woman together and while one is talking the other one is physically close, yet somehow the speaker realizes the other person is not involved with him in meaningful dialogue. Presentness is absent in all these examples!

*Love.*    This component of dialogue may seem strange at first glance. Connotatively "love" is a word that conjures up a variety of meanings. For instance, many of you might first get inner images of persons you

---

26. Ibid.

love, others might get feelings and thoughts which are sexual in nature, while still others might focus on a religious concept, ideal, or figure.

Love in our intentions is an important and inherent aspect of the I-Thou relationship. Psychologist Jess Lair describes love in this way: "I don't know of anything that I have seen that is more loving that one person can do for another than to tell that other person how it is *really* with them in their deepest heart. To give, in a sense, a part of yourself."[27] Now examine Lair's statement very carefully and ponder it in light of what we have been saying about dialogue in interpersonal communication. Being loving is telling the other how you really feel deep inside yourself. Another helpful perspective of love comes from existential theologian Paul Tillich. In discussing love, and the range in quality for essential meanings associated with the word, Tillich speaks of a quality of love which expresses a self-transcending element. One participates with another beyond mere identification.[28] "Love is one," an expression of a multidimensional unity, which is a person. Love in this sense, and as described by Lair, is congruent with counselor and priest John Powell's concepts of "gut level" communication and "peak" communication. Gut level communication emerges from *deep within* a person, and peak communication is based upon absolute openness and honesty. As Powell indicates, in our human condition peak communication can never be a permanent experience.[29] There should and will be, however, moments when encounter attains perfect communication. At these times the two persons will feel an almost perfect and mutual empathy. We feel this idea is a loving one, in communion with Lair's idea of communication, to give, in a sense, a part of yourself.

Examples of this component of dialogue can be found in marital relationships. We cite marriage as only one example even though the separation and divorce rate often runs as high as the rate of marriages today. In their comprehensive and popular book, *Open Marriage,* anthropologists Nena and George O'Neill place a tremendous amount of emphasis for successful open marriage on healthy and loving interpersonal communication.[30]

27. Jess Lair, *I Ain't Much Baby, But I'm All I've Got* (Garden City: Doubleday, 1972), p. 39.
28. Paul Tillich, *Morality and Beyond* (New York: Harper & Row, 1963), pp. 40–41.
29. John Powell, S. J., *Why Am I Afraid to Tell You Who I Am?* (Chicago: Argus, 1969), p. 62.
30. Nena O'Neill and George O'Neill, *Open Marriage* (New York: Avon Books, 1973).

*Recapitulation.*     Interpersonal communication is dialogic, by consisting of the components we have examined, and will thus produce in a communicative setting what Johannesen calls a "supportive psychological setting." Essentially this means communicators will feel free to express themselves. They will have both the capacity and the desire "to listen without anticipating, interfering, competing, refuting, or warping meanings"[31] into preconceived interpretations. Dialogue with these components will at least achieve the lowest level of misunderstanding.

The components of dialogue in interpersonal communication which serve to bring about an I-Thou relationship are, at least:

1. Courage
2. Genuineness in self and image projection
3. Accurate empathic response
4. Unconditional positive regard
5. Realistic communicative equality
6. Presentness
7. Love.

Now, to examine dialogue in a different light let us contrast it with monologue. You must be willing to set aside general meanings you associate with the term monologue, especially the notion that monologue is restricted to one person addressing a large audience where the speaker seems to be doing all the talking.

## Monologue

Much of the writing on monologue stems from Buber's conception of the I-It relation which often manifests itself in monologue, propaganda, or pseudo-dialogue.[32] Earlier in this chapter we spoke briefly about the I-It relationship when we introduced Martin Buber's work *I and Thou.* When we speak of monologue we agree with Johannesen that it is a conception which stems from the I-It relationship.

Basically, when a communicator experiences the other as an object, a thing, one to be used or manipulated, the communicator establishes an I-It relationship.[33] In such experiences we find a lack of the characteristics of dialogue, and in their place individuals who seek to exploit others in interpersonal communication or to seduce others to serve

---

31. Johannesen, "Emerging Concept," p. 376.
32. Ibid., p. 377.
33. Buber, *I and Thou,* pp. 3–7, 38–72.

self-indulgent ends. A good analysis of monologue applicable to human communication, whether the form is an experience in an interpersonal setting or a public address situation, is in the essay by Johannesen or in the work of Reuel L. Howe. The monologic communicator aims at:

1. Primary concern for power over the other
2. Primary concern with persuasion for profit, regardless of whether or not ends justify means
3. Primary concern with personal prestige and status
4. Primary concern with shaping the other's image regardless of the other's concern for developing a unique self
5. Primary concern with self-aggrandizement.

Obviously, then, monologue is a self-centered process of communication.

Howe tells us that in monological communication the communicator is so preoccupied with himself that "he loses touch with those to whom he is speaking."[34] Moreover, one engaging in monologue often seeks the obliteration of another person through communication. We can think of many instances where we have confronted another person with a proposal or a resolution we believed to be worthy of experiencing dialogue, only to be put down, or have our views obliterated by the monological attitude and form of the other's communication.

Clark, Bock, and Cornett tell us of a kind of dialogue which is not really dialogue but merely monologue disguised as dialogue: "Monologue/Dialogue is our attempt to satisfy our own private needs by using the other for our gain without giving anything in return. It is a conversation in which we really do not care about making contact with the other. We talk to satisfy our need to talk. ... When we engage in monologue/dialogue we are never really aware of an other that really exists apart from ourselves. We see everything in terms of ourselves."[35]

Thus, we can see monologue is different from dialogue in interpersonal communication. Both kinds of communication can be of significance to us if we are seeking strong and meaningful relationships through interpersonal communication with minimal or no effective barriers to mutual understanding. Obviously, dialogue is highly desirable for communication while monologue is to be avoided, for it can destroy rather than create rich human experiences.

---

34. Howe, *Miracle of Dialogue,* p. 32.
35. Clark, Bock, Cornett, *Is That You Out There?,* p. 107.

## Summary

You have now been introduced to the concept of dialogue in the process of interpersonal communication. After examining several definitions, we describe dialogue as a process which initially takes place within ourselves and is eventually extended to another person. The communication is purposeful and truth-seeking, open and honest, but nonmanipulative and not imposing. The person with whom we communicate shares in this view of communication so that both reach out to join each other in a communion of meaning to bring about mutual understanding or a solution to a problem. In the dialogic experience of interpersonal communication a relationship is brought into existence which seems to the communicators to have a unique spirit and is realistic and genuine.

To fully understand dialogue in interpersonal communication and to deal authentically with the need for dialogue we must become aware of its essential components. Once we develop this awareness we may choose to embody these components in our own communication behavior and encourage others to do likewise. The characteristics are courage, genuineness, accurate empathic response, unconditional positive regard, realistic communicative equality, presentness, and love.

With these characteristics internalized, we can recognize monologue and not confuse it with or practice it as a form of dialogue. Monologue is a self-centered, manipulative, and exploitive communication which is the opposite of dialogue. The communicator engaged in monologue is preoccupied with himself and has little or no genuine regard for the other person.

We ought to keep the words of Howe in mind throughout the next two chapters as we work to be dialogic in interpersonal communication: "The purpose of dialogue . . . is to restore the tension between vitality and form, to bring parties of a relationship into a communicative relation with one another, to shake them free of their conformity and make them available for transformation. Only through dialogue can the miracle of renewal be accomplished in a relationship."[36]

---

36. Howe, *Miracle of Dialogue,* p. 63.

# 8

# The Need and Conditions for Dialogue

Our exploration in defining dialogue leads us to draw the conclusion that dialogue is an especially unique sort of communication which is far more authentic than remarks frequently labeled by communicators as "mere rhetoric." Because our society generally reflects in both public and private discourse varieties of "mere rhetoric" and superficial communication, we feel that a need for dialogue exists.

For example, Jerry Rubin, social activist and one of the defendants in the Chicago Seven Trial, which took place as a result of turmoil at the 1968 Democratic National Convention, once appeared as a guest speaker at a mass lecture period of a basic course in speech communication at a large university.[1] He immediately told the students he would not "make a speech." Instead he said, "Let's just talk." Immediately hands went up and for fifty minutes Jerry Rubin and students interacted interpersonally. Although it was difficult for one person to establish any interpersonal relationships with 300 others in a fifty-minute period, the speaker made a genuine attempt to transcend the traditional speech-making format. It was as if he sensed a need for dialogue when he entered the room and faced the large audience.

---

1. The appearance of Mr. Rubin was on February 20, 1972 and the communication was recorded and transcribed by one of the authors at Ohio State University.

In order to reach a mutual understanding through accurate communication the need for dialogue had to be met. Excerpts from the interaction reveal how communicators felt a need to open up to each other.

> *Questioner:* You mentioned the media awhile ago and I know people who get public attention have images created by the media. I heard Bill Russell interview George Wallace recently, and Wallace said TV distorted his image. How do you feel after the trial of The Chicago Seven about what the media has done to you?
>
> *Rubin:* Reporting is the nature of the media. It isn't that reporters aren't honest or they are out to get you. I don't believe that. It's the nature of television that it reduces a person whether it's me or George Wallace to a TV commercial, you know. To the American people my name is a TV commercial. It could be reduced to kill your parents or burn buildings down or whatever it is. I basically think my image is positive. I think that in effect I step aside and look at my image, you know, because there is such a thing as an image. It does exist. I think the image is very revolutionary and inspires young people. Besides I think it's a good image. But what gets me is that it is personally hard because people act very strange toward me on a face-to-face level. First of all they expect me to be a superman. That's the first expectation. Second of all, their attitude is I'm making a revolution and they're watching it. And then, you know, people have a strange attitude toward me. I'm not treated as a person, I'm treated as a name in a newspaper. That's disturbing when potential friends treat you that way.
>
> *Questioner:* Do you see any hope, based on your youth-oriented image, of reaching older people, or do you place all your stock with younger people?
>
> *Rubin:* Well, I'm going through changes on that. It used to be I only talked to young kids and when I went on television, I didn't care about anybody but young kids, and I was consciously trying to project an image of freedom and rebellion to young kids. Now I realize I'm getting old and the prospect of getting old shouldn't send you into an old age home. Realizing how Americans oppress people after they get old and how Americans hold this thing of young, young, young. Nobody wanted the Beatles to break up because everyone wanted those young kids to remain as an example of our youth. That's the whole thing. It's the whole sick attitude that Americans have

toward youth which is very oppressive in a most subtle way and it's related to capitalism in a complicated way. I think it's important to talk to everybody. I went on the Mike Douglas show last week and failed. I was trying to talk and just started screaming and yelling. I'll never live that down.

*Questioner:* I have never heard you speak before and I have talked to a lot of people who have. They've characterized you as someone being very emotional, a lot of yelling and screaming. How can you or have you changed your approach? You seem very logical and reasonable. Hearing you in the past, you were excitable, emotional—perhaps to get people aroused? Why are you today softspoken and reasonable?

*Rubin:* (laughing a little) I'll have to ask my psychiatrist.

These excerpts from an hour of interpersonal interaction with members of a large group, in light of what we said about the need for dialogue, serve to show how communicators can recognize a need for a dialogue.

Contemporary song writers at times suggest the need for dialogue in their songs. For example, Paul Simon wrote in the "Sound of Silence" about a lonely individual who wants meaningful dialogue, and sees the need for it in society as he perceives it.[2] This song concludes the need is not being filled. At one point the lonely voice describes ten thousand or more people, "talking without speaking," "hearing without listening." Why? Because "no one dare disturb the sound of silence." The lonely voice even cried out to generate dialogue: "Hear my words that I might teach you, Take my arms that I might reach you." But for him there was no response and there continued to be a need for dialogue. Who among us, faced with our own perceptions and interpersonal communication settings, would deny *there is a need today for dialogue?* Our task is to recognize the need and to utilize dialogic interpersonal communication to eliminate, or at least minimize that need on a day to day basis.

Everywhere we look we see social change, as well as political, scientific, and technological advances. Yet a close examination of human activity surrounding areas of achievement reveals that misunderstandings often result as people talk with each other, integrity is often lacking in human communication, and time, talent, energy, and resources are often wasted in large part because of problems arising

---

2. The entire lyrics to the "Sound of Silence" are printed in a chapter titled, "The Need for Dialogue," in John J. Makay and William R. Brown, *The Rhetorical Dialogue* (Dubuque: Wm. C. Brown, 1972).

out of interpersonal communication settings. These general views serve to confirm for us that there is a need for dialogue.

Dialogue is most likely to result under certain conditions. Therefore, it is essential for us to review these conditions before moving more deeply into a consideration of dialogue with ourselves and others. The list of conditions could be excessive but essentially there are ten.[3] All ten may not be required in every interpersonal setting, and a dialogic experience can emerge when only some of these conditions permeate the atmosphere. If none of the conditions needed for a dialogue is allowed, then it simply will not develop. These conditions are directly related to the characteristics of dialogue, and we can blend the dialogic characteristics and conditions in our own thinking as we deal with the list:

1. Involvement from a felt need to communicate
2. Atmosphere of openness, freedom, and responsibility
3. Mutual trust and respect
4. Sincerity and honesty in attitude toward communication
5. Appreciation of individual differences and uniqueness
6. Acceptance of disagreement and conflict with a desire for resolution
7. A willingness to admit error and allow persuasion
8. Dealing with issues and values
9. Effective feedback and use of feedback
10. A positive attitude for understanding and learning.

## Involvement

Dialogue, as we can see by this point, is often a serious and intense process in interpersonal communication. An important condition for facilitating dialogic communication is that the partners in dialogue experience internally *a strong personal need* to communicate with each other. Furthermore, this condition requires that each communicator be willing to commit himself to speaking and responding at whatever levels of awareness and depths seem warranted in the communicative relationship.

Instructors of communication courses have often served courses which required students to engage in classroom speech communica-

---

3. The ten conditions for dialogue are adapted from the conditions listed in Makay and Brown, *Rhetorical Dialogue,* p. 27.

tion activities which were to be interpersonal, one-to-one, or small group experiences. These experiences fall into one of two general categories: the involved and uninvolved! Involved communicators are able to transcend the idea that the classroom setting is merely another academic assignment to complete for a grade in a trek toward a degree. On the contrary, involved students usually take time and find strong motivation to recognize particular intrapersonal and interpersonal needs genuinely so that the classroom situation becomes dialogic. Involvement and need keep communication from becoming part of a dreary drama of superficiality.

To explore this condition further, consider the case of Bill and Sandy. Their relationship began early in their days of taking courses together and studying in the same major program. After several months, Sandy discovered she was deeply in love with Bill and Bill discovered he had mixed feelings about Sandy. He simply could not tell her he was in love with her. Still the relationship was kept alive with Sandy asking Bill to spend a great deal of time with her, and Bill developing a resentment toward the demands for his time. Eventually frustration developed between the two, in a large part because they could not be dialogic with each other. Each felt a deep need to get involved in dialogue; still neither would "get it together" and begin. One evening, after seven months of tension, an emotional crisis occurred. Sandy launched a barrage of verbal attacks to which Bill responded with additional attacks. Their individual defense mechanisms sought to protect their personal stances. This case is not unusual. Had the essential conditions for dialogue been present early in their relationship when trouble seemed to develop, when they felt need initially emerged, the eventual outburst and ill feelings which followed could have been avoided. Instead, they spent months in growing disappointment and dissatisfaction because they did not create and take advantage of dialogic conditions.

## Openness, Freedom, and Responsibility

If Sandy and Bill had developed the dialogic atmosphere in their interpersonal communication, the condition of *need* and *involvement* would have resulted. A dialogic atmosphere within an interpersonal setting coupled with openness, of course, should be full and genuine and give the communicators a sense of freedom while including personal responsibility. Consider this condition in the case of the Barnes, an upper-middle-class family residing in a "commuter community" located near a large midwestern city.

Dave Barnes was an investment counselor who had effectively climbed a corporate pyramid and had a very comfortable income and sense of personal satisfaction. He supplemented his income with additional fees earned as a consultant to various professionals. Barnes was married to an attractive woman who taught in a neighborhood elementary school, and had two teenage children, a sixteen-year-old son and a fifteen-year-old-daughter. He gave his children material rewards to reveal his affection for them, but then manipulated the things he gave them in an effort to control their social behavior. For example, the son, Tom, received a Porsche for his birthday and every time his social behavior displeased one or both of his parents, the keys to the automobile were taken from him for a period of time. In another instance, when the parents returned home early one night after a dinner party and discovered their daughter in bed with her boyfriend, they angrily lectured her and announced a list of punishments she would suffer rather than talking to her in depth about her behavior. Furthermore, the father frequently picked up the extension phone when the teenagers were talking to friends. Mrs. Barnes seldom confronted her children when she was displeased so she channeled her messages through her husband, who then dealt with the children. Does this home seem to have an atmosphere of openness, freedom, and responsibility for dialogue in the family?

The interpersonal communication patterns of interaction in the family were stifling and bred complex games instead of meaningful dialogue, in part because the Barnes' home did not possess an atmosphere of openness, freedom, and trust. The parents were *monologic* in dealing with behavior they disapproved of, and the children consequently felt as if they were in a domestic prison and certainly not a house which encouraged or rewarded dialogue! Furthermore, the parents assumed responsibility for themselves, their children, and the objects and opportunities centered in the lives of their children.

## Mutual Trust and Respect

In viewing communication barriers which have existed unnecessarily, we find that two important ingredients for dialogue are mutual respect and trust.

A communicator who lacks respect for himself or for another is going to encounter considerable difficulty. This is because respect is a liking, an appreciation for "the person," and in many instances, a recognition of authority and/or expertise which is important to the realization of goals. If trust is missing in dialogue, suspicion or ambiguity are likely to exist. A person goes to a psychotherapist or some sort of professional counselor because he has a problem or cluster of related problems which he does not understand how to cope with and needs to talk with someone about. Perhaps he does not feel that he can trust anyone in his family or circle of friends to keep his problem privately, and he believes he can both respect and trust the professional listener to guard the privacy of the problem and guide his behavior in dealing with it.

Obviously there can be a great deal of personal value in private counseling but we can learn to respect and trust others around us if we are going to engage in authentic dialogue. Admittedly, this can be risky business for a communicator, especially in a society filled with mistrust and suspicion. When we are especially reluctant to allow this condition to exist we could ask: "What is the worst thing that can happen to me by respecting and trusting the other in interpersonal communication?" Almost always the intrapersonal response will be "nothing much," or "more goals can be helped than hindered when such a condition is created." Nothing catastrophic will result (a catastrophe is thought to be in line with an earthquake or a tremendous business loss rather than being rejected by a statement like, "If that's how you really feel you can go to hell!"). The communicator wanting to respect and trust another must likewise be one whom others can always respect and trust unquestionably. These essential qualities lead us to a discussion of a fourth condition for dialogue.

## Sincerity and Honesty

Two dimensions of self which seem essential to the creation of a dialogic atmosphere are sincerity and honesty. In order to eliminate any possibility of monologic behavior, spurred on by mistrust, seduction, and manipulative expectancies, communicators must be totally in earnest while speaking and listening, and do so in a way which is consistent with those premises within their personal value systems. We cannot hide, disguise, or falsely invent information for interpersonal communication. Sincerity and honesty entail risks to the communicator. Consider the case of a group of students who were discussing a required course over coffee one day. A big complaint seemed to be the dreary and out-of-date text required for the course and edited by the chairman of the department. No one in the group seemed willing to go to the course instructor or department chairman to engage in dialogue about this matter because this would require sincerity and honesty in an attitude toward communication. Each seemed afraid some punishment would be suffered by the person who undertook the task. Finally, one woman agreed to speak to both the chairman and the instructor. She took the risk, and found instead of punishment a willingness on the part of those responsible for the course to study and act upon the problem.

"Tell it like it is," was a popular challenge in public and private communication of the 1960s, and the phrase continued to be used by many persons in the years which followed. "Tell it like it is," is a call for sincerity and honesty so that dialogue can take place. A group of seminarians taking a course in homiletics each provided input to every sermon prepared and preached by a member of the class. Early in the course one message seemed especially weak to the class in general. An artificial discussion, which seemed designed not to offend the class or hurt the feelings of the student speaker, followed the preaching. Finally, one man stood up in the discussion, looked at everyone, and declared, "Bull shit!" Following this statement was an in-depth exploration of the message and its presentation and the seminarians were willing to be far more honest and sincere than they were initially.

## Appreciation of Individual Differences and Uniqueness

To understand the next condition of dialogue, study this excerpt from a discussion between two university students and a United States congressman. The conversation took place several years ago is relevant to our concern with this condition for dialogue.

> *Congressman:* I suppose, too, that differing life styles add to the problem. As I travel around . . . talking to all kinds of people, I find that many of them have no sympathy for the ideas and reforms suggested by the young, simply because they say that it's hard to believe that young people are idealistic or serious when they insist on trying to shock older people. They look at young people's long hair, different styles of dress, use of language. And they wonder if all these things aren't better indica-

> tions of young people's attitudes toward society than all their
> demands for improvement.
>
> *Student 1:* Adults make a false assumption that long hair and
> unconventional dress are designed to shock older people. You
> talked about arrogance earlier; there is nothing more arrogant
> to me than someone who discriminates against other persons
> because of the length of their hair or style of dress. . . .
>
> *Student 2:* We are all victims of generalizations gone wild. One
> young person may wear long hair because he likes it—and he
> may be more conservative politically than his parents. . . .[4]

If communicators allow differences or uniqueness in ideas, appearances, environment, or other matters to stand in the way of dialogic communication, maximum understanding cannot be realized in interpersonal communication.

Often people are afraid of differences in other people to the extent that dialogue simply cannot take place. Still others harbor resentment because of the differences and uniqueness of people they need to deal with. History indicates that men and women became martyrs because persons in power could not tolerate their differences and uniqueness. Socrates and Jesus, for example, were killed for their differences and uniqueness in contrast to established expectancies of leaders and followers who possessed the power, authority, and will to try to destroy them and their ideas. Today hostilities exist among persons because of differences in life styles and viewpoints centered in generation and economic gaps.

A dialogic atmosphere requires, ultimately, that communicators appreciate each other's uniqueness and differences so interaction can result in rich and in-depth communication.

## Acceptance of Disagreement with a Desire for Resolution

We can consider in our own lives the degree of intensity existing in situations where there is significant disagreement and conflict. Although we often wish we did not have to encounter much disagreement we all know that disagreement is a daily part of our reality and

---

4. "Bridging the Generation Gap: A Conversation Between Rep. Morris Udall and Three Interns," *The New Republic,* 1970.

that conflict has to be faced realistically. Dialogue can lead to both satisfying and peaceful resolutions of difficulties.

Consider the example of Tom and June, a couple in their late twenties. Although they had been married for nine years, their relationship was rocky, stormy, and frequently threatened by the walkout of one or the other. At the height of any extremely hostile, explosive, and dramatic argument Tom would go to his hobby room, put classical music on his stereo, and turn up the volume. June always turned to tears, picked up the phone and sought the comforting ear of a close friend. One day the friend did not listen passively, but instead advised emotionally, "Go upstairs, knock on his door until you have his attention, then ask him to turn the music off, get together and then you two talk to each other!" Accept disagreement and conflict. Then try to create and act upon an earnest desire to resolve your disagreement. When this acceptance and desire became a part of the communicative atmosphere for Tom and June, dialogue became a reality and helped them to bring about growth and a stronger relationship. Conflict resolution is entwined in the next condition for dialogue.

## Willingness to Admit Error

Do we think of ourselves as being openminded? Being human and therefore subject to error? Most of us probably contend we are neither dogmatic nor closeminded. Yet in many instances we may have encountered biased resistance from friends and acquaintances (and ourselves) when controversy began to develop in conversation to the extent that opposing feelings and points of view emerged.

Our society does not oppose argumentation and advocacy. We teach and defend its principles. We may also find within ourselves intrapersonally, as well as in our interpersonal communication with others, that for authentic dialogue to take place, an essential condition to meet is a genuine willingness to admit, "I can be wrong," coupled with a fearless and open mind which can be persuaded—changed—when evidence (whether facts or values) and reasoning seem to warrant a shift or modification in view.

Communication journals and books are replete with information about being human, attitudinal and counter-attitudinal change, bias in language use, dogmatism versus open-mindedness, persuasibility and immunization to persuasion, as well as a variety of related research concerns. We recognize the meaning of these messages. We also see that if we want a dialogic experience, and want to avoid becoming monologic, there must be a willingness on our part to admit error and be open to persuasion.

## Feedback

Feedback is a term we have used or referred to frequently in our discussion. For instance, we mentioned that it was an important variable in the first chapter, and we placed it prominently in our communication models.

We know that as communicators we generally are not oblivious to each other, but instead invite response when we speak, and give off cues, clues, and other indicators when we react to what we hear. Yet if clarity, understanding, maximum meaning—in short, relationship and content goals—are to be realized in a dialogic atmosphere, then each communicator in a setting must provide effective feedback and make use of the feedback in the setting so that this important condition for dialogue is established.

Certainly dialogue cannot take place when communicators are not sensitive to each other during the symbolic interaction. Often in face-to-face communication another communicator may appear to be staring through or past someone talking as if the listener is merely waiting, without *really* listening, for the speaker to stop so the listener can make a point without even considering what has just been stated.

Consider informal conversation with a group of friends. Have you ever been in a setting in which you were so eager to make a contribution to the flow of ideas that you failed to listen to what another said because you were busy inwardly rehearsing what you wanted to say? In class discussion we find that those who are so eager to make their point give off every indication that they are not providing desirable feedback to the person currently speaking. One who speaks also must read the expressions, nonverbal and verbal, of those who listen and respond! This sort of feedback behavior can encourage all communicators to concentrate on each other and really become involved in the sort of dialogue we spoke about in chapter 7.

## Positive Attitude

We have discussed the nature of attitudes, values, beliefs, and opinions. In the context of our conditions for dialogue we refer to attitude as a positive or negatively charged psychological construct which exists in a cluster of similar and related constructs. Attitudes, then, are directive forces which tend to shape and steer our feelings and subsequent behavior. This force is implied in such comments as, "I don't like your attitude about doing this work," or "You have a good attitude about the army, soldier, and it will help you enjoy your enlistment period far more than if you had a bad attitude." We contend that, if meaningful dialogue is to take place in a communication setting, communicators must have a positive attitude, one charged forcefully to encourage them to want to enjoy and benefit from dialogue which leads them to maximum understanding and learning.

Students are required to take courses they believe they would not take if they were given a choice. When this happens, they may enter the course with hostile or negative attitudes which are not likely to help them reach maximum understanding and learning. We have found this attitude too often in required speech courses. "Why should I study speech? I've been doing it all my life! I want to take courses in my major, courses which I can benefit most from." As long as this sort of attitude is influential in one's approach to a communicative setting, the chances of full dialogue are slim.

## Summary

In chapter 7 we focused on the nature and elements of dialogue in interpersonal communication. Here we examined both the need and conditions for dialogue. The conditions are:

1. Involvement and a felt need to communicate
2. Atmosphere of openness, freedom, and responsibility
3. Mutual trust and respect
4. Sincerity and honesty in attitude toward communication
5. Appreciation of individual differences and uniqueness
6. Acceptance of disagreement and conflict with a desire for resolution
7. A willingness to admit error and allow persuasion
8. Dealing with issues and values
9. Effective feedback and use of feedback
10. A positive attitude for understanding and learning.

In this chapter we sought to introduce you to the basic conditions which ought to prevail if dialogic interpersonal communication is to take place. Review them by *thinking* about them.

# 9

# Dialogue with the Self and with Others

Dialogue results when we are authentic with ourselves and with others. Without authenticity the components and conditions for dialogue are not likely to exist, and the need for dialogue is not likely to be met. In this chapter we will focus on authentic intrapersonal communication. Not only is this important in and of itself, a "fact" which we hope will become clear in the following pages, but authentic intrapersonal communication—honesty with self—is essential and prerequisite to authentic interpersonal communication—honesty with others. As you remember, honesty with others (or authenticity or genuineness) is one of the necessary conditions for dialogue, our most rewarding and fulfilling communication.

In chapter 2, we introduced the basic concepts inherent in intrapersonal communication: self-awareness, self-acceptance, self-assertion, and self-actualization. We described what we find when we analyze these stages in intrapersonal communication. In this chapter, we will examine what some psychologists, counselors, teachers, and communicologists have found works best for most people in developing authentic intrapersonal communication.

## Stages of Personal Growth

Before exploring more fully ideas about achieving the quality of dialogue with self, we will consider an example in order to see what stages, phases, levels, or progression can be discerned.

Elaine entered counseling with feelings of frustration and anxiety. Her main problem appeared to be one of efficiency and organization —she never finished any of her term papers until the very last minute and not infrequently turned them in late. She was a straight A student, so her modus operandi was obviously not affecting her grades or standing with her professors. When asked what was motivating her to change her behavior, she replied that she's always wanted to write, but she was afraid that, until she learned to discipline herself, she'd never get around to it. Having determined her goal, that of becoming more efficient so that she could find time for and learn the discipline necessary to creative work, she and the counselor set about achieving it.

Through discussions of the feelings she experienced when she tried to work and had difficulty in concentrating, she realized that she had internalized her father's admonition that there was only one right way to do a thing—and that she'd have to discover it; he'd let her know afterwards if she was right. Once she understood this, she concentrated on experiencing this feeling when it arose and on giving herself permission to do her work on time rather than spending most of her energy to find the "right way." The counselor suggested to her that she experiment with different forms of organization and different unifying themes for her papers. She said that she would, and she and the counselor worked on some specific techniques she could try out.

This approach began to produce results. She found the organizing technique which suited her. Soon her papers were turned in on time, some even early. As she progressed, not only did she discover new organizing principles which made her writing easier and even at times, enjoyable, she also found that she had time to undertake some creative writing. From time to time, she stops and reevaluates her approach now, trying to discover even more efficient ways to complete her work and embark on a creative writing career.

This illustration serves as an introduction to the *stages of growth:* awareness, exploration, commitment, skill development, skill refinement, and reassessment.[1] As we discuss each of these stages, it is important to remember that no one stage is inherently any better than another, that each one can be a legitimate "place to be" in our per-

1. Donald J. Tosi, *Youth: Toward Personal Growth: A Rational-Emotive Approach* (Columbus, Ohio: Charles E. Merrill, 1974), pp. 13–19. Developed and adapted from J. J. Quaranta, "Conceptual Framework for Career Development Programming," in *Guidance for Planning and Evaluative Career Development,* ed. R. McCormick and J. Wigtil. Project sponsored by the Division of Guidance and Testing (Columbus: Ohio Department of Education, 1971).

sonal growth. Also, the stages of growth obviously take place over a person's life as well as in a single role. You might at one level be in the stage of developing the general life skills of coping and functioning and *at the same time* be, for example, at the awareness stage in marriage, the commitment stage in a profession, the skill refinement stage in being a student.

The stages we grow through are intimately bound up with authentic intrapersonal communication. We need the ability to be completely honest with ourselves in order to discover what stage we are in in any particular role in our lives and perhaps more importantly, where we want to go from there.

### Awareness

The first stage of growth is awareness. This is mainly a cognitive process, one that occurs "in your head." The four substages involved are intuition, consciousness, attention, and decision. In our example, Elaine was intuitively aware, through her feelings of frustration and anxiety, that she had a problem. In articulating these feelings (mainly a cognitive process) she became conscious of the fact that her problem was centered in an old parental "tape," that is, she was replaying injunctions and admonitions from her father when she was young and allowing them to direct her behavior as a student today. Once conscious of the underlying reason, she attended to her thoughts and feelings when this problem obstructed her productivity. Finally, Elaine decided to take steps to remove the problem by giving herself permission to experiment with various ways of organizing and developing her papers.

In any new role that we try out, we almost invariably begin with the awareness stage. We are all right now at the awareness stage in some area of our lives. Perhaps you are becoming aware of what it would mean to be a businessman, an instructor, a marriage partner, a friend to a new person in your life, or a member of a new organization. You might even be in an awareness stage that pervades your entire life, that of a newly emerging "self." That is, you might be attempting to become aware of what it would mean to become a slightly different you, perhaps one more in tune with your ideal self-concept.

The important thing to note about the awareness state is that we have not yet engaged in or entered into our new role. Awareness is a mental rather than actual experimentation with a new role or life style.

*Exploration*

Whereas the first stage of growth was primarily cognitive, the second stage is primarily emotional and physical. This stage involves risk and some possibility of failure.

In our illustration, Elaine's exploration stage occurred when she and the counselor discussed various techniques of organizing and developing term papers and when she experimented with some of those various techniques. Exploring these possibilities involved risk and possible failure for Elaine—she might have discovered that even with her new insights and techniques she couldn't overcome her problem.

We can explore at various levels. One way of exploring is *vicarious;* that is, we watch someone else do it to try to feel what it would be like. Elaine used this type of exploration when the counselor showed her how he, personally, organized the things that he wrote.

Another way of exploring is through *simulation.* We play "as if" the situation were real. Elaine used this when she tried developing themes that were not going to be actual papers to be handed in; she was playing "as if" they were real.

The final way of exploring is *experiential.* In this case, we actually try it out in a real situation to see if it will work for us, as Elaine did when she actually had a paper due for a course.

You are probably in or entering the exploration stage of your career role. Let's say that you think you want to become a teacher. You are already pretty much mentally aware of what the textbooks suggest is involved in teaching and so you've moved into the exploration phase. You notice teachers you have and try to understand the role better by vicariously feeling with them in a classroom encounter. In some of your education courses, you role-play or simulate the teacher role by presenting a lesson to a class of your peers. Then, you student teach; you actually experience, as much as is possible without being a teacher, the emotions and actions involved in that role. All of these means are progressively risky for you as you might fail to be able to empathize with your teachers, to feel right and natural when acting "as if" you are a teacher, or to facilitate learning in an actual classroom situation.

*Commitment*

The third stage of growth is commitment. It is here that the role we are about to engage in is fairly clear and definite to us. We can attach a name to it that we understand, feel comfortable with, and are willing to acknowledge as our role; such as husband, wife, friend, mother, father, teacher, counselor, minister, demonstrator, etc. At this point we make a private or public decision to enter a new role on a more general commitment to full and fulfilling living; that is, we articulate to ourselves or someone else that we are "going to take the plunge."

In Elaine's case, she entered the commitment stage when she publicly announced to the counselor that she would make an effort to try these organizing techniques in a real situation, for a paper that was actually due in class. This is different from experiential exploration in that she not only tried out the new behavior in a real situation but she was also committed to *follow it through* despite obstacles such as first time failure, anxiety, and frustration.

To make clear that this is a very real and important difference and to show how crucial this stage of growth is, here is a further example. Don was having difficulty in achieving professionally in his business what he desired to achieve. He'd talk about how much he wanted to and had the potential to sell, but in spite of further awareness of his job through educational seminars, exploration of new selling approaches and techniques, he didn't make any significant progress. Why? Because he failed to make a commitment. He would explore new techniques experientially in a real live selling situation but after a failure, he would not try again.

Goals, whether goals in life or in specific roles, can seldom be achieved unless a public or private commitment is made. Joseph Quaranta, a professional counselor who has identified and developed these stages of growth, suggests that only when both public and private commitments are made are you really living and growing, because only then have you taken the step to gain some sort of control over your life.[2]

The importance of this stage is very clear. We realize, for example, that in order to offer this book we had to make a commitment to ourselves, to each other, and to our publisher. We were past the stage of exploration; there was no room for forgetting it when the ideas or words failed to come for a particular page or chapter; we had to try again.

Counselors often see how crucial the concept of commitment is in dealing with student problems. Some students want to come in and just talk about their problems; they want to gain insight into their thoughts and feelings. Unfortunately, that is where many of them

---

2. From notes taken in a seminar on Counseling and Guidance, taught by J. Quaranta, Fall, 1973, Ohio State University.

want to stop—at the thinking and feeling stages. Unless a person commits himself to *doing* the necessary things to solve his problem, be it a personal, academic or professional problem, and to taking the necessary actions *again after failure,* there is no way that anyone can be of help.

This stage is the test of determination and desire. There is little continued success, achievement, or growth without commitment.

### Skill Development

The fourth stage of growth is skill development. Having committed ourselves to a new role or new ways of behaving, we embark upon that path, perform the necessary activities, and continue to develop the skills we have and learn new ones.

Elaine did just that. She performed the necessary activities such as taking notes, recording references, and outlining and continued her development of these skills until they could be performed almost automatically.

A student enters college and begins performing the necessary skills involved in being a college student. He attends classes, learns to take notes, and write papers and exams. Perhaps he also learns the skills involved in communicating with classmates and professors. Many of those skills become automatic to him, and he is ready to move into the next stage of growth.

### Skill Refinement

The fifth stage is skill refinement. Here we move into higher level development of skills and creativity.

In our example, Elaine began experimenting with new and different techniques. She created and developed some of her own methods and transferred these to the creative writing situation.

At this stage we go beyond what we were taught and mold the particular role to our own personalities and life styles. We can all, hopefully, think of teachers who made the subject "theirs," who created a classroom atmosphere that fit their personalities (for better or worse), who experimented with new materials and approaches that indicated they were beyond what textbooks had taught them about teaching.

In one sense this is the last stage of development in the role, as we entered it. It is at this point that boredom usually sets in and changes are called for if enjoyment and excitement are to be recreated. Boredom, at this stage, is not bad. On the contrary, it is usually a very healthy sign that we have gone about as far as we can with this particular role in its present form. When boredom sets in, if growth is to continue and not turn into stagnation (which is too often the case), we must move into the transitional stage of reassessment/redirection.

## Reassessment/Redirection

When we reach this stage, we need to be in tune with our thoughts and feelings about our role or behavior in its present form, and also about alternatives to that role or behavior. The two movements we can make at this point if we are not to continue being bored and sink into stagnation are reaffirmation or redirection.

We may reaffirm our present role at a higher level. A student may say to herself, "Okay, so I'm bored a lot and I wish I were somewhere else, but I need this degree for more important goals and I'll just stick it out." A homemaker who has been exposed to some consciousness-raising feminist literature may decide that yes, she's bored, but considering alternate possibilities, she'd rather be where she is than any place else, so she'll just accept her role and make the most of it. Now this really doesn't sound like any change is involved. There is, however, a change in *attitude about* the role. When the role is reaffirmed in its present form the change comes through the way we look at that role rather than in the role itself. Acceptance is present where none existed before and because there is acceptance, boredom is decreased.

We may redirect. The change can be some modification of our present role or behavior. A student may decide to change her major, or to develop interpersonal relationships with her professors, or to attend the cultural activities her college provides. The homemaker might decide to work part-time or full-time, or return to school to earn an advanced degree, or learn a new domestic skill such as wine-making, macramé or decoupage, or join a volunteer organization. In this case, at least part of the former role is kept intact; something new and different is added to it, or another role, which ameliorates the boredom, is added. The change can be complete redirection into another role. The student may drop out. The homemaker may get a divorce.

Growth can be erratic. These stages may not follow in such logical order. For example, a person may find himself committed to marriage before he knows what it entails and how he is going to feel about it. It seems safe to say, however, that the more closely our growth pattern follows these stages the smoother our growth will be.

We have spent a great deal of time on these stages. Understanding them and being able to identify where we are in life and in any particular role or behavior is essential to understanding and being honest with ourselves through authentic intrapersonal communication. We can see how these stages are applicable to the development of authentic interpersonal relationships. Having discussed the stages of growth, we can now relate them to the four concepts of intrapersonal communication.

## Intrapersonal Concepts

At this point we wish to go back through the stages of growth and intrapersonal development. In each stage, we will find some relevant humanistic psychological concepts which will aid us in further understanding these stages, and how to make the most of each.

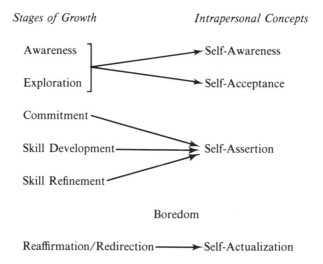

### Self-Awareness

Self-awareness, or knowing what we think and feel and "are," encompasses the cognitive awareness and the emotional and physical exploration stages of growth.

We all have thoughts, feelings, and tendencies which affect our behavior. Therefore, we should try to understand or be aware of what is influencing our daily actions in order to redevelop more efficient, rewarding, and exciting communication with ourselves and others.

The theory of transactional analysis[3] can be an aid to self-aware-ness. This theory speaks to thoughts and emotions and behavioral inclinations. TA is concerned with three ego states: parent, adult, and child. The parent state is the *taught* concept of life. It is the internali-zation of parental messages we received directly and indirectly and absorbed consciously and unconsciously during the first five years of our lives. The parent is full of admonitions, warnings, threats, and "should" and "ought" statements. It is generally in the parent that we will find our life's script or what we have been "programmed" to carry out in our lives such as, "You'll never amount to anything," or "You can do anything that you set out to do." Everyone really has two parents in the parent state: the *loving* parent who says, "Be the way you are," and *critical* parent who says, "Be the way I want you to be." Being aware of our parental ego states can aid us in under-standing many of our thoughts and emotions. For example, when you study hard for a test and fail to do well you will be able to recognize a critical parental message if you are hearing things like, "You should have taken better notes," or "You'll never get a 3 point that way." On the other hand, you might hear a loving parental message such as, "That's all right—you're doing so well in all your other subjects and are in so many worthwhile activities." It seems safe to say that the more critical the message from our parents the more destructive our life scripts (unless our adult intervenes—a possibility we'll discuss later in the chapter); the more loving the messages, the more winning our life scripts.

The next ego state is the child. The child is the *felt* concept of life. It is in this ego state that all the feelings from childhood are kept, ranging from positive emotions of joy to negative emotions of guilt. As with the parent, we really have more than one child. There is the *adapted* child who has learned to "Thank Aunt Mary for the coloring book." There is the *little professor,* who has learned to manipulate, both creatively by tearing apart a clock to see how it runs, and controllingly by climbing on her Daddy's lap and hugging him to get him to buy her an ice cream cone. Finally, there is the *natural* child, who expresses emotion uninhibitedly, be it screaming in rage or laugh-

3. See for example, Thomas A. Harris, *I'm OK—You're OK: A Practical Guide to Transactional Analysis* (New York: Harper & Row, 1967); Eric Berne, *Games People Play: The Psychology of Human Relationships* (New York: Grove, 1964) and *What Do You Say After You Say Hello?* (New York: Grove, 1972) and *Transactional Analysis in Psychotherapy* (New York: Grove 1961); Muriel James and Dorothy Jongeward, *Born to Win: Transactional Analysis with Gestalt Experiments* (Reading, Mass: Addi-son-Wesley, 1971).

ing with delight. Understanding this ego state will help us identify such reactions as saying we like someone's new outfit when we really don't to avoid hurting their feelings (adapted child), or stopping in to see our boss in the hopes of getting a raise (little professor), or running laughingly through a pile of autumn leaves someone has just raked into a heap (natural child).

The final ego state is the *adult*. The adult is the *thought* concept of life and is responsible for processing incoming data and using it to solve problems intelligently. The adult asks the questions what? where? when? how? who? and why? (and takes the answers and does something with them). Understanding our adults will help us recognize such actions as asking directions, reading the editorial page of the newspaper, and balancing our checkbooks.

Once we can easily identify these three ego states we will be able to understand better where we are "coming from" in any thought, emotion, or action.

Another theory helpful in self-awareness is rational-emotive therapy.[4] This theory suggests that it is not what happens to us that causes our emotions, but what we are telling ourselves about what happens that controls any subsequent feelings. For example, it isn't your friend yelling at you that makes you angry, it is your telling yourself that he-has-no-right-to-yell-at-me-I-didn't-do-anything-and-I'm-such-a-good-friend that makes you angry.

Ellis explains the process which occurs in ABC form.[5] First, you have an activating act or agent (A). Then you have a belief about that event (B) which can be rational or irrational. Finally you have the consequences of that belief (C) which will be rational or irrational emotion and perhaps action corresponding to the type of belief involved. Usually we first have a rational belief such as "I don't like it when my friend yells at me"; but all too often this rational belief is immediately followed by an irrational one such as "I can't stand it when my friend yells at me. He shouldn't do that," so that instead of a rational consequence which can be dealt with intelligently such as mild frustration, we might experience uncontrollable anger which may leave us unable to deal with solving rather than increasing the problem.

RET helps us understand how what we are thinking disturbs us and produces unpleasant emotions. Following are the irrational ideas

---

4. See Albert Ellis, *Humanistic Psychotherapy: The Rational-Emotive Approach* (New York: 1973); with Robert A. Harper, *A Guide to Rational Living* (Hollywood, California: Wilshire Book Company, 1961); Tosi, *Youth.*
5. Ellis, *Humanistic Psychotherapy,* pp. 57–60.

which cause most of our intra- and interpersonal problems.[6] You'll have no trouble in identifying at least half a dozen irrational beliefs that you are telling yourself to disturb yourself.

1. I must be loved or approved by everyone for virtually everything I do—or if not by everyone, by persons I deem significant to me.
2. I believe that certain acts are sinful, wicked, or villainous and that people who perform such acts should be severely punished and blamed.
3. I can't stand it when things are not the way I would like them to be.
4. When I am unhappy, it is because something external to me such as persons or events causes me to be that way.
5. I should be terribly concerned about things that may be dangerous or fearsome to me.
6. Although I want to face difficult situations and self-responsibilities, it is easier for me to avoid them.
7. I need someone stronger or greater than myself on whom to rely.
8. In order to have a feeling of worth, I should and must be thoroughly competent, adequate, intelligent, and achieving in all possible respects.
9. When something once strongly affects me, it will always or indefinitely affect me.
10. I don't have much control over my emotions or thoughts.
11. I should never be angry or express my anger because such expression is bad and a sign of personal weakness.
12. I should rarely confront other people or assert my own thoughts or feelings about another person because people are fragile and are hurt easily. I don't want to hurt anyone.
13. Most of the time I will please other people even if I have to forego my own pleasure.
14. I am happiest when I just remain inactive and passive.
15. In order to be perfectly fulfilled as a human being, I need (must have) a close personal, involved, and intimate relationship with another person, especially a member of the opposite sex.

---

6. Donald J. Tosi, "Self-Directed Behavior Change in the Cognitive, Affective, and Behavioral Motoric Domains: A Rational-Emotive Approach," *Focus on Guidance,* December 1973, p. 10.

When we find ourselves overly disturbed about something and experiencing anger, anxiety, dullness, self-pity, resentment, or some other equally negative emotion, perhaps there is an irrational belief underlying the emotion.

Another theory that is helpful in self-awareness is Gestalt Therapy as conceived of by Fritz Perls. As a matter of fact, Perls suggests that awareness is practically the whole ball game. He says: "And I believe that this is the great thing to understand! *that awareness per se—by and of itself—can be curative.* Because with full awareness of this organismic self-regulation, you can let the organism take over without interfering, without interrupting; we can rely on the wisdom of the organism."[7]

Through such techniques as dream therapy, in which one role plays the various people, objects, and events in his dreams; nonverbal awareness, in which the person role plays various parts of the body such as a tapping the foot or taking a trip through the body; identifying top dog and underdog, in which one carries on a conversation between two opposing desires; and deathbed fantasy, in which one can project what he will say and will feel and will want to say when he is about to die, Gestalt therapists lead their clients to self-awareness. Barry Stevens recounts a self-awareness experience:

> I must notice myself, and when it is time for me to go to bed. Sometimes I have to make myself quiet before the time when I lie down. And in the morning, I must know that even the slightest movement of mind or body breaks up my awareness. I have to live with my half-sleep (half-waking) gently, and let myself simply notice what is going on in me. . . . I once dreamed that a long scroll was moving before my eyes. . . . On the scroll were written all sorts of charges . . . made against me, and to some extent accepted by myself. I felt more and more guilty as they reeled off . . . I was the most worthless creature on earth. When I awakened . . . I stayed with the dream. . . . The last accusation was: "*And furthermore:* you are a sloppy housekeeper." Suddenly all the other accusations fell into their proper place: they were, in the same way, absurd. What does my housekeeping have to do with anyone but me and the people who live with me? Why should anyone even waste life having an opinion about it? . . . Only we, the permanent residents, can see it "whole." And I am the only person who can know me in my entirety.

If I had not let this dream roll on, I would have lived with the feeling

---

7. Fritz Perls, *Gestalt Therapy Verbatim* (Toronto: Bantam Books, 1969), p. 17.

of guilt which I had when I awakened, instead of arriving at what the dream was telling me.[8]

This is another way of getting in touch with our thoughts and emotions.

A final means that has been helpful in achieving self-awareness is the technique of role stripping.[9] The theory is that by mentally removing each of the roles we play we fill find out what is left, and what is left will be "pure self."

Try drawing a diagram similar to figure 10 for yourself with the roles that you are now engaged in. Rank the roles from the least important to the most important. Start with the least important, and cross it out. At the same time try to imagine what it would be like not to be engaged in that role and the thoughts, feelings, and actions which accompany it. Continue this process with each role you have identified until you reach the one most important to you. Eliminate it. What is left? Theoretically this is *you*. If you have been able to do this successfully (it's very difficult, especially with the most important roles), you have achieved a great deal of self-awareness.

### Self-Acceptance

The next stage of intrapersonal growth is self-acceptance. In this stage we move beyond identification and increased awareness of our thoughts, emotions, and actions to an acceptance of them.

It is rather difficult to explain self-acceptance clearly and meaningfully, much less achieve it. If we accept ourselves, we "let ourselves

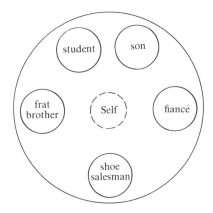

**FIGURE 10. Self with Roles**

8. Barry Stevens, and Carl Rogers, *Person to Person: The Problem of Being Human* (New York: Pocket Books, 1971), pp. 251–52.
9. Perls, *Gestalt Therapy Verbatim,* p. 17.

be." We acknowledge the thoughts and feelings we have as our own and accept them *without evaluation,* on that basis alone. We say, "Yes, this is what I am right now and that's the way it is." We don't hassle ourselves for thoughts and emotions we "shouldn't" (by whatever standard) have. Ellis focuses clearly on self-acceptance when he tells his clients, "You are not *good* and you are not *bad*—you are merely *you.*[10]

It is important to distinguish, at least from our point of view, that acceptance does not necessarily mean approval. Failing to keep these two concepts distinct leads people to say, "That's the way I am. I'll never change. Take it or leave it." The point here is that it is possible (and we believe, preferable) to accept what we think and feel and "are" at any given point in time and still see and be willing to work with our potential for change, development, and growth.

If the explanation seems a bit vague and ambiguous at this point, that may be because it is. Complete self-acceptance is one of the most difficult things in the world to accomplish, and we, ourselves, have not yet achieved it. So our lack of clarity may be due not only to some inherent fuzziness of the concept, but to our own lack of full experiencing. Still, we do believe that it is possible to achieve some measure of self-acceptance by working with some of the following ideas. Before we do anything else we must make the decision to move from awareness to acceptance. Awareness of thoughts and even of emotions is primarily a cognitive process that is all in our heads. As Westerners and especially as cognitively-oriented college students and instructors we are often accused of "intellectualizing," and insofar as concentration on awareness excludes acceptance, this is an accurate accusation and should be taken into consideration. Staying "in our head" prevents us from fully experiencing ourselves as total human beings. So to the extent that "head" focus excludes "being" focus, acceptance and therefore growth is inhibited. This move from awareness to acceptance is a risky choice to make. For example, the advice of one friend to another was, "When you are forced to move out of your head into experiencing your deeper emotional responses, I don't 'hear' anything," which means, "You are so out of touch (unaccepting) with your feeling self that you cannot possibly communicate that self to me."

The first step to self-acceptance is to acknowledge the fact that we are fallible human beings and that we sometimes do things that would have been better left undone. If we must evaluate ourselves, it should be evaluation of specific performances rather than a holistic judgment

---

10. Ellis, *Humanistic Psychotherapy,* p. 24.

of our persons. For example, if you oversleep and miss an important class, try not saying something like, "I'm a lazy good-for-nothing"; but rather, "What I did was unfortunate, I'll try not to do it again." Or on the other hand, if you did well on a test, try saying, "It's good that I studied hard and did well on the test," rather than, "I'm a terrifically intelligent person." The focus is on *actions,* rather than personhood. As we can see from the example, it doesn't matter whether the personality evaluation is positive or negative, because if we concede that it's all right to evaluate ourselves rather than our actions then a positive judgment can always be withdrawn and replaced by a negative judgment. Self-evaluation is, of course, related to self-esteem. It appears that something in our nature dictates that we evaluate ourselves in some way.[11]  An appropriate suggestion drawn from theory is: accept yourself as being you in the here and now, without evaluation. Insofar as you must evaluate to maintain a sense of self-esteem judge your actions and performance as they occur, in isolation. For example, once you have evaluated the speeding ticket you got as unfortunate and suggest to yourself that you'll try not to let it happen again—forget it—getting that ticket says nothing in a predetermined way about future driving behavior, and it definitely says nothing about you as a whole person.

The second step toward self-acceptance is understanding the difference between *having* thoughts and feelings and *acting* on them. Quite a few people tend to equate the two and fail to realize that they can choose *not* to act on those emotions. John Powell clarifies this point well. He suggests that we must understand

> emotions are not *moral* but simply *factual.* My jealousies, my anger, my sexual desires, my fears, etc. do not make me a good or bad person. Of course, these emotional reactions must be integrated by my mind and will, but . . . before I can decide whether I want to act on them or not, I must allow them to arise and I must clearly hear what they are saying to me. I must be able to say, without any sense of moral reprehension, that I am afraid or angry or sexually aroused.
>
> Before I will be free enough to do this, however, I must be convinced that emotions are not moral, neither good nor bad in themselves. I must be convinced, too, that the experience of the whole gamut of emotions is a part of the human condition, the inheritance of every man.[12]

11. Ibid., chapter 2, "The Value of a Human Being: A Psychotherapeutic Appraisal."

12. John Powell, *Why Am I Afraid To Tell You Who I Am?* (Chicago: Argus Communications, 1969), p. 71.

Jack, for example, will never admit that he is feeling negative emotions because not only should he *not* feel that way because he'd be a terrible person if he did, but also he thinks that feeling and acting are the same. The potentially dangerous thing about his confusion is that he fails to express his thoughts and feelings, with the possible result that he will lose the ability to feel.

So as well as accepting that we do execute some unfortunate events, we need to accept the fact that we have negative thoughts and emotions. Jess Lair explains how acknowledging his human imperfections worked for him: "This helped me to see deeper within myself, accept myself and tell more about how it was with me. All this came out of an acceptance of myself as I was. I had to throw away as much of the fake as possible and recognize all my feelings and all my actions as me. So I was able to see and accept: I ain't much, baby—but I'm all I've got."[13]

Carl Rogers suggests that one cannot "move forward in the process of becoming" unless one is accepting of himself.[14] So it appears that if we want to become more self-accepting we need to try taking these two steps.

## Self-Assertion

Self-assertion is the affirmation in action and communication of what we are. It is the harmonious acting out of those thoughts and feelings that we choose to act on, based on our own standards of choice. In relating self-assertion to the stages of growth, we see that self-assertion involves a commitment to those thoughts and feelings we will act on, and development and refinement of not only our actions but the ideas and emotions which lead to them.

Although external circumstances may seem to overwhelm us, we can be "the captain of our fate." The key concept here is responsibility, which was introduced in chapter 3 (responsibility is the willingness to accept the consequences of our thoughts, feelings, and behavior). Humanists think it far more important to stress accepting consequences than dictating any "correct" ideas, emotions, or actions.

William Glasser, the originator of Reality Therapy, believes responsibility to be such an important variable that he suggests that

---

13. Jess Lair, *I Ain't Much, Baby—But I'm All I've Got* (New York: Doubleday, 1969), p. 17.

14. Carl Rogers, *On Becoming a Person: A Therapist's View of Psychotherapy* (Boston: Houghton Mifflin, 1961), p. 63.

unhappiness and inappropriate behavior do not cause irresponsibility, but rather that irresponsible behavior is a *cause* of unhappiness and inappropriate behavior.[15] One of Glasser's favorite tactics is to get the client to develop a concrete plan to initiate "constructive thinking about what he is doing right now and about his future."[16] This is not used to tie the person inflexibly to any particular course of action, but rather to stimulate the person to commit himself or herself responsibly to the present and future existence. For example, if you are "responsible," you will probably have some plan or plans about what you intend to do when you finish school. That doesn't mean that you *have to* be an accountant or teacher, it merely means that you are thinking ahead and planning to take responsibility for your own life in *some way*.

Now let's look again at the P-A-C model to see another approach to commitment and acceptance of responsibility. It seems safe to infer that responsibility, to the transactional analyst, consists of keeping our adult in control. This does not mean always *acting* from our adult (unless we choose to live a rather emotionless life), but rather having our adult act as mediator between the parent and the child. There are times when parental messages such as, "Don't touch that stove," are not only appropriate but life saving. And there are times when child messages such as, "Wow, the flowers are blooming!" are not only appropriate but joy giving. The point is that the *adult* is to make the decision, based on incoming and stored data, about what action is appropriate at any given moment. For example, my adult, based on the data that I'm moving right along in writing this chapter and have more than adequate time to meet my deadline, may let my child out to play—my adult might give me permission to watch M.A.S.H. on TV or go get a Dairy Queen. To the extent that we keep our adult in control, letting it decide what thoughts, feelings, and actions are situationally appropriate, we will be acting responsibly.

Finally, the RET person would suggest that acting responsibly involves disputing our irrational ideas. To begin this process, we need to consider the possibility that other people don't disturb us, we disturb ourselves. There is no room in rational-emotive therapy for extricating ourselves from a situation by saying the devil made us do it. We are responsible for the thoughts we have and the emotions resulting from and actions based on them.

---

15. William Glasser, *Reality Therapy: A New Approach to Psychiatry* (New York: Harper & Row, 1965), p. 30.

16. Ibid., p. 31.

We can dispute our irrational ideas with the following rational beliefs. Each one corresponds directly to the previously mentioned irrational ideas:

1. While it is desirable to be approved and accepted by others, it is not an absolute necessity. My life doesn't really depend upon such acceptance, nor can I really control the minds and behavior of other persons. And, furthermore, a lack of total acceptance is certainly not catastrophic or horrible and doesn't at all mean that I am worthless or a louse.

2. Many persons do commit acts that are inappropriate, self-defeating, or antisocial. It is desirable to try to induce such persons to act more effectively than to spend needless time and energy blaming, accusing, and becoming upset over their acts. Moreover, needless blame and punishment rarely stop such persons who are usually ignorant, emotionally disturbed, or stupid from committing such acts. Demanding that persons should not commit stupid acts often is nothing more than a demand that reality be different—reality is reality. The crucial question is, what constructive actions can I initiate to modify reality?

3. When things don't go the way I want them to go, it is too bad or inconvenient—but not catastrophic. And, it may be in my best interest to change them or arrange conditions so that they may become more satisfactory. But, if I can't change or modify situations to my liking, I would be better off accepting their existence rather than telling myself how awful they are.

4. While most people are taught that external events are the direct cause of one's happiness, in virtually most cases human unhappiness is caused by one's thoughts, appraisals, evaluations, or perceptions of those events. That is, I create my own disturbance. Since I am human, I can expect to disturb myself often. But, that doesn't mean I have to continually disturb myself forever.

5. If something is or may be dangerous or fearsome, it is probably in my best interest to face it and try to render it less dangerous and, if that is impossible, I should stop dwelling on such fears —especially when little evidence exists that such horrible things will, in fact, occur.

6. While it is humanly normal to want to take the easy way out —such things as avoiding life's difficulties and self-responsibilities—in the long run, I would probably be better off confronting openly such difficulties, facing them squarely, and trying to solve them.

7. Although the sociocultural system teaches and reinforces one's tendencies to be dependent on others and things, I would be better off standing on my own two feet in facing life. Moreover, if I fail to be independent in the short run, that doesn't mean that I will fail in the future. After all, am I not a fallible person?

8. Since I am a human being with biological, sociological, and psychological limitations, I cannot reasonably expect to be perfect in any endeavor. But, I certainly can strive to perform well in those tasks I deem as significantly contributing to my self-development. In those areas I am deficient, I certainly can strive to improve. If I fail—tough, too bad.

9. Although I have been influenced greatly by my past experiences and specific instances of the past greatly affect me today, I can profit by such experiences but not be overly prejudiced or biased by them. Nor do I need to be dominated by them in the future.

10. I could probably develop the skills necessary to control enormously my own emotions or feelings if I decide to commit myself to that process. And, it would be in my best interest if I would take the necessary risks in order to achieve a greater control over my own destiny. Of course, I don't really expect to develop these skills overnight.

11. Anger is a normal human emotion and its expression is not a sign of personal worthlessness. Moreover, being aware of my anger and expressing it as a communication of current feelings without indiscriminantly attacking the personal worth of others may be in my best interest. Denying my anger is rarely in my best interest.

12. If I share most of my thoughts and feelings (negative or positive) honestly and openly, it will probably help me communicate more effectively with others in the long run—even though in the short run I might experience some temporary discomfort.

13. Striving to know and to accept others for their humanness is a reasonable goal. Moreover, it is in my best interest to try to act fairly with others so I may receive the full benefit of their humanness. However, trying to please others at the expense of my own well-being is not personally growth enhancing. Therefore, I can only do my best in trying to please others. If I fail —tough.

14. Human beings, including myself, are happiest when they are actively involved in creative pursuits or when they devote themselves to people or projects outside of themselves. Long-term withdrawal from the world or inaction rarely are associated with happiness. Therefore, it would be in my best interest to force myself into productive or creative activity.

15. It is desirable for me to be able to develop meaningful and intimate relationships with persons, especially those of the opposite sex. However, if I demand intimate and satisfying relationships with others, I will tend to focus on the outcome of such interpersonal relationships rather than the process of getting to know and accept another person. Therefore, I would be better off not demanding but trying to be spontaneous, responsive, and accepting toward significant persons.[17]

Furthermore, we can check the rationality of our ideas by seeing if they meet the following three criteria. According to these criteria, thinking is rational when it

> ... leads to constructive actions that are likely to preserve the individual's life; it stimulates actions that have a greater likelihood of achieving the individual's personally defined goals; and it does not result in significant and sustained personal, emotional, or environmental conflict.[18]

We hope it is clear that by assertion we do not mean doing or saying *anything* we feel like at the moment, regardless of circumstances. It could, of course, but only if we are willing to accept the consequences that attend such action. Some people refuse to accept this responsibility, like the person who says something and when asked to clarify the statement completely absolves himself of responsibility for the communication by saying, "Oh, that didn't mean anything," or, "I don't know what I meant. I just talk."

It is important for us to realize that control over our lives resides in us, that we shouldn't find anything else responsible but our own actions or lack of them when failing to do something. For example, when we fail to get to class on time—is it the alarm clock, the car, the traffic, the weather, the parking, the elevator?—do we blame external circumstances? Do we see control of our lives as external rather than internal?

Responsibility is not easy to take, but if we do assume it, we have a legitimate right to give ourselves credit for positive achievements. It makes little sense to assume that we control our successes, but other things control our failures.

---

17. Tosi, "Self-Directed Behavior Change," pp. 10–11. Used with permission.
18. Maxwell Haultsby, "Systematic Homework in Written Psychotherapy," *Rational Living* 6 (1971): 16–23.

### Self-Actualization

In chapter 2 we discussed Maslow's hierarchy of needs. At the top of that hierarchy stands self-actualization. Self-actualization can be defined, paradoxically, as a *state* of continued *growth*. In this state we reaffirm/redirect our present state in life with the result that we escape boredom and are at peace with ourselves. Maslow expresses it this way: "A musician must make music, an artist must paint, a poet must write, if he is to be ultimately at peace with himself. What a man *can* be, he *must* be. He must be true to his own nature."[19]

The theory, as you recall, is that we don't move toward self-actualization until the other physiological, safety, love, and esteem needs have generally been satisfied. Maslow points out, however, that each level will not be fulfilled 100 percent before we move to a higher level.[20] It is possible then that we might still be working on the fulfillment of, say, esteem needs when we embark on self-actualization.

Maslow's characteristics of self-actualizing people can be reviewed in chapter 2. To indicate the interest that currently exists in the process of growth, we'd like to share two other similar descriptions of the self-actualizing person. Carl Rogers terms the growth process that of "becoming a person." This is how he describes the process and characteristics of self-actualization:

> I have pointed out that each individual appears to be asking a double question: "who am I" and "how may I become myself?" I have stated that in a favorable psychological climate a process of becoming takes place; that here the individual drops one after another of the defensive masks with which he has faced life; that he experiences fully the hidden aspects of himself; that he discovers in these experiences the stranger who has been living behind these masks, the stranger who is himself. I have tried to give my picture of the characteristic attributes of the person who emerges; a person who is more open to all of the elements of his organic experience; a person who is developing a trust in his own organism as an instrument of sensitive living; a person who accepts the locus of evaluation as residing within himself; a person who is learning to live in his life as a participant in a fluid, ongoing process, in which he is continually discovering new aspects of himself in the flow of his experience.

19. Abraham Maslow, *Motivation and Personality* (New York: Harper & Row, 1954), p. 46.
20. Ibid., pp. 53–54.

These are some of the elements which seem to me to be involved in becoming a person.[21]

The characteristics of self-actualizing people are described in another way by Donald Tosi, an RET counselor. Drawing from Everett Shostrom's Personal Orientation Inventory, he lists the following as dimensions of personal growth that he sees as goals of the counselor-client relationship.

> *Time Competence* refers to one's ability to live his life in the "here and now" ... [it] also implies a balance between the immediate gratification of one's desires ... and being able to delay gratification for the sake of long-term rewards and satisfaction. ...
>
> *Inner-directedness* is the ability to be positively self-oriented and self-directed in contradiction to being directed by others. ...
>
> *Existentiality* is the ability of a person to react to new experiences without rigid adherence to unsound, unscientific, or unproven principles ... [it is] an openness to experience. ...
>
> *Feeling Reactivity* refers to one's awareness and sensitivity to his thoughts, feelings, and desires. ...
>
> *Spontaneity* is the freedom to react or act in a nondefensive, reasonable manner in a variety of interpersonal situations. ...
>
> *Self-regard* ... refers to a person's being able to affirm himself because of his self-defined sense of worth or value to himself.
>
> *Self-Acceptance* refers to one's ability to accept himself fully in spite of his biological, sociological, and psychological limitations. ...
>
> *Nature of Man* ... depicts one's affirming a rational-realistic, constructive view of man. ...
>
> *Synergy* is a cognitive ability ... to transcend seemingly opposite positions or to synthesize them into a meaningful concept. ...
>
> *Acceptance of Aggression* is the capacity to accept one's natural aggressiveness as opposed to defensiveness, denial, and repression of aggression.
>
> *Capacity for Intimate Contact* is the facility to develop close interpersonal relationships with others unencumbered by expectations and obligations.[22]

As we look at these attributes of the self-actualizing person it is important that we not despair, thinking that this is a perfection we

---

21. Rogers, *On Becoming a Person,* p. 123.
22. Tosi, *Youth,* pp. 19–20.

will never achieve. Self-actualization is *continuing* growth. This implies that there will always be plateaus, and even regression. The important thing is that there is movement, and it is forward and upward. Maslow, as intrigued as he is with self-actualizing people, reminds us:

> What this (studying self-actualizing people) has taught me I think all of us had better learn. *There are no perfect human beings!* Persons can be found who are good, very good indeed, in fact great. . . . And yet these very same people can at times be boring, irritating, petulant, angry, or depressed. To avoid disillusionment with human nature, we must first give up our illusions about it.[23]

These descriptions are all very nice, but they don't really tell us how to move toward self-actualization, do they? It is not usually a simple, painless process. Many take the stand that growth comes only through suffering and conflict. If we make the decision to grow, we will find that some pain is inherent in growth. But perhaps the rewards are worth the costs involved. Although there is some disagreement as to whether self-actualization is achieved or the natural outcome of the first three stages, Maslow lists some ways we can work toward (achieving) self-actualization.[24]

First, we can try to experience things with total concentration and involvement, forgetting about ourselves except as we interact with the object of concentration. We all have had moments when we are totally unaware of our surroundings, be it playing cards, reading a good novel, or sharing with a cherished friend. We can increase the number of "experiencing moments" by forgetting about what "other people might think" and becoming totally involved in what we are doing at the time.

Second, every time we must make a choice where one of the good alternatives involves some risk, we can try to make that choice, the growth choice, rather than another safer, defensive choice. Choosing to come to college may be a growth choice for some, involving the risk of leaving familiar surroundings. On the other hand, if parents had planned college for their child, choosing to follow that path rather than risk disapproval or maybe even disinheritance is a safety choice.

Third, we can try to get in touch with what we really think and feel about things, not what our parents, or friends, or "society" thinks and feels. We need to turn off those messages from childhood and listen

---

23. Maslow, *Motivation,* p. 176.
24. Abraham Maslow, *The Farther Reaches of Human Nature* (New York: Viking, 1971), pp. 45–50.

to ourselves. Do you really want to be a doctor like your father? Do you really want to get married and have children? Do you really like Chinese food or expensive wine?

Fourth, we need to be honest and take the responsibility for that honesty. Except in situations where it will do much more harm than good (such as John's announcing proudly to deeply religious parents that he is now an atheist), we can strive for authenticity—making our words match our thoughts and feelings. As we are honest we should avoid making a game of it by saying something like, "I'm only trying to be open and sincere."

Fifth, we need the courage to be different. This suggestion relates to the previous ones and obviously involves risk, honesty, and listening to self.

Sixth, we can work hard at the thing we really want to do. In other words, we can discipline ourselves to do the rather routine parts involved in every life goal. For example, we can't experience the joy of victory in winning a race if we don't work out and run many extra miles, just as we can't have attractive builds if we don't exercise and watch our caloric intake.

Seventh, we can let peak experiences happen. Peak experiences are the highest, most fleeting, most at-one-with-the-world-and-yourself type of self-actualizing moments. They can occur when listening to music, reading a poem, or making love. Because it is difficult even for Maslow to describe what a peak experience is, it is even more difficult to explain how to achieve one. The best that can be suggested is that we create the conditions for peak experiences by ridding ourselves of prejudices and myths, learning what we like and can do, and expanding our awareness by experimenting with new ideas and activities.[25] Try reading Vonnegut or learning yoga or listening to Chopin.

Eighth, we can attempt to identify and remove our defenses. In line with what we have said previously, we can try not repressing our anger or sublimating our artistic inclinations. Most of all, Maslow suggests, we must try to rid ourselves of the defense that there are no such things as values or principles, a defense mechanism developed because too often we have seen values and principles thwarted or laughed at. Redeveloping a value for life and love and family and honesty, as hokey as it may sound, seems to be an inherent part of self-actualization.

---

25. For a number of ways to promote personal growth, see Herbert A. Otto and John Mann, *Ways of Growth: Approaches to Expanding Awareness* (New York: Viking, 1968).

Many of these steps are included under self-awareness, self-accept-ance, and self-assertion. We find repetition here because these stages must be worked through in order to embark on the process of self-actualization. Maslow sums up:

> Put all these points together, and we see that self-actualization is not a matter of one great moment. It is not true that on Thursday at four o'clock the trumpet blows and one steps into the pantheon forever and altogether. Self-actualization is a matter of degree, of accessions accumulated one by one. ... People selected as self-actualizing subjects ... go about it in these little ways: They listen to their own voices; they take responsibility; they are honest; and they work hard. They find out who they are and what they are, not only in terms of their mission in life, but also in terms of the way their feet hurt when they wear such and such a pair of shoes and whether they do or do not like eggplant or stay up all night if they drink too much beer. ... They find their own biological natures. ...[26]

As we suggested before, authentic *inter*personal communication begins with authentic *intra*personal communication, and authentic intrapersonal communication results from knowing yourself, accept-ing yourself, asserting yourself, and realizing yourself. Let's assume momentarily that we have been authentic with ourselves. How do we go about bridging the gap between ourselves and the other? We will find in our final section that self-disclosure is one of the most impor-tant means of communicating in a meaningful way, of becoming aware of another, and, in the process, of becoming even more aware and accepting of ourselves.

## Bridging the Gap: Self-Disclosure

John Powell answers the title question of his book, *Why Am I Afraid to Tell You Who I Am?* by saying "If I tell you who I am, you may not like who I am, and it is all that I have."[27] Self-disclosure, or telling what is in your deepest heart, involves not a little risk, but it is necessary for dialogue.

When we share information about ourselves, we give the other a certain amount of power over us because of the information he now

---

26. Maslow, *Farther Reaches,* p. 50.
27. Powell, *Why Am I Afraid,* p. 27.

possesses. Giving the other this power involves basically two risks: one to our self-esteem and one to our reputation. Let's say that a woman discloses that she has had an abortion. What if the other person, given this new information about her responds, "Why that's murder. That was an immoral way to handle your problem." The image of "murderer" will be very damaging to her self-esteem. Suppose further that this other person "spreads it around" that she has had an abortion, telling people who agree essentially with his opinion on the subject. The damage is then extended to her reputation.

Because of these risks, we do not advocate self-disclosure of everything to everyone. That could be as foolish, inflexible, and as dangerous as withholding everything from everyone. We really must be able to *trust* the other person and trust that he cares enough about us to treat the information we give him judiciously and tenderly. Generally, it takes time and a certain similarity of values in a relationship to establish this kind of trust. It is accomplished in small steps, which Sidney Jourard, a psychologist who has written extensively about self-disclosure, calls the dyadic effect.[28] When the dyadic effect is operating, we disclose a certain amount about ourselves and the other discloses a similar amount, then the process begins again. Powell describes the dyadic effect this way.

> I open myself and my world to you for your entry, and you open yourself and your world to me for me to enter. I have allowed you to experience me as a person, in all the fullness of my person, and I have experienced you in this way. And for this, I must tell you who I am and you must tell me the same about yourself.[29]

Another way to understand the process of self-disclosure is to look at the Johari Window.[30] There are four types of information in relation to others knowing us. There is information (1) known to self and others—the *free* area; (2) not known to self—the *blind* area; (3) known to self and not to others—the *hidden* area; (4) known neither to self or others—the *unknown* area.

Theoretically, through self-disclosure we move information about ourselves from the hidden area into the free area. Not only do we let the other know what we know about ourselves, but we discover through the other's feedback things we did not know. The other may

---

28. Sidney M. Jourard, *The Transparent Self: Self-Disclosure and Well-Being* (New York: Van Nostrand Reinhold, 1964), p. 179.

29. Powell, *Why Am I Afraid*, p. 47.

30. William D. Brooks, *Speech Communication* (Dubuque: Wm C. Brown, 1974), p. 72.

| I | II |
|---|---|
| FREE | BLIND |
| III | IV |
| HIDDEN | UNKNOWN |

expose us to something that is in our blind area and, together with the other's help, we may discover something not known to either one of us at the beginning of the relationship.

Before we illustrate this process a distinction between *self-description* and *self-disclosure* needs to be made. Self-description involves information that the other person could gain about us in some way, other than our telling him; for example, age or occupation. Self-description is usually nonthreatening; telling someone where we went to school involves little risk. Self-disclosure, on the other hand, provides information which the other person can usually get in no way other than by our disclosing it to him. Of course, it could be said that one man's description is another man's disclosure. For example, we may know someone who treats revealing age as a very important and threatening disclosure.

To illustrate, Tim initiates a disclosing relationship with another by telling him that he is really terrified of asking questions in class. Tim takes information from the hidden area and brings it into the free area. As he explores this phenomenon with the other, hopefully the dyadic effect is operating and the other is sharing some of his own fears with Tim. In this process he tells Tim that he always appears most confident when posing a question. Tim thought he looked as scared as he felt—material has moved from the blind area into the free area. Through further mutual probing into his problem Tim discovers that the reason he is frightened is that his father always told him that what he said was silly. Tim shares this insight with the other person. Newly discovered information has moved from the unknown area into the free area.

The theory further suggests that we move as much information as possible into the free area, so that the Johari Window looks like this:

| I | II |
|---|---|
| III | IV |

Obviously, the larger our free area with a greater number of people important to us, the more honest and authentic we are being in communicating with ourselves and others.

Jourard suggests that the healthy person will "display the ability to make himself fully known to at least one other significant human being."[31] This statement reminds us that the risks we mentioned are real; that it takes caution and time and effort to establish a disclosing relationship; that a healthy balance needs to be struck between over-concealing and overrevealing. There are not that many significant others in our lives. Disclosing with them is challenge enough. We do not have to accost strangers on the street and tell them our life's story to be a healthy individual.

It is at this point that we would like to again bring in the stages of growth. They are intimately tied to the building of a trusting relationship in which we can freely self-disclose and allow another to do likewise. We become aware of what self-disclosure is and involves—that it is more than self-description and involves material about ourselves that we have kept hidden and also material of which we are not yet cognizant. We *explore* self-disclosure by experiencing it in very low risk situations with nonthreatening people, to see how it feels. Next we *commit* ourselves to self-disclosure with a particular person; we decide to take the risks involved even though we are afraid, and we decide to take the responsibility for what we disclose. Then, we *develop the skills* of self-disclosure; we learn what types of things are beneficial to disclose without being afraid or guilty afterwards. Finally, we *refine the skills* of self-disclosure; we learn how to "brainstorm" with the other to get at things in the unknown area, or we allow ourselves to fantasize freely and creatively with him by, for example, sharing strange dreams. If *boredom* sets in, perhaps we will want to reaffirm the process of self-disclosure with this person and decide to end the relationship because there is nothing more to be gained or to continue it with modification by bringing in a third party, or just to allow it to remain as it has become—hopefully a close and intimate friendship that can be reaffirmed with new experiences, thoughts and feelings to be shared.

We have mentioned the risks. What are the rewards? We think, obviously, that they are greater than the risks or we would not even have focused on this vehicle of authentic communication. Generally we see three basic rewards to be gained from self-disclosure.

31. Jourard, *Transparent Self,* p. 25.

First, self-disclosure is a way to promote continued personal growth. As Jourard puts it: "It is not until I *am* my real self and I act my real self that my real self is in a position to grow."[32] We have had this experience of continued growth through disclosing with people significant to us. This is achieved because by acting our real selves, we provide the conditions where additional insights to our beings might be found. Through increased knowledge about ourselves, discovered mutually through disclosure, we are in a more favorable position to grow. For example, revealing to a close friend, "I honestly feel that when it comes right down to it, nobody really cares. You really can't rely on anyone but yourself," is not easy especially because it is an indirect indictment of that person, too. However, by pursuing the subject, additional insight as to why this feeling existed, whether it was true or whether it was the person's own feeling projected onto everyone else, can be gained and growth can be facilitated.

Another reward from self-disclosure is that of finding certain commonalities among people. Sometimes thoughts and feelings that we believe are really strange are being experienced by others. For example, many students think they are the only ones ever to have experienced stage fright before giving a speech. Then we share with them feelings similar to theirs, sometimes experienced just before giving a lecture. Another example is that many men and women feel that they are singular in their inability to understand and explain and predict the actions and reactions of the opposite sex. Through disclosure with the same sex, they find that others do, indeed, encounter similar problems: "Does your husband/wife do that, too? Doesn't that just aggravate the hell out of you? Gee, I thought I was the only one who had that problem." Through self-disclosure we may find that we are not so weird after all.

The final reward to be gained from self-disclosure is establishing the type of I-Thou relationship discussed in chapter 7. These relationships may be of short or long duration—some will last a few months, others, a lifetime—but there is something deep and beautiful to be gained from each of them. That something is the essence of dialogue and all the conditions which surround it: presentness, spontaneity, authenticity, empathy, positive regard, experiencing, congruence, "letting be."

32. Ibid.

## Summary

In this chapter we have provided a framework for achieving more authentic communication with ourselves as a basis for achieving more authentic communication with others.

We began by describing stages of growth which we believe operate not only intrapersonally in both the general progression of living and in specific roles we engage in at various times, but also operate in interpersonal communication. The stages of growth are awareness, exploration, commitment, skill development, skill refinement, then boredom and reaffirmation.

We saw the stages of growth as being related to the processes of intrapersonal development introduced in chapter 2: self-awareness (cognitive awareness and exploration), self-acceptance (emotion and physical awareness and exploration), self-assertion (commitment and skill development and refinement) and self-actualization (reaffirmation). In probing more deeply into these concepts we shared some psychological theories. Among them were theories of transactional analysis, rational-emotive therapy, Gestalt therapy, reality therapy, and self-actualization.

Finally, we suggested that once being honest with self, we could move toward greater honesty with others through self-disclosure, a process explained by the Johari Window. We suggested that although risks were inherent in self-disclosure, the rewards of moving unknown, blind, and hidden information into our free areas were well worth the risks involved.

In the next part of this book we will move from theoretical underpinnings to some discussion of various types of interpersonal experiences: routine, dyadic, and group.

# PART FOUR

# Interpersonal
# Experiences

# 10

# Routine
# Experiences

To this point, we have discussed intrapersonal and interpersonal communication and their dialogic components. Now we can apply this knowledge in exploring various types of experiences which we encounter each and every day of our lives.

Every day we participate in routine, dyadic, and group experiences. It is not enough to be a participant in these experiences—anyone can be an unwitting partner in what, on the surface, appears to be an automatic, natural activity. We need to be fully aware of the nature of those activities we take part in, because awareness of our behavior can bring control of it, and therefore greater fulfillment in even the most trivial and transient communication encounters.

This section of the book logically begins with routine experiences, for it is routines which we are least aware of and yet engage in most often. Study the following transactions:

*Tom:*  My dad gave me a hassle last night about my hair being too long again.

*Jim:*  You too? Man, everytime I go home for vacation I get it. It's really a bummer.

*Karen:*   Yeah, you just can't win. If its not the hair, its the music you play, or the hours you keep.

*Brent:*   Hi, How's it going?

*Kim:*   Okay, I guess, and with you?

*Brent:*   'Bout the same. See you around.

*Kim:*   Yeah, later.

*Bev:*   Tim hasn't called for two days. I bet he's on to some other girl.

*Sandy:*   Don't worry. He'll call and I bet he'll take you out this weekend. You know he's holding down a job and carrying eighteen hours.

*Doug:*   I just can't seem to get the courage to break up with my girl, even though I know it's never going to work out.

*Bill:*   Why don't you just come right out and be honest with her?

*Doug:*   Yeah, but she'd cry and I can't stand that. I really freaks me out.

*Bill:*   Well, why not write her a letter?

*Doug:*   Yeah, but that would be a chicken way to end it, a real cop out!

*Susie:*   Excuse me, do you have an extra pen?

*Bert:*   Sure, here.

*Susie:*   Thanks a lot. I'll give it back right after the lecture.

*Bert:*   Sure. Think nothing of it.

We have all engaged in similar experiences. Though they may be of different styles, they are the same as routine interpersonal communication. By the end of this chapter, we will be able to distinguish different types of routine experiences and at the same time see the similarity of purpose and effect among them.

## Definition

For our purposes, *a routine experience is an interpersonal transaction in which we seem to engage automatically and yet purposefully in every day communication with others.* An experience is routine when it is synchronized, reciprocal, regular, and culturally conditioned. Before proceeding to detail different types of routine experiences, consider characteristics of phatic communion, social ritual, pastimes, games, and P-A-C transactions.

*Purpose.* Each routine in which we engage has a specific, though often unconscious, purpose. We will find that routine activities function primarily "as social cement and lubricants."[1] Their purpose is to keep persons together and help persons to communicate smoothly.

*Synchronization.* Each routine in which we engage is synchronized, timed to flow smoothly for its duration. We will find that routine activities are characterized by a rhythm, by a patterned give and take. The entire exchange is patterned to last a specified amount of time and each of our exchanges within are patterned to be of a certain length and intensity.

*Reciprocity.* Each routine in which we engage is reciprocal, which means designed so that all participants are a party to the exchange in approximately equal degrees. As communicologist Leonard Hawes explains: "We act *as if* others will act in concert with us. . . . We act *as if* he knows we are enacting a routine . . . and he acts *as if* we are acting *as if* it is a routine."[2]

Reciprocity implies the functioning of roles, role expectations, and role performance. Each of us, in a routine experience, has a well-defined role to perform according to certain expectations inherent in the specific type of routine. And, as each role we play assumes a complementary role played by others, there are certain expectations that need to be met by the other participants in the exchange.

*Regularity.* Each role in which we engage exhibits regularity; it is nearly predictable in its outcome if the purpose for each participant is identical, and synchronization and reciprocity are present. Routines

---

1. Leonard Hawes, "Interpersonal Communication: The Enactment of Routines," in John J. Makay, ed., *Explorations in Speech Communication* (Columbus, Ohio: Charles E. Merrill, 1973), p. 73.
2. Ibid., p. 73.

are certainly not random, and they are unlikely to vary from one set of exchanges to the other. From each routine, a recognizable pattern emerges which appears to be more important than what each of the participants is doing individually.

*Cultural Conditioning.* Routine interpersonal communication is culturally conditioned, characterized by its adherence to certain social norms and standards. Social norms affecting routine experiences function for the participant in two ways: "As an obligation that requires him to do (or refrain from doing) something in regard to others, and as an expectation that leads him to anticipate righteously that something will be done (or specifically not done) by them in regard to him."[3]

Having defined and identified the major characteristics of routine experience, we now turn to the different types of routines in which we engage.

## Phatic Communion

As communicologist Kim Giffin affirms, "The initiation of a communicative event carries with it an implied request: 'Please validate me'."[4] It is this seemingly inherent human desire for the other's recognition that leads us to engage in the routine called phatic communion.

*Phatic communion is a routine which validates another's existence, which implies recognition of another's presence.* Another term for phatic communion, coined by Eric Berne, is "stroking."[5] A stroke is a verbal (or sometimes nonverbal) unit in an exchange which serves the function of validating the other. Before we proceed to study examples of phatic communion, decide which of the exchanges given at the beginning of the chapter involved stroking.

As a saying goes, we have "different strokes for different folks." For example, you may owe only a nod to a classmate you see in a big lecture hall twice a week. You incline your head in a nonverbal acknowledgment of his existence and he likewise recognizes your presence. Someone who lives in the same apartment deserves a solitary verbal stroke, such as, "Hi." An acquaintance may demand a

---

3. Erving Goffman, *Relations in Public* (New York: Basic Books, 1971), p. 96.
4. Kim Giffin, "Social Alienation by Communication Denial," *Quarterly Journal of Speech* 56: 351.
5. Eric Berne, *Games People Play* (New York: Grove, 1964), p. 15.

greater number of strokes: a hi-how-are-you-how's-it-going pattern. A very close friend (whether regular date of permanent mate) requires the greatest number of strokes as indicated in the following interchange.

*1 Mary:* Hi (kiss on cheek).

*2 John:* Hi (kiss on cheek).

*3 Mary:* How was your day?

*4 John:* Fine, and yours?

*5 Mary:* Okay. Traffic bad?

*6 John:* Same as always.

*7 Mary:* Uh-huh.

The important point to notice about this exchange (and of all phatic communion that goes beyond the hi-hi stage) is that although it *appears* that information is being transmitted, this is not the *function* of phatic communion at all. What is really being transmitted, if put into words, would be something like this.

*1 Mary:* I know you exist.

*2 John:* I know you exist, too.

*3 Mary:* Are you going to be predictable tonight?

*4 John:* Yes, are you?

*5 Mary:* Yes. I hope you're okay.

*6 John:* I am.

*7 Mary:* Good. Things are normal. Now we can exchange information.

Phatic communion serves as a basis for real communication, and perhaps every dialogue. Although some people decry phatic communion as shallow, trivial, and meaningless, we think it necessary and *prerequisite* to a real exchange of thoughts and emotions. Phatic communion must precede communication at deeper levels where we create meaning about ideas, attitudes, beliefs, and values.

Perhaps you doubt this viewpoint. Even if you wish to take it at face value, we hope that you will test out the assertion. Try the following experiments. For an acquaintance who usually receives three strokes, subtract two. Instead of saying (1) Hi (2) How are you (3) How's it going, say merely (1) Hi. If he doesn't ask you later if something was wrong that day, you can be surprised. Or, try eliminating phatic communion altogether as a basis for further communication. The next time you see a friend, say immediately, "I want to talk about my math course," or something similar. We do not guarantee that the reaction will be negative, only that there will be a reaction—the person will probably be taken aback because you did not "pave the way" for this statement in the normally accepted manner, or expected routine.

Phatic communion is a necessary routine. As Clark, Bock, and Cornett express it, "We 'mill around' each other, trying to discover some way of getting beyond milling around, looking for ways to break the ice, to get deeper, etc. But it *always happens;* we begin phatically (italics ours).[6] Let's investigate other routines that "cement and lubricate" human relationships.

## Social Ritual

A *social ritual in interpersonal communication is a set of conventions functioning to support the roles, expectations, and outcomes of social interaction, and to remedy a social situation if something goes awry.* We can see here that although phatic communion is "ritualized," i.e., patterned, its main function is to validate existence; social ritual is, as we shall discover, more inclusive and comprehensive of patterns of social interaction.

After we have recognized the other and made contact with him, according to Erving Goffman, we perform two basic types of ritual: supportive and remedial.[7] Goffman, having devoted most of his professional career to studying forms of human interaction, has discovered four types of supportive ritual which regulate the roles, expectations, and outcomes of human interaction.

The first type is the *ritual of concern.* This ritual is manifested in signs of identification, sympathy, and consideration exhibited toward the other person. An example of this ritual is the host/guest relationship. Usually when we visit another's home the host inquires, "What will you have to drink?" or, "Can I get you anything?" This is a

6. Tony Clark, Doug Bock, Mike Cornett, *Is That You Out There? Explorations in Authentic Communication* (Columbus, Ohio: Charles E. Merrill, 1973), p. 144.
7. Goffman, *Relations,* pp. 65–84.

ritualized way of saying, "I am concerned for your comfort and well-being. I want to make you welcome." Some people are so concerned with their guests' comfort and well-being that they feel that they have failed in their social duty if the guest doesn't leave either drunk or five pounds heavier. How often have you heard your mother or father express concern over the arrival of unexpected company because there was "nothing in the house to offer them." This helps us understand more the flurry of activity that occurs in every home before guests arrive. It's Operation Ritual-of-Concern.

While the host/hostess feels a certain duty to exhibit consideration, the guest, on the other hand, has certain expectations. Have you ever visited when you were not offered something? How did you feel? Did you resent it? Or perhaps you visited with the expectation of being a guest and found that you were required to help with the preparation of a meal, or that your host/hostess decided to go out to dinner and you were expected to pay your own way. You may have felt uncomfortable and resentful, concluding that a lack of consideration existed that was something you would not do in your role as host/hostess.

The second type of supportive ritual is the *ritual of ratification.* This ritual is practiced to reassure a person who has changed status. In effect, the ritual of ratification socially legitimizes a person's new status or role.

There are many examples of changes in status and the roles and rituals connected with them. One most obvious is marriage. When we are presented with the fact of a person's new marital status and the accompanying new husband or wife role, what do we do? Perhaps first we say, "congratulations," or, "best wishes." We might use appropriate titles and ask appropriate questions about where *they* are living now, where did they go on *their* honeymoon, etc. All of these ritualized reactions *confirm* the status of the new couple; we aid them in legitimizing the "couple image."

A divorced status must also be ratified. For most people this ritual is less codified and therefore a bit more difficult to master. We're pretty sure of what not to say, "How are Sara (or Dick) and the kids?" or, "Would you and Dick (or Sara) like to go to dinner with us and two other couples?" We're not quite certain of what should be said, however. What is safe? Usually the divorced status of a woman is ratified by addressing her by her maiden or at least her first name, instead of her husband's as in "Mrs._____," (if she took her mate's name in the first place). The new "single" is also recognized by being somewhat left out of "couples" activities, unless it is possible to be paired with another "single."

Many professional changes in status are ratified simply by a change in title, such as "doctor," "reverend," "professor." The ritual can be carried further by appropriate questions and references to the person's particular job and particular expertise in a certain area, for example, "Oh, ask Judith about wills, she just got her law degree."

The ritual of ratification should not be treated lightly. To some people it is extremely important and expected to be enacted. Perhaps you have encountered the new degree holder woman who becomes quite upset when not addressed as "Doctor." On the other hand, we may encounter more women who want to be ratified in their status as "persons" and prefer the title "Ms." or simply their first and last names.

The third type of supportive ritual is the greeting or *access ritual*. This occurs when people enjoy increased access to each other; they are in each other's company, a minimum number of distractions and expectations external to the encounter exists, and therefore a greeting is in order. This ritual is the one that is similar to phatic communion: once eye contact has been made with another, access to them exists, and the necessity for validating their existence, for greeting them, occurs. The greeting ritual includes phatic communion but can go beyond it. We initially give the other "strokes," but then move on to more interesting matters.

Access is an important and interesting idea. It is directly related to the establishment of eye contact and the consequent necessity of "greeting" as mentioned above. Sometimes we go out of our way to create access to a person we really want to talk with or get to know. On the other hand, we may walk down the other side of the street or along the other side of the hall to preclude access to someone we especially don't want to greet or converse with at that particular time.

The greeting ritual involves the minimum expectation of an exchange of hellos and, if the relationship warrants, an exchange of information pertinent to the people involved. Neighbors may exchange information about their kids; businesspeople, information about the market; students, information about classes and professors.

The fourth type of supportive ritual is the *leave-taking ritual*. This ritual brings the interaction to a definite end by summarizing the meaning of the exchange and providing support for a period of no contact. Comments such as, "it was good seeing you," "We must get together soon," "Drop over sometime," "Give me a call," indicate that the relationship will be able to continue on the same grounds and bolster it for the lack of contact that is to follow. Of course "goodbye," "bye," and "see you" bring the interaction to a definite close.

It is easier to see the importance of this ritual by looking at what occurs when something inhibits the usual routine of exchange. For example, have you ever said your good-byes, taken your leave, and then remembered that you left your car keys behind? Or, you have completed the leave-taking ritual with the expectation of meeting at a later date, only to see the person five minutes later in another part of the store, library, or airport. You probably felt very uneasy because what you expected to be concluded at this point in time was opened up again. Access exists and there is the need for re-enacting the greeting and then leave-taking rituals for a second, and surely anti-climatic time.

These four supportive rituals, as all routine experiences, give structure and support to our social interaction. Goffman describes these positive rituals: "One individual performs for and to another, attesting to civility and good will on the performer's part and to the recipient's possession of a small patrimony of sacredness."[8]

The second major type of ritual is the remedial ritual. This ritual functions primarily to make what could appear as an offensive act seem acceptable. Goffman has discovered three types of remedial rituals.[9]

The first type of remedial ritual is the *account*. This ritual uses explanations, justifications, rationalizations, and excuses to make an offensive act seem acceptable. For example, if you failed to return a call within a specified time, you don't just call up with no excuse a few days past the expected deadline. You provide a reason: you were busy or you were sick or you were out of town. That absolves you of blame, removes the offense, and allows the relationship to continue as before. You have, in effect, acted out this ritual so as to maintain the original structure of the interaction.

The second type of remedial ritual is the *apology*. The apology usually includes an "expression of embarrassment and chagrin: clarification that one knows what conduct had been expected and sympathizes with the application of negative sanction; verbal rejection, repudiation, and disavowal of the wrong way of behaving along with vilification of the self that so behaved; espousal of the right way and an avowal henceforth to pursue that course; performance of penance and the volunteering of restitution."[10] We've all been in routine interpersonal situations where we have had to apologize for something

---

8. Ibid., p. 63.
9. Ibid., pp. 109–43.
10. Ibid., p. 113.

we have said or done. The simplest example of this ritual is when we inadvertently bump into someone and automatically say, "Excuse me." Or, we have pulled absent-mindedly into another lane of traffic only to hear brakes screech and a horn blow. We make nonverbal gestures of apology: we may shrug our shoulders, cock our heads and raise our palms in a what-can-I-say? fashion. Statements such as, "I should have watched where I was going—I'll be more careful next time," or, "I didn't mean to say that—I wouldn't blame you if you didn't forgive me. I promise never to mention it again," are apologies rejecting what was said or done, recognizing that it deserves punishment, and indicating that we will not deviate from the right path in the future.

The third type of remedial ritual is the *request*. This ritual is prior to the act and indicates that we know that we are going to ask something which the other has a right not to grant, leaving him the option to refuse. When this ritual is performed completely and to expectations, it has four parts:

| | |
|---|---|
| Request: | Can I see your notes? |
| Relief: | Sure, here. |
| Appreciation: | Thanks a lot. You've saved my life. |
| Minimization: | Nothing at all. |

The *request* is asking a favor which may infringe on the other's rights. The *relief* is the magnanimous granting of the favor. The *appreciation* is the glorification of the person who didn't view the act as an offense. The *minimization* is acceptance of the appreciation and completion of the ritual.

The importance of this ritual can be best understood when the established pattern is not followed. Though we give the other the option not to grant a request, we do not really expect that he will not do so. If you have ever said, "Is it okay if I sit here?" and the other replied "no"; if someone has granted you a favor and when you expressed appreciation remained silent, we're sure that you felt a sense of uneasiness because the expected pattern was not completed.

Another interesting way to view rituals is from the concept of "face-work." All the rituals explained here can be considered face-work which combines "the rule of self-respect and the rule of considerateness [so that] the person tends to conduct himself during an encounter so as to maintain both his own face and the face of the other participants."[11] Goffman further explains that one's face has sanctity; to maintain this sacredness of our own and others' faces we must enact rituals.

When we "have face" we have a definite role with definite expectations that we are enacting. For example, a person may "have face" as a student; he knows that the role entails certain expectations of class attendance, reading, listening and test-taking. To "be in face" means that he is playing the defined role by fulfilling its expectations properly at the moment; that is, he is "in face" as a student when he is fulfilling the above expectations. Furthermore, when "in face" not only is he aware of playing the role correctly, but the other people in the interaction (professor and other students) are also aware that he is meeting his expectations. When he "maintains face" he stays in face for the *entire* interaction.

When we are unsure of what our role expectations are we are said to be "out of face." For example, if the student goes to an informal gathering at a professor's house, is he still supposed to be in his "student face"? What is his role? What do others expect of him?

When we calculate our role incorrectly, we are "in the wrong face." We are assuming a role that is not appropriate to the situation and for the other participants. Suppose, for example, the student goes to the informal gathering at the professor's house, and assumes the role of peer. Chances are he would be in the wrong face and not fulfilling the expectations of those around him.

Not only is it important for us to be in the right face and maintain it, it is important for us to help others maintain their faces. This is what the rituals are all about—the mutual maintenance of each other's faces in a social situation. Think of the number of times each day we say, "That's all right," "Okay," "No problem," "Don't worry about it." In effect we are helping others maintain their faces and thus preserve the social relationship *with the expectation* that when the time comes that we are in need, others will do the same for us. The you-scratch-my-back-I'll-scratch-yours agreement occurs not only in politics, it is the sum and substance of social ritual.

As we found phatic communion, social ritual, though appearing superficial and trivial, is a necessity in interpersonal interaction. Ritual makes the initiation of dialogue easier. As Dean Barnlund explains: "Having mastered the rules of social interaction, men are

11. Erving Goffman, *Interactional Ritual* (Chicago: Aldine, 1957), p. 11.

capable of using this structure to give form to impulse, organization to action, and humanity to their relations with others."[12]

## Pastimes

*A pastime is a semiritualistic interaction focusing on a special area of discussion for the purpose of structuring time and defining roles.*[13] It is semiritualistic because it is not as predictable as a social ritual. A pastime is conducted socially, of course, but as social ritual moves beyond phatic communion, so do pastimes move beyond social ritual. There is more leeway within the interaction for originality and spontaneity of thought. This occurs because we single out a special area for discussion. The purpose is no longer just to validate the other's existence or to support social interaction, but to structure time and further define our roles as participants.

Everyone engages in pastimes: from talking about the weather to the price of hamburger. We've heard our mothers engage in the pastime of "recipes," our fathers engage in the pastime of "football scores," and our little brothers and sisters engage in the pastime of "trading cards." But let's see if we can't identify some of the pastimes that we engage in to structure our time.

The major pastime, in which we all take part in its various forms, is "ain't it awful." "Ain't it awful" involves picking a subject, any subject, about which to complain. Students have any number of reference points from which to begin this game. The most obvious is school. This subject area can include the amount of work, the professors, the administrators, the physical conditions, etc., as areas of discussion. Let's listen to some of them.

*Bruce:*   I've got so much to do, I can't see straight.

*Bev:*     Yeah, they really lay it on thick at this place. I've got two midterms and a paper due next week.

*Bruce:*   I've got three tests next week. They must think we're intellectual robots the way they expect us to crank things out.

*Candy:*   Have you ever had Dr. Mannix for history?

---

12. Dean C. Barnlund, *Interpersonal Communication: Survey and Studies* (Boston: Houghton Mifflin, 1968), p. 171.
13. Berne, *Games,* p. 41. Also see Goffman, *Interaction Ritual,* who uses similarly the term "social encounter," p. 135, to describe what we have been discussing as pastimes.

*Jerry:* Yeah, what a waste. All he does is lecture straight from the book. But he counts attendance so there's no way you can cut.

*Candy:* I know. Hey, did you ever catch the way he peers over his glasses at the end of every sentence?

*Jerry:* Yeah, he looks like a pigeon. Up and down, up and down. Drives me crazy.

*Ted:* Did you hear what that stupid registrar's office is doing this quarter?

*Sherry:* Well, it couldn't be any dumber than it was last quarter when they let freshmen register before seniors.

*Ted:* Well, it is. This time we have to get a new identification form processed before they'll release our schedule cards.

*Sherry:* I think they lie awake at night trying to think of ways to make things more difficult for us.

*Ben:* Have you been in the cafeteria lately? They bolted down the chairs.

*Mike:* Why the hell did they do that?

*Ben:* So that we couldn't seat a large number at a table to play cards. They wanna increase the turnover.

*Mike:* Damn! As miserable as they make it for us in every other way you'd think they'd let us have some fun. This joint's like a prison every day.

So that you don't think that we're singling students out as the only pastime players, listen to some of the faculty versions of "ain't it awful."

*Dr. Tucker:* That new dean must have graduated from West Point. He sure doesn't cut us any slack does he?

*Dr. Stewart:* Are you kidding? My paperwork's increased three fold since he came. Reports for this, questionnaires for that—committee for everything. You'd think he was gunning for president or something.

*Dr. Brown:* Did you eat lunch at the faculty union today?

*Dr. Hicks:*        Yeah, what *was* that stuff in the luncheon special?

*Dr. Petrie:*       Did you fall for that, too? It looked like a regular hamburger, but I swear it was soy bean meal, and very aged at that!

*Dr. Brown:*        Yeah, they must be fattening *us* up for the kill instead of the cow.

*Dr. Smith:*        Have you had that guy Hensley in your class yet?

*Dr. Schwartz:*     You mean the big man on campus that can never come to class or get things in on time because he has so many "important" meetings to attend?

*Dr. Smith:*        Yep, you've had him, too. I swear I've never heard so many excuses in my life, the guy is a real bullshitter.

We all play forms of "ain't it awful." The subject is a free choice as long as you complain about whatever it is. "Ain't it awful" is probably the pastime to which we devote most effort in structuring our time and defining our roles. There are many others which we can identify and describe from our own experiences: "sports," "clothes," "cars," "clubs," "men," "women," "money," "sex," "political bureaucracy," etc. So there aren't different types of pastimes, there are only different subjects about which to pass the time. Now that we can identify a pastime, let's look more closely at some of the characteristics involved.

We said that a pastime involved a specific area of discussion and we've seen the wide variety of subjects which pastimes can treat. The *scope* and *depth* of the subject is of major importance when we are involved in these conversational pastimes. The subject must be broad enough so that everyone can participate and yet narrow enough to establish rapport and the opportunity to be creative and original in participation. For example, if the pastime subject is "professors I have known," and two of the three participants are in the same department at the same school, the third participant will probably feel left out because the subject area will be too narrow. On the other hand, if the subject is "entertainment," it may be too broad to allow the participants to give and take properly by preventing them from picking up each other's leads. The depth of the subject is significant, too. If we begin to go too deeply into a subject such as "politics," then the rapport of the pastime situation may be in jeopardy. When conversation moves to controversy, we move from pastimes to games.

Second, pastimes *structure time*. They give us something to *do* at a party, at a restaurant, before a class, in a line, etc. They help us fill the time until we accomplish our goal, such as getting a chance to meet a new person, getting served, sitting down to take notes, or making our way to the ticket counter.

Third, pastimes help to *define roles*. These roles aren't complementary in the normal sense of the term, such as when we speak of husband-wife, employer-employee, teacher-student, etc. Usually, in a pastime, roles are the same and what needs to be determined is not what complementary roles each will take, but what role they will have in common, such as students, fathers, girlfriends, etc. Although within the pastime specific roles might exist, such as definer of the subject, straight man, comedian, etc., the role-in-common is of most importance.

Finally, pastimes are more *spontaneous* than the other types of routine experiences. They consist of verbal play and admit of much more individual style than the other routines. Each of us, as long as we stick to the subject and keep it within its proper scope and depth, is free to be original and creative with our contribution. For instance, in the example where the student said, "Did you ever catch the way he looks over his glasses at the end of every sentence?" what would your response have been? It would probably be unique and indicative of your own personal style. Equilibrium in the pastime routine is kept by a proper balance between spontaneity and the rules of scope, depth, achievements of passing time, and common role.

As with our other routine experiences, pastimes are important to human existence. As Erving Goffman explains, pastimes "differ a great deal in the importance that participants give to them, but whether crucial or picayune, all [pastimes] represent occasions when the individual can become spontaneously involved in the proceedings and derive from this a firm sense of reality. And this kind of feeling is not a trivial thing, regardless of the package in which it comes. When an incident occurs and spontaneous involvement is threatened, then reality is threatened."[14]

---

14. Goffman, *Interaction Ritual,* p. 135.

## Games

Although there are a number of different approaches to games, most theorists would agree with Dean Barnlund that a game as "a social system in microcosm. As such it offers another perspective on interpersonal performance. . . . In games like monopoly, hide-and-seek, or poker there are official players, game objectives, rules of combat, prizes and penalties and prearranged outcomes. Many if not all social encounters . . . share some of these qualities."[15]

Our primary concern in this section is with the type of interpersonal game popularized by Eric Berne in his now famous book *Games People Play.* Here is his definition of an interpersonal game:

> *A game is an ongoing series of complementary ulterior actions progressing to a well-defined, predictable outcome* . . . it is a recurring set of transactions, often repetitious, superficially plausible with a concealed motivation . . . a series of moves with a snare or "gimmick" . . . clearly differentiated from procedures, rituals, or pasttimes by . . . (1) *their ulterior quality* and (2) *their payoff.* . . . Every game . . . is basically dishonest, and the outcome has a dramatic, as distinct from merely exciting, quality.[16] (italics ours)

Berne differentiates the game from other routine experiences. While phatic communion, rituals, and pastimes are ongoing, complementary, recurring, and repetitious, only the game has an ulterior quality and a payoff. For example, in phatic communion while we don't explicitly state that we are seeking recognition, we are not attempting to *conceal* it. We also are not seeking a payoff, winning *at the expense of the other;* that is, we normally don't seek validation from the other so that we can turn around and refuse it to him. Because of their particular differences from the other routine experiences we have discussed, games are, in essence, antidialogic. Whereas other routine experiences can help pave the way to dialogue, continuing games will only prevent dialogue.

You may wonder then why we have included a discussion of games. One reason for this is that a game has the characteristics of other routine experiences. It has a purpose: the player initiating the game wants to win. It is reciprocal: the game takes two players. It is regular: we all play games which have predictable patterns. It is culturally conditioned: the games we choose to play are influenced by our up-

15. Barnlund, *Interpersonal Communication,* p. 157.
16. Berne, *Games,* p. 48.

bringing and present environment. Another reason is that it is only through awareness of participating in a damaging sort of routine experience that that damage can ever be corrected. It is only by knowing the sorts of things we do that block dialogue that we can eliminate them and grow if we choose dialogic experiences.

The two differentiating factors of games need to be emphasized. The first factor is that a concealed motive is present. If you've ever had anyone pay you a very nice compliment, your reaction may have been, "Now I wonder why he said that." Any type of response like this indicates the search for an ulterior motive, a reason for the interaction that is *underlying the apparent reason* that he perhaps thought you looked nice and wanted to pay you a compliment. What did he want? A date? Money? Your notes from class? The second factor is that there is a payoff—someone is going to win in the exchange. As a matter of fact, when we are searching for a concealed motive we are at the same time asking ourselves what the other will gain (at our expense) from the exhange. If we fall for the come-on, we may end up relinquishing possessions, time, or psychological well-being.

Most of the games with which we are concerned are those that are psychologically rather than physically damaging. An important point here is that games are destructive to *all* concerned, not just the loser in the exchange.[17] The "winner" also loses, according to principles of dialogue, because he is allowed to perpetuate dishonesty and control with himself as well as others, thus preventing his growth.

Perhaps you have been involved in a game similar to this one:

> The initiator makes the challenge that you can't trust anybody, that everyone's out to screw you, that you have to look out for yourself and not get involved with anyone else. The victim, who happens to believe in dialogue, maintains that that just isn't the case, that people can be trusted if only given a chance, that a trusting person is a happier person, and that he, the victim, will begin by demonstrating that he is trustworthy. What ensues can occur in the period of one interaction or a number of interactions over time. An attempt at trust is made on the part of the victim; for example, he might tell the skeptic that sometimes he feels insecure in his position as an instructor and is not always sure that he is relating well to the students. He reveals this information to demonstrate that he trusts the skeptic. If the game is played "properly" the skeptic will then

---

17. This is a somewhat different perspective on what is usually described as a zero-sum, or an I-win-you-lose outcome, described by game theorists.

use this or other delicate information to hurt and abuse the victim. The victim is thus put in a double bind. If he just sits there and takes it, the initiator can say "See you can't trust anybody. You trusted me and look how I'm hurting you." If the victim refuses to tolerate the abuse and either strikes back or ends the relationship, the aggressor responds in the same manner. "See you can't trust anybody. I trusted you to be good to me and now you are turning on me." Anyway you look at it, the initiator of the game gets to play "Now I've Got You, You Son-of-a-bitch."[18]

From this brief example, we can look at the components of any game.[19] (1) Every game can be *named* and the name provides some sort of description of the winner's payoff. "Now I've Got You, You Son-of-a-bitch" describes the revenge gained by the winner. The "Yes, But—" game, used in one of the examples in the beginning of this chapter, describes the control gained by the winner in continuing to maintain that his problem is incapable of solution. (2) Every game has an *aim* or purpose in being played. In the above example, the aim was justification or revenge. Other aims might include reassurance, self-derogation, or mutual admiration or destruction. (3) Every game has *roles.* There are always an aggressor and victim, and at times, a third party, the rescuer, might intervene to save the victim. In the above example, a rescuer could have exposed the aggressor's hand by explaining the obvious dilemma in which he was holding the victim. (4) Every game is initiated because of some *need* on the part of the aggressor and at times on the part of the victim. In our example, the aggressor had a need to lash out at someone, perhaps to make himself feel superior and in a controlling position. The victim may have a masochistic, self-destructive need to be used. In other words, there is a tension that requires reduction on the part of the players. (5) Every game has *moves.* In the example, there were basically two moves: provocation and, once provocation produced a reaction, accusation and punishment. (6) Every game has some sort of *apparent advantage.* In the example an internal psychological need for revenge was temporarily reduced. Perhaps there was also an external social advantage gained through embarrassing the victim by putting him in a dilemma. Games can provide biological, psyhological, social, and existential advantages to the players. These advantages are only temporary and illusory. The needs and driving forces which produce them are never eliminated by playing the game, so that playing games becomes self-

18. Berne, *Games,* p. 86.
19. Ibid., p. 52ff.

perpetuating—the more games we play, the more we must play. Fortunately, (7) every game can be *ended.* This final factor is much more difficult than *playing* the game. This is the main reason we continue to play games of one sort or another. Playing games is much easier and often less painful than searching for and discovering what is causing us to engage in such deceptive, closed, and controlling behavior. The only way the game can be ended is through our own insight, understanding, and acceptance. We may need others' guidance in ending game playing, but the decision to desengage, to refuse to play, is our own.

If you are interested in the games you might be playing, Berne's *Games People Play* has an exhaustive list of games played in life, in marriage, at parties, etc. A simpler, relatively jargon-free classification of games can be found in Powell's *Why Am I Afraid to Tell You Who I Am?* Powell categorizes and describes games ranging from the "braggart" and "clown" to the "loner" and "martyr."[20] While Berne maintains that, given the human condition, some sort of game playing is necessary and desirable, we tend to agree more with Powell's attitude toward games: "They mask and distort the truth about the one most important thing that I could share with you: myself. I must ask myself: which of these games do I play? What am I seeking? What am I hiding? What am I trying to win!"[21]

## P-A-C Transactions

The final section in this chapter is not concerned with a different *type* of routine, but rather with a construct from which all routine experiences can be viewed. This construct is called a *transaction,* and its simplest definition is that of a *unit of social interaction.* Berne describes it as follows:

> The unit of social intercourse is called a transaction. If two or more people encounter each other in a social aggregation, sooner or later one of them will speak, or give some other indication of acknowledging the presence of the others. This is called a *transactional stimulus.* Another person will then say or do something which is in some way related to this stimulus, and that is called the *transactional response.* [22]

20. John Powell, *Why Am I Afraid to Tell You Who I Am?* (Chicago: Argus Communications, 1969), pp. 122–67.
21. Ibid., p. 121.
22. Berne, *Games,* p. 29.

From this explanation, you can see that the nature of transaction encompasses phatic communion, routines, pasttimes, and games.

At this point, we want to relate transactions to what we discussed about ego states in the last chapter. You will remember that description of an individual's ego states is called *structural analysis.* One description of communication between two or more individuals is called *transactional analysis.*

In brief review, according to this view, we all possess the "taught" ego state of *parent,* the "felt" ego state of *child,* and the reality-oriented, information processing ego state of *adult.* When we communicate we are communicating from one of these ego states. Our communication serves as a transactional stimulus to one of the other's ego states. He will react from this or another ego state, and this reaction is the transactional response. To illustrate, read the following example.

*Roommate One:*   Have you seen my English notebook?

*Roommate Two:*   It's with your lit book.

This exchange is an adult/adult transaction because it is dealing with information processing. It can be diagrammed as follows:

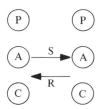

Now, look at another example.

*Roommate One:*   Oh, I've done it again. I've gone and lost my note-book.

*Roommate Two:*   I'll look for it for you.

This exchange is child to parent/parent to child, because one individual is seeking help and support and the other is giving it.

These types of transactions are called complementary because the response is to the stimulus as transmitted. The child speaks to the parent and the parent answers the child. Berne suggests that this type of transaction, because one ego state is complementing the other, can

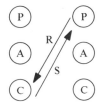

go on indefinitely. On the other hand, interaction tends to be terminated or at least disrupted when the transaction is crossed.[23] A crossed transaction occurs when the ego state that was addressed does not respond. For example:

*Roommate One:*   Have you seen my English notebook?

*Roommate Two:*   Can't you ever get organized?

We can see that this is a crossed transaction because the adult addressed the adult, but the parent responded to the child. Either the exchange will be terminated or the person addressed as a child will respond in anger.

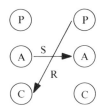

An important point is that there is nothing inherently healthy about transactions that are complementary just because they can proceed indefinitely. For example, it would seem that a relationship where one individual consistently responded from his parental ego state and the other consistently responded from his child ego state would not be a healthy, growth-producing relationship. On the other hand, a crossed transaction, just because it disrupts communication, is not inherently unhealthy. Let us say that you know a person who consistently acts from his child ego state by appealing to the other's parent for guidance and support. When the other refuses to play father or mother and responds from his adult to the other's adult, communication may be

23. Ibid., pp. 29–30.

disrupted momentarily, but at least the opportunity for growth is provided. For example:

*Roommate One:*  Oh, why can't I ever do anything right? I haven't studied enough for my test tomorrow and I'm going to flunk it.

*Roommate Two:*  How much time do you have left? How much material do you have to cover? Can you schedule it so that you can at least look over all of the material before the test tomorrow?

This crossed transaction (A) would seem to be a healthier communication than a complementary transaction (B) that would allow Roommate One to continue being a child by responding: "You do do things right. You've just had a bad week. Don't worry about it. The test isn't that important anyway."

Before we characterize each type of routine experience by analyzing it transactionally, we need to point out that there are overt and covert levels of transaction. For example, the overt level might be adult/adult while the covert level is parent/child.

An illustration of the difference between overt and covert transactional levels follows:

*Dick:*  Will you pick me up at 7 P.M.?

*Jane:*  I'll pick you up at 8:30.

On the overt level this appears to be an adult/adult exchange of information. On the covert level, one individual is taking charge of the situation from a superior position. These two levels can be diagrammed in this way:

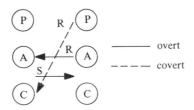

Now let's look at the different kinds of routine experiences to see if we can determine generally what type of transactions they are. Phatic communion, on the overt level, is adult to adult because a request for information is made and responded to. On the covert level, it is child/parent because the request is really for validation of the self. Ritual is overtly adult to adult, again because there is exchange of information. This, too can be seen as a child to parent transaction on the covert level, because the requests (May I intrude? May I leave?) are made from an inferior to superior position. . Pastimes are adult/ adult on the overt level. On the covert level, because of the enjoyment involved in verbal play, the transaction is child to child.

It is nearly impossible to generalize about games, except to say that there is always a covert level because there is always an ulterior motive. So the notion of transaction can pull together and give us a framework for viewing and analyzing all types of routine experiences.

As we have indicated throughout this chapter, these routine experiences are important and necessary to the stability and growth of our interpersonal relationships. Hopefully, we are more aware of and understand better the function of our everyday encounters. The more skilled we become in these experiences, the better able we are to maintain harmony with others and create the opportunity for dialogue.

Social psychologist Michael Argyle found that most socially skilled people possessed the attributes of perceptual sensitivity, warmth, and the ability to establish rapport with the other, flexibility and ability to adapt to the encounter, energy and the willingness to initiate interactions, a large repertoire of social techniques and smooth response patterns.[24]

24. Michael Argyle, *The Psychology of Interpersonal Behavior* (Baltimore: Penguin, 1967), pp. 103–4.

Argyle has offered five rules for skillfully engaging in routine experiences. These are, if read with the proper attitude, similar to some of the conditions of dialogue.

1. Try to establish rapport with the other; stroke rather than antagonize him.
2. Try to keep the other in the interaction; keep him involved in the conversation.
3. Try to motivate the other person to participate and enjoy the interaction; show him what he can gain from participating.
4. Try to minimize any fears, anxiety or defense.
5. Try to be aware of the impression you are making on him so that you can more clearly read his responses and know how to act toward him.[25]

## Summary

In this chapter, we have defined a routine experience as an interpersonal exchange in which we engage automatically and yet purposefully in our everyday communication with others. We explained the five characteristics of every routine experience: purpose, synchronization, reciprocity, regularity, and cultural conditioning.

There are various types of routine experiences ranging from the simple to the complex: phatic communion, which seeks validation of self; social ritual, which seeks to support social interaction; pastimes, which seek to pass the time and define a role in common; and games, which seek to win a payoff. Transactions were viewed as a construct from which to analyze all routine experiences. We indicated some of the social skills necessary to carry out routines effectively.

Throughout this chapter we have stressed the importance of being aware of engaging in routine experiences. We feel that awareness leads to skill in and better control of our participation in routines. We hope that you will choose to use this understanding as a means of creating dialogue in everyday communication experiences.

---

25. Ibid., pp. 96–100.

# 11

# Dyadic
# Experiences

Dyadic experiences, involving our deepest thoughts and most intense feelings, are highly charged discussions. We get so bound up in them that often we cannot view them objectively (especially if they are our own) much less speak about them without being biased by our personal opinion.

## The Experience

Our focus is primarily on that part of the interaction between two people which involves communication. However, since we have defined communication broadly enough to include both verbal and nonverbal messages, we'll find that everything that two people say to each other and nearly everything that they do to or with each other might be considered dyadic communication.

The dyadic experiences in this chapter are those involving family, friendship, marriage, and work. These particular experiences were chosen because all of us are now or will in the future be engaged in them. Most of these relationships can probe the deeper levels of communication. John Powell identifies five levels of communication:[1]

1. Cliché conversation
2. Facts about others
3. Personal ideas and judgments
4. Personal feelings (gut level)
5. Peak experience.

The first and second levels are ones which were discussed under routine experiences. The last three levels are tapped in dialogic communication. Since dialogue is possible and usually desirable in dyadic experiences, we can concentrate on these last three levels. Moving from the first to the fifth level involves a progressively greater investment of self, and therefore, a greater risk. As an example, consider the greater amount of self-disclosure and the greater amount of trust in the other that is needed in the following levels of communication.

1. "How's it going?"
2. "John says he wants to see *The Sting* Friday night."
3. "I think Robert Redford is tremendous."
4. "It bothers me that you don't like the same kind of movies I do."
5. Touch, eye contact, mutual sharing of movie experience non-verbally.

We believe that there are certain approaches that best facilitate dyadic communication at these levels. Before we look at these, however, we ought to deal with "getting into" and "getting out of" dyadic experiences. As a matter of fact, the following can be considered rule-of-thumb number one: "Don't get into a dyadic relationship that is not mutually beneficial and valuable; if you find yourself in one that isn't, get out." The appropriate *goal* of any dyadic relationship is to promote our happiness in one form or another—it should make us feel good, right with ourselves, free to grow and glad to be alive and present to the other person. The *purpose* of the relationship is to create that type of atmosphere which will promote our happiness and growth.

If we follow this principle, it seems likely that the other steps will be easier because we will be maintaining and enhancing a relationship

---

1. John Powell, S. J., *Why Am I Afraid to Tell You Who I Am?* (Chicago: Argus Communications, 1969), pp. 54–61. We have switched the numbering on these levels. When we speak of "deeper" levels of communication, it seems that it is more appropriate to talk to the fifth level than the first.

that we really *want* to exist and continue. It isn't always necessary to perpetuate a relationship that holds very little pleasure for us. If we are maintaining such a relationship to avoid pain (rather than to produce pleasure) or to enable us to reach some larger long-term goal, perhaps we need to question the value of avoiding pain and the value of our goal. Is it really worth sticking with a relationship from which we derive more frustration than enjoyment?

Harry Browne speaks to this question perceptively. He suggests that we should determine three things: (1) the price we are paying to remain in a relationship we find distasteful, (2) what it would cost us to get out, and, most importantly, (3) what we could do once we are out and free.[2] Freeing ourselves from nonsatisfying relationships allows us to devote time and energy to those that are truly valuable to us. In other words, we are acting positively to maximize pleasure rather than negatively to minimize pain.

Assuming that we are now free to "get into" such relationships, what are some ways we can go about it? Browne has some helpful suggestions here, too. First, we can *advertise ourselves honestly.* In doing this, we wouldn't leave *Atlantic Monthly* out for people to see when we really read *Popular Mechanics.* Or, we wouldn't go to the opera when we'd rather be at the Grand Ol' Opry. Or wear Hart Schaffner & Mark suits when we'd rather wear Levis. Chances are we won't attract those people with ideas, values, opinions, and tastes similar to ours if we don't let other people know what ours are.[3] Second, once we have found someone with a similar interest, we can *limit the relationship to what those interests are.*[4] We can try to avoid making the relationship all-inclusive. For example, sharing enjoyment of Chinese food does not mean you will both want to see Ted Kennedy as the president of the United States or that you would enjoy living together. Finally, remembering that everyone *is* unique, we can allow our relationships to reflect and thrive on that uniqueness. According to this approach, we shouldn't try to make the other like us—we should *let him or her be free to be what he or she is.*[5] We need, therefore, to build the relationship on those things the other is that we find valuable. If there are things we don't find valuable (or that are even distasteful), rather than trying to change them, we can maintain the relationship in such a way that they are not a concern. If the other

---

2. Harry Browne, *How I Found Freedom in an Unfree World* (New York: Macmillan, 1973), p. 126.
3. Ibid., pp. 175–77.
4. Ibid., p. 183.
5. Ibid., p. 187.

is messy and you are not, you might try living apart or in a place big enough to accommodate different life styles.

Let's assume that we can now get out of nonproductive relationships and into rewarding ones. How do we maintain and enhance them? Psychologist David Johnson, author of *Reaching Out,* has some principles which can be beneficially applied to any dyadic relationship which we want to be dialogic and based on the deeper levels of communication mentioned previously.[6]

Generally speaking, *the focus of communication can be on the person's behavior rather than on the person.* Remembering what we said in chapter 9 about a person being more than his actions, focusing on behavior does not involve the danger of holistically judging the person. Rather than saying, "You are really a slob," we can say something like, "It upsets me when you don't pick up your belongings." Not only does this avoid the pitfall of evaluating personhood rather than behavior, it also makes clear that we are speaking from *our* feelings and perception of the situation. This is an important point. Saying, "There is a mess of junk next to your chair," implies our perception of behavior. It may not be his. To him it might be the height of creative existence.

Closely related to this principle is a second one: *the focus of communication can be on observation rather than inference.* In chapter 6 we talked about "checking things out." This notion applies specifically here. Rather than *assuming* intent or emotional and mental state, we can ask. Rather than saying, "You just don't care about me," perhaps we could try, "When you forget my birthday, I feel as if you don't care. Is that true?" We can avoid assuming or infringing on the other's freedom by trying to read his or her mind.

*The focus of communication can be on the here and now rather than the there and then.* We can avoid dragging out old hurts and irritations that are past facts because they are over and nothing can change them. Instead of using the present situation as a stimulus to reopen old wounds by saying, "You didn't hear what I said. You've never listened to me, like when I told you that I wanted money for graduation and you didn't remember and got me pajamas," we could try saying simply, "I feel as if you aren't hearing me and I get upset when I think you're not listening." This might prevent a completely defensive posture on the other's part and could enhance the possibility of a more open search to resolve the problem at hand. In terms of these

---

6. David W. Johnson, *Reaching Out: Interpersonal Effectiveness and Self-Actualization* (Englewood Cliffs, New Jersey: Prentice-Hall, 1972), pp. 16–17.

three principles, we have been very careful to begin what we consider the better response with, "*I* feel as if—." We might remember that (according to rational-emotive therapy) the other person really doesn't *do* anything *to* us, that it is our perceptions and interpretations of him and his actions that cause our emotional responses. We need to take responsibility for that response and not shift it to him. This in no way prevents discussion of the stimulus, however; it may have been better and nicer if the stimulus had not occurred.

*The focus of communication can be on exploration and information rather than on advice and solution.* It is a common-sense rule that people don't change until they want to, and then they will change only in the way they think best. Not only is giving advice and offering solutions somewhat preemptive of the other's freedom to be creative, it is generally a waste of time. Even when someone ostensibly seeks our advice, he might just want reinforcement for what he already believes, feels or wants to do. But, assuming that he really will follow our solution to his problem, what are we doing by accepting that type of responsibility? Accepting responsibility for someone else's decisions often has adverse additional consequences, especially if our advice doesn't pan out. We could be blamed for the other's failure. So instead of saying, "I think you ought to go to med school," we might say, "What do you enjoy doing? What job could provide that enjoyment for you?" If advice is given, the focus could be on advising to explore many alternatives rather than advising to choose a particular one.

*The focus of communication can be on the amount of information the other wants, not on what you want to give.* Overloading the circuit is usually unproductive because the other might filter out the information he didn't care about in the first place and he might also not be able to detect that information in which he was interested. If someone asks, "Is Dr. Dunlap a hard grader?" it might be better to respond with a simple "yes" until further questions arise and examples are sought, rather than going into a long-winded monologue about how we worked millions of hours and handed in eighty typewritten pages and had to do it all over again because he didn't like it and never even knew what he wanted because his syllabus was so ambiguous but we would've failed the course if we didn't redo the papers, etc. That's probably more than everything he wanted to know about this particular professor and not exactly what he asked.

We believe that following these five simple principles will go a long way toward enhancing the quality of any dyadic relationships we have and increasing the chances that they will, if desired, endure.

Now let's look at specific dyadic relationships and the communication involved. In doing so, we'll try to apply what we have discussed about "getting into and out of" relationships and about maintaining and enhancing those dyadic relationships in which we are engaged. Rather than attempt to discuss all possible dimensions, we'll look at some common and recurring problems involved in that type of relationship and then apply the principles we've discussed to try to resolve it. The assumption here is that the problem is to be resolved so as to create an atmosphere in which growth and happiness can best be achieved.

# Family

A family relationship, from a dyadic point of view, is any one which involves us and one other member of our families and in this section will be concerned with "us" and our mother or father. Many of you reading this book will not yet be parents, and so we won't approach the relationship specifically from that viewpoint, although what is dealt with here could be transferred later.

It is important for us to speak of a *member* of our families in discussing dyadic relationships, rather than of parents or brothers or sisters. Though we may interact together, when it comes right down to it we are still interacting with one individual at any one time. Our "parents" do not have a single identity, our mother or our father does.[7]

Unfortunately, a family relationship is the only one of those we discuss that we can't choose to get "into"—only "out of." As with anything else in which we have no initial choice, the possibility for resentment exists. If you have ever said, "I didn't ask to be born" you are probably expressing that resentment. We don't have control over who our mothers, fathers, brothers, or sisters are, we do have some control over what to make of that reality.

The most common family-oriented problem can be labeled, vaguely, the "generation gap." This "gap" usually involves a lack of communication, a lack of understanding, and therefore, a lack of acceptance of the other's life style. Let's look at an example.

Tim complained loudly and long that his parents didn't understand and accept him. He wanted to stay out all night periodically and play

---

7. Browne, *How I Found Freedom,* pp. 183–86, also chapter 2, "The Identity Traps."

softball during every other waking hour. His parents gave him a hard time. They wouldn't leave him alone. They wanted him to be something he didn't want to be—a businessman earning a respectable living instead of playing amateur softball which they viewed as unexciting and unproductive. They complained that he was never home and never helped around the house like his brother did. He couldn't talk to them. He was miserable because he wanted acceptance and approval. What was he to do?

Instead of viewing this problem from the point of view of what the parents are "doing wrong," let's look at it from his point of view, that is, what *he* can do to remedy the situation. Tim was attaching a single identity to his mother and father, always complaining of what his "parents" were doing to him. On closer examination, he acknowledged that his mother complained about his never being home and staying out all night; his father complained about his playing softball and not earning a "decent living." So he really had two separate problems with two separate relationships.

Looking at the method for getting into and getting out of a relationship, we see that he was advertising himself honestly; he was doing pretty much what he wanted to do and wasn't trying to make it appear any differently. But was he limiting the relationship to those interests held in common and was he giving his mother and his father freedom to be what they were? Not really. Not only did he want freedom to do what he wanted to do without hassle, he wanted his mother and father both to accept, be interested in, and approve of his activities. He was trying to make the relationship with each of them something it wasn't and probably could never be.

He was paying a high price to remain with those relationships. The home atmosphere did not promote his happiness or growth in the direction he desired it. To get out of the relationship he had to go to work, get his own apartment, and pay his own way. If he followed this course he would be free to pursue his individual life style without censure and judgment. He eventually decided that the price to get out was not too high to pay. He was much happier when he chose to terminate an arrangement that was not pleasurable and growth-inhibiting for him. He wanted to continue communication with his mother and father (just because we can't live with someone doesn't necessarily mean we don't love them). So the principles we discussed to facilitate communication in dyadic relationships can operate here. Now when Tim is with his mother or father, he tries to communicate his thoughts and feelings honestly. He explains to them that he gets irritated and upset when they judge him and try to control his life. He tells them that he feels as if they are unwilling to accept him as he is, and feeling this way hurts him. He tries to express regret that his mother didn't attend his latest softball tournament without bringing up all the other times she didn't come to see him. He doesn't tell them how to run their lives. He tries sincerely to answer their questions about his life without going into details they don't need to know that would only upset them. As a consequence, deeper levels of communications between him and his father and him and his mother are being reached. He now feels somewhat freer to express "gut level" reactions because he has learned a more appropriate way of communicating.

It is interesting to note that Dr. Haim Ginott's advice to parents can be reversed and utilized well by sons and daughters. He lists "Seven Roads to Trouble," barriers to communication that parents ought to avoid.[8] It is advisable (and only fair) that sons and daughters avoid these hazards also. One can only add to a problem by:

1. *Reasoning.* "There is nothing inherently wrong with sex before marriage. How can twenty minutes in a wedding ceremony all-of-a-sudden make sex okay?"
2. *Using Clichés.* "You've got to let me do my own thing. My bag isn't yours. You've got to cool it and get off my case."
3. *"Take me for instance"*—"*I'm* not afraid to be different. It doesn't bother *me* what people think of my clothes and my hair. *I* don't care what other people do."
4. *Minimizing the situation.* "I don't see why you should be upset. So I'm not going to be here for your birthday. Big deal. You have one every year."
5. *"The trouble with you."* "The trouble with you is you never listen. You never want to hear what I have to say. You're bigoted and dogmatic and authoritarian."
6. *Self-pity.* "I can't help it I'm not getting good grades in math. The prof is lousy. He doesn't like me. The course is too hard."
7. *A "Pollyanna" approach.* "Everything'll be okay. I'll keep in touch even if I'm away at school. I'll write and call. You'll see."

If one has difficulty understanding what is wrong with these statements, perhaps the following "roads to trouble" as used by *parents* will make it clearer:

1. *Reasoning.* "Did you expect the first girl you ever asked for a date to accept? Life isn't like that."

---

8. Dr. Haim G. Ginott, *Between Parent and Teenager* (New York: Avon Books, 1969), pp. 66–67.

2. *Using Clichés.* "You've got to tow the line, keep your shoulder to the wheel and nose to the grindstone to get ahead in this world."
3. *"Take me for instance"*—"When I was your age, I had to work for every penny I got!"
4. *Minimizing the situation.* "So you didn't make the team. They had a lousy schedule this year anyway."
5. *"The trouble with you."* "The trouble with you is you think you know everything."
6. *Self-pity.* "We can't help it if you didn't make fraternity. Everyone's against us because we don't have a college education."
7. *A "Pollyanna" approach.* "Everything happens for the best."

Any one of these statements (either version) in a given situation would not only *not* solve a problem, it would probably create more. Ginott suggests one path to effective communication. That is the nonjudgmental reply which identifies feelings, recognizes wishes, and acknowledges opinions.[9] Statements such as, "It upsets you that I get bad grades in math," "You are unhappy that I am going away to school," "It frustrates you to try to communicate with me," are nonjudgmental and will probably facilitate dyadic communication rather than destroy it.

Ginott sums up by speaking directly to our concern with interpersonal communication:

> It should be emphasized that the suggested methods are not merely techniques but interpersonal skills, helpful only when used with empathy and genuineness. They are effective when applied selectively and appropriately. Teenagers (substitute "parents") vary in their response to our communications. In words and acts they tell us what they like or dislike. A wise application of . . . skills will not ignore individual differences in temperament and personality.[10]

People seldom change the way we want them to. And it seems that, for better or for worse, a parent is the least likely of all to change to be the way we would like them to be. We will probably find that once we accept a parent the way he is and give him *his* freedom to be, ignoring and avoiding those traits which upset us and concentrating on those which bring us pleasure, we will receive acceptance and freedom from him.[11]

9. Ibid., p. 68.
10. Ibid., pp. 72–73.
11. Albert Ellis, *How to Live with a Neurotic* (New York: Universal, 1969).

## Friendship

One of the most rewarding types of dyadic relationships is that of friendship. Friendship, as it exists between the same or opposite sex, is difficult to define in other than a poetic manner. It is "a special kind of love," as one greeting card suggests, the sort of love which is essential in dialogue. Probably the most acceptable line of demarcation between friendship and romantic love is drawn along the lines of sex. Friendship is love without sex; romance is love with sex. Of course, defining what one means by sex or sexual attraction is another problem, as it is often difficult to determine where affection ends and sex begins. Theodore Reich shares and describes our confusion:

> The human language, otherwise so discriminating and differentiating, often proves that it has remained a poor medium of expression. Do you love your friend? You feel tempted to answer, "Yes." At the same time you feel that love is not the word to express your emotion adequately. It is certainly not the same feeling a man has for a woman. No, it is not the same, but it is, nevertheless, something similar. You try to distinguish between the two feelings. . . . The fact that the object belongs to the other sex makes, of course, a great difference. But is it the only factor? You discuss other matters with the girl you love than you do with your friend, and even if you discuss the same things you do it in a different way, in another spirit. And why is it more difficult to have a friend who belongs to the other sex? Is it that the sexual element disturbs the development of such a relationship? It is certainly untrue that sexual desire differentiates love from friendship. . . . It seems it is difficult to find the differences between love and friendship even between persons of the same sex. . . . And how should we understand a sentence which states that there is more love in friendship than friendship in love? We feel that there are emotional shades and nuances which are hard to grasp.[12]

We could easily avoid the whole problem by saying, "Well, we're just going to talk about same-sexed friends," but friendships with the opposite sex are too important to ignore for the sake of convenience.

There are problems that arise in friendship as well as in other dyadic relationships. Here is Sharon speaking of a friendship problem.

> I have this friend. I know she cares about me, but every time we're together, she tries to put me down by laughing at what I say or by

---

12. Theodore Reich, "Friendship and Love," in Robert Cummins, *Friendship* (Winona, Minnesota: St. Mary's College Press, 1971), p. 68.

finding fault with the way I do things. It's very difficult to talk about personal things with her as she avoids revealing her true feelings about anything, especially the way she feels about our friendship. I know she'll do anything for me, but I wish that she'd express herself verbally.

Let's look at this problem from our suggested approach. From Sharon's point of view, honest advertisement existed. What she was and wanted was expressed. The relationship was limited to similar interests—for example, her friend liked to drink and she did not, so the friend chose another person for that particular activity. But was there "freedom to be"? No, it appears that Sharon was intent on wanting the friend to conform to a certain mode of expression.

So Sharon took stock. The price being paid to remain in the relationship was one of periodic frustration and resentment. The cost of getting out of the relationship was the loss of an intelligent, interesting, and perceptive friend who could be depended on in any crisis. The gain of freedom from the relationship would be the time and energy to devote to finding and developing a friendship where the modes of expression of affection were similar and compatible. In this case the decision was made to continue the relationship, as the cost involved in ending it was too high. Sharon concentrated on accepting the friend as she was and attempting to avoid situations where the verbal expression of affection became a paramount concern.

When communication took place Sharon focused on observable behavior rather than inferred intent. Statements such as, "You don't really give a damn about our friendship," and "You are never serious," "You are a cold person," were terminated. Long lectures on the value of verbal expression were stopped. What remained of any frustration and attendant problems were mutually explored when they arose. Using this method of communication combined with the willingness to let the friend "be" virtually eliminated all problems in the relationship. Maslow suggested that a healthy individual will self-disclose to at least one significant person. Usually this person is a friend.

Possibilities for closeness, the deepest levels of communication, and the widest area of self-disclosure and perhaps even peak experiences exist in a good friendship. A friendship in which total openness and intimate sharing are present is called an A to Z friendship because no barriers to thoughts, feelings, or actions exist.[13] Although one's part-

---

13. Arnold A. Lazarus, *Behavior Therapy & Beyond* (New York: McGraw-Hill, 1971), p. 135.

ner in marriage can often be considered one's "best friend," psychologist Arnold Lazarus suggests that "marriage is intimate sharing whereas friendship is shared intimacy."[14] In marriage the close proximity of the two partners and the necessary responsibilities they share dictate that there be some emotional privacy. Because most friends do not live together daily, they can afford to share "what is in their deepest hearts." For example, a wife might share the fact that she resented certain expectations her husband had of her to her friend before she would reveal this resentment to her husband.

It is extremely important that we remember to allow our friend his freedom. This means not attempting to make our relationship all-inclusive, assuming that our friend should enjoy doing everything that we want to do and being hurt when we discover otherwise. From this it follows that neither will our friendship be exclusive; both we and our friend will expect to have other friends, some of whom may be common to both of us, some not. We will try to avoid turning the friendship into an institution by establishing a binding contract in a flush of affection that cannot be broken without hurt or sorrow. As one writer expresses it:

> Friendship establishes a bond between two persons which can be broken if one wishes to break it. This ever present possibility of it being broken along with the fact that it isn't broken, is what creates the peculiar faithfulness which is typical of authentic friendship.[15]

Finally, the kind of friendship which allows this freedom is particularly of value because it seems to promote growth as few other relationships can.

> Life must be seen, accepted, and challenged. Friends do this to each other. They don't allow for mediocrity or stagnation. The love they share demands that they both constantly seek growth.[16]

You see, we *have* waxed poetic over friendship. Touching our innermost, indescribable feelings, probing our deepest levels of communication as friendship does, we, who believe we have experienced the best of such friendships, can turn to little else than poetry.

---

14. Ibid., p. 135.
15. Cummins, *Friendship,* p. 2.
16. Ibid., p. 47.

# Marriage

Marriage is probably an unfortunate term for this section. It implies only that two people are living together legally. A better term might be "partnership." Using this term allows us to talk about the process of "becoming partners" and "marriage and its alternatives."[17] So when we use the term "partner," we don't mean exclusively a husband and wife in the legal and traditional sense, but rather two people who are living and loving together and attempting to grow in the process.

A very important place to begin is at the point where we "get into" the relationship. Probably no decision (or series of decisions) is any more important than the choice of a partner, be it for life or for a limited, but intense and intimate, period of time. What we have discussed before about "advertising yourself honestly" is crucial in this type of dyadic relationship. Bach and Deutsch, in their book *Pairing,* speak specifically to the general lack of honest advertisement in the quest for an intimate partner:

> They present themselves in a ritualistic way. They try to behave appropriately according to the setting in which they appear. On the beach they flex their muscles. At meetings they concentrate on the problems of the business at hand. On the dance floor they concern themselves with dance style. Under the masks, one may be sure, are interesting and lonely faces. But the intimacy-hunter is busy preserving his own facade in order to hide his fear of being rejected. He is afraid to expose his genuine self and too self-concerned to elicit reality from others. So he and his peers become accommodating mirrors for one another, *things* for mutual convenience—to make a quorum, fill out a foursome, dance with, display beauty and power for, or warm a double bed.[18]

Bach and Deutsch see this maintenance of a facade as a defense against being rejected. They suggest that open and honest presentation of self cannot be developed until we learn to meet rejection without fear.[19] The most significant technique that they offer as a means of reducing this fear and of "getting into" a relationship hon-

17. See Carl R. Rogers, *Becoming Partners: Marriage and Its Alternatives* (New York: Delta, 1972) for exploration of alternative approaches to 32 marriages by case study.

18. George R. Bach and Ronald M. Deutsch, *Pairing* (New York: Avon, 1970), p. 32.

19. Ibid., p. 38.

estly is the art of *impacting.* Basically, impacting is "successfully asserting one's wishes, feelings, or identity to a paring partner."[20] Instead of attempting to create an image or illusion of what we think the other person expects and wants, they suggest that we try to come on straight and level with the other about what we are really thinking and feeling.

For example, instead of sitting next to someone with gorgeous eyes and saying, "Do you think the midterm in this class will be objective or essay? I can't stand objective tests, they are no measurement of knowledge" and trying to create the image that we're hip, we don't like multiple choice tests just like most other college students, and we know that an educational system that fosters that type is inadequate, we can say what we are really thinking, "You have beautiful eyes." This may sound a bit extreme, but many psychologists and communicologists believe that this approach of openly revealing our thoughts and feelings can be beneficial, not only because it is honest, but because it dispenses with the need for establishing an image which we may not be willing to live up to at some future date, it signifies trust and acceptance of the other person, and it involves us immediately in the deeper levels of communication.[21]

At this point we might question: "Won't the person think I'm weird and reject me?" This is really two questions. Yes, the other person may perceive that we're weird. As much as talk about openness and honesty pervades our conversation, little seems to exist, and employing it may make one something of a rarity. No, it doesn't necessarily follow that the other will reject us because of our "unusual" approach. And what are the consequences if he or she does? We could tell ourselves irrationally (according to rational-emotive therapy) that it's terrible and we can't stand it because everyone should love us. However, if we talk to ourselves rationally we might realize that while it would be nicer if he or she didn't reject us (but there's really no moral or natural reason why he or she shouldn't), we'll be okay. Besides, if he or she does, we'll know that relationship probably wasn't meant to materialize anyway. Initial and immediate openness and honesty has a way of weeding out people who eventually may prove unsuitable for us and it's best to find out who they are as soon as possible.

Before moving on to the actual partnership, the "being in" a relationship, here are three techniques for impacting with a potential

20. Ibid., p. 281.
21. Ibid., p. 137.

partner that Bach and Deutsch suggest.[22] They sum up what we've been saying here and are consistent with our approach to establishing and developing any dyadic relationship.

1. *Use a role and stereotype free approach.* We should try not to ask a potential partner what he *does,* but begin the conversation by asking about his opinion about the decor, his beliefs about the energy crisis, his feelings about meeting strangers-in-a-place-like-this. The ice-breaker should be what we really want to know about him or something that we really want to say to him right then. If we are asked what we *do,* we might suggest that it may not make a difference and move on to discuss what we wish at that moment. (There is the possibility, of course, that we might really, because of sincere interest and enthusiasm rather than the need to label, want to talk about our work or his. In that case, we wouldn't hesitate.)

2. *Introduce an authentic reservation.* An authentic reservation is some negative feeling we might have about the potential partner which is preventing us from being on the same "wave length" with him. This needs to be preceded by a request such as, "Would you mind if I said something negative?" The reservation serves the purpose of demonstrating immediate openness, beginning the relationship on an honest basis, and taking us and our potential partner directly to the "gut level" of communication. An authentic reservation might be, "It disturbs me when you look all around the room when we're talking."

3. *Explore differences.* We believe that exploring differences is one way to begin focusing on uniqueness in a developing relationship, though Bach and Deutsch do not mention such an advantage specifically. When we explore differences, we tend to remember the fact that this potential partner is an individual with an identity all his own, and when we remember that we are much more likely to allow him his freedom to be unique. So rather than talking about what we might have in common such as both attending college, we can talk about differences in background, interests, tastes, and goals.

We now turn from discussing potential partnership to actual partnership. We're going to assume that even if we enter a partnership openly, honestly, and with a mutual sense of freedom, problems will arise.

Partnerships can get bogged down in seemingly the stupidest, most trivial, and most senseless matters. This seems to be an unavoidable and very real part of living and spending time together. Joe came

22. Ibid., pp. 104–5.

home from an exhausting day's work of soliciting house listings for his real estate business. Anne, an interior designer, likewise was tired after visiting a number of homes she was to redecorate. Dinner was not prepared. Joe began by complaining that Anne's work certainly took precedence over her home life. Anne said she wanted to go out to eat. Joe said he wanted to relax at home. Anne replied sure he could relax while she did all the work. Joe countered with she just didn't know how it was in the real world just talking to housewives all day long. Anne screamed that he didn't think her work was important and who did he think provided security when he was off looking for his "ideal" job? Off and running. By now you can probably find many communication errors that were committed.

Let's take a look at this example from another approach. Bach and Wyden, authors of the *Intimate Enemy,* suggest ways to "fight fair in love and marriage."[23] Beginning with the premise that "verbal conflict between intimates is not only acceptable . . . it is constructive and highly desirable,"[24] they suggest that constructive fighting is open, game-free communication at its best; it is a way of resolving realistic conflicts, dissipating resentment and aggression, and clearing the way for positive and loving sharing. Perhaps we can make our example conform to the specific suggestions for constructive conflict Bach and Wyden make.[25] The initiator should:

1. Begin with a specific objective, not a general observation.
2. Specify the real issue underlying this fight.
3. Size up the results of the fight periodically and gain feedback.
4. Seek a common ground based on shared premises.
5. Accept a compromise offered by your partner.
6. Offer details of an exact solution.
7. Confirm the plan and specify when it will begin.

If these suggestions had been followed the incident may have occurred as follows. Joe and Anne both came home tired. Anne hadn't prepared dinner. Joe stated specifically that he wanted dinner on time. Anne explained why this might be difficult to accomplish, said that it was difficult because they both arrived home at different times every day, she wasn't sure what "on time" was. Joe revealed that his real concern was that she cared more for her work than she did for him. Anne, explaining her point of view, said that she cared for her work

23. George R. Bach and Peter Wyden, *The Intimate Enemy: How to Fight Fair in Love and Marriage* (New York: Avon, 1968), p. 17.
24. Ibid., pp. 17–34.
25. Ibid., pp. 66–68.

as much as him, not more, and she didn't see why the two loves necessarily had to conflict. Joe sought feedback; he asked if it was correct that she was not averse to fixing his dinner, but that at times it was difficult. Anne replied that she did not mind fixing his dinner but that it would be helpful if he prepared the meals part of the time. Joe tried to establish common ground by suggesting that it would be ideal if work did not interfere with their time together. Anne agreed with this in principle and suggested that they plan dinner for later in the evening when it was certain they would both be home. Joe accepted this compromise solution and suggested that they eat at 8:00 every night alternating responsibility for preparing dinner and when a home evening meal was impossible they would go get a late pizza together. Anne thought that a terrific solution. Joe then suggested that they begin immediately.

Now, in a real situation there would probably be much more give and take before arriving at a mutually agreeable solution. The point is that following these suggestions for "fight communication" works toward clearly understanding our partner's position and solving problems, rather than merely stirring up trouble. This "round" did not speak to some problem issues, such as regard for the partner's work brought out in the first example. That is not to say that these issues will never be uncovered—they will when they are the true underlying issue rather than just additional ammunition. Speaking to one conflicting issue at a time is probably the best way to proceed if problems are to be solved and tension reduced.

Fair fighting is only one of the elements involved in a happy partnership. We have taken the factors most mentioned as necessary to and evident in ideal partnerships by Rogers, Maslow, Bach and Wyden and the O'Neills and compiled them under six headings.[26] They could be said to represent "intimacy" (Bach and Wyden), "open marriage" (the O'Neills), "love in self-actualizing people" (Maslow), and "the partnership revolution" (Rogers).

*Commitment.*    There seems to be a commitment to each other and the relationship, not in the restrictive sense, but in the sense suggested in our "stage of growth"—a responsibility for our actions vis-à-vis our partner. Along with commitment, there is a synergistic type of dedication, meaning that the dichotomy between selfishness and altruism is

---

26. See Rogers, *Becoming Partners,* pp. 199–210; Bach and Wyden, *Intimate Enemy,* pp. 324–27; Abraham H. Maslow, *Motivation and Personality,* 2d ed. (New York: Harper & Row, 1970), pp. 181–202; Nena and George O'Neill, *Open Marriage: A New Life for Couples* (New York: Avon, 1972), *passim.*

transcended. In other words, many things that we may do for our partner, such as reading something he has written and giving him feedback, constitute enjoyment rather than sacrifice for us.

*Communication.*    We have already discussed the necessity of clarity, openness, and honesty with our expression of thoughts and feelings. It is difficult for this to occur, of course, if a trusting atmosphere has not been established. Learning the rules of constructive conflict so that we do not hit "below the belt line" is relevant here. If our partner can trust us to use what he says constructively for better under-standing and the mutual solving of problems, rather than to misuse disclosed information by turning it against him, the conditions for deep level communication and self-disclosure have been established.

Another factor which is relevant here is humor, the ability to laugh at oneself and the situation, and with our partner. In fact, we tend to believe that an honest (as opposed to vicious) sense of humor is one of the most important elements in a mutually beneficial partnership. For example, rather than blame someone because the toilet gets stopped up five minutes before company arrives, it is helpful to be able to laugh at the situation; rather than get defensive because we forgot to feed the cat (which we didn't want to do in the first place) and he ate part of a tuna casserole sitting on the stove, laugh at the cat's ingenuity and suggest going out to dinner; rather than getting angry with our partner because she forgot to meet us for lunch, treat it as a charming example of her absent-mindedness and get some enjoy-ment out of it.

*Individual Identity.*    Having a separate self implies all sorts of other conditions in a partnership. This means that we have a right to our own physical, mental, and emotional privacy if we so desire—we are not required to maintain "togetherness" or a couple image, spending every free moment together. For example, we do not have to attend cocktail parties together just because everyone there will be married. It also means that we have a right to be independent of each other. If one partner wishes to earn his/her own living, have his/her own possessions, even retain (if a woman) her own name, that person can. It means freedom for *"open companionship,"*[27] the enjoyment of other relationships outside marriage; for example, if one partner likes West-erns and the other doesn't, he has the freedom to go with someone who does. Finally, it means the ability to pursue our personal growth

---

27. O'Neill, *Open Marriage,* Chapter 12.

in our desired direction; for example, if one partner wants to be a ditch digger or a free lance artist or a college student at the age of forty, nothing other than her own values should inhibit her.

*Role Flexibility.*    In an ideal partnership, rigid man-woman roles do not exist. Where is it written that man shall mow the lawn and woman shall do the ironing? Roles are chosen by what is most enjoyable (or least distasteful) to each partner and an equal division of labor according to criteria of time, energy, effort, and satisfaction is attempted. Role flexibility implies equal authority and responsibility in and for the partnership. Decisions that affect a partner individually, such as what type of clothes he will wear, are made by that partner; decisions that affect both, such as the location of a new house, are made mutually.

*Change.*    The realistic expectation that the relationship will change as the partners do is acknowledged. The woman who was content to stay at home and keep house the first year of marriage may later wish to explore other possibilities; the man who began a career as a rising young executive may quit the organization to stay home with his growing children. In an ideal partnership, change is not only accommodated, it is often encouraged as providing variety and stimulation in the relationship.

*End Experience.*    Admiration, wonder, and awe exist in the ideal partnership. These are attitudes not only toward the partner, but toward the relationship itself. The partnership is seen as an end in itself, not as a means of security or material gain. Often the partners feel lucky that their paths have crossed.

These are the factors that have been found. You probably do not, at this point, believe that all of them are possible, much less desirable. We urge you to consider them and to adapt them as they meet your particular goals and life styles. Partnership is a dynamic process, not an institution. In its ideal form it is

> . . . not just a matter of a new freedom for marriage partners, for its true goal is the mutual growth that such freedom fosters. . . . The key . . . to understanding open marriage as a dynamic process, is the concept of *synergy.*
>
> Synergy occurs when two organisms, or people, are brought together, or combined, in such a way that the end result is enhanced —that is, when the combination of the two produces a quality or

effect that is more intense than what either of the two contributing parts originally had or could independently attain. Thus in synergy one and one makes three, not just two. It is this special effect, this enhancement, that makes it possible in open marriage for husband and wife to exist and grow as two separate individuals, yet at the same time to transcend their duality and achieve a unity on another level, beyond themselves, a unity that develops out of the love for each other and each other's growth. In a synergistic, cooperative way, each one's individual growth enhances and augments the other's growth, pleasure and fulfillment. The more of a whole person each one becomes, the more self-actualized, the more he has to offer his mate. The better he feels within himself, the more he can love; the more he can give freedom, the more he can take pleasure in seeing his mate grow; the more both partners grow, the more stimulating and dynamic each one becomes for the other.[28]

# Work

Work relationships are those involved with one's job. We can have a working relationship that is superior, subordinate, or equal to another person. A working relationship is usually task- rather than relationship-oriented; that is, we are usually more concerned with meeting deadlines, quotas, and production goals and with communicating information relevant to these than we are with developing and maintaining a close interpersonal relationship.

This appears to be one section in the chapter where attempting to probe the deepest levels of communication is not really realistic and perhaps not even desirable. However, as in any other dyadic relationship, open communication, emphases on individual uniqueness, and granting of maximum possible freedom are important. Since the most likely relationship one will have at this stage of her or his life is employer-employee that is the one to devote our attention to.

The three rules for "getting into" a relationship seem appropriate here as elsewhere. It is obviously very important that we advertise ourselves honestly; failing to do so may not only lead to a personally distasteful but also practically unachievable working relationship. If we falsely indicated during the course of interviewing that we were aggressive and liked to sell, we might get a job where we were expected to be very productive sales representatives. The probability that we and our employer would be unhappy is high. Limiting the relationship

---

28. O'Neill, *Open Marriage,* pp. 257–58.

to interests held in common is also relevant. If we view the working relationship as one in which the job at hand is to be completed (the main interest we both have in common), we won't fall into the trap of thinking that we necessarily have to like each other and socialize together, unless, of course, there is mutual benefit from such an arrangement. Finally, we can give our employer freedom to be by allowing him eccentricities of tapping his pen on the desk, looking out of the window when we talk to him, or giving an order in a circuitous manner. These are things that are in our control. Before we decide to enter a working relationship, however, we can be clear about those aspects of the job which are not in our control, such as rigid organizational structure, expectations of working overtime without pay, or few fringe benefits, and ask ourselves if the price we must pay to earn a livelihood in this way is worth it to us. Will it promote our individual happiness and growth? Maslow suggests that a self-actualizing person transcends the dichotomy of work and play; that is, he is so involved in his work and finds it so fulfilling and enjoyable that he ceases to differentiate it from play.[30] Ideally, we should seek those working relationships which create conditions facilitative of such an attitude toward our jobs. It has been found that those conditions which lead to the greatest job satisfaction are a sense of achievement, deserved recognition for work accomplished, interesting, challenging and varied nature of work, responsibility for outcome, and potential for growth and advancement.[31]

Consider the case of Brian to illustrate some of the communicative aspects of a dyadic employer-employee relationship. Brian, a full-time instructor, made an appointment with his departmental chairman to discuss his assigned class hours for the following quarter; he was upset because they had been changed from morning to afternoon meeting times for no apparent reason. When he expressed his dissatisfaction, the chairman unexpectedly stated that if he had his way Brian would not be rehired for the following year. Brian became emotional and visibly upset. He managed, however, to ask the reason for the chairman's statement. The chairman replied that he did not spend enough time on campus, that he did not talk to his colleagues enough, that he spent too much time with students. Brian countered that while it was true that he left at 2 P.M., he did come in at 6 A.M., he kept more than adequate office hours, did a great deal of work for the department

---

30. Maslow, *Motivation and Personality*, p. 179.

31. Aubrey C. Sanford, *Human Relations: Theory and Practice* (Columbus, Ohio: Charles E. Merrill, 1973), pp. 175–76.

that no one else wanted to do, and received good ratings on his instructor evaluations. Brian continued by saying that the chairman was a manipulator and authoritarian administrator who wanted to control others and make them conform, reciting in the process a number of examples that had occurred over the quarter. The chairman voiced some other faculty members' complaints about his being "an efficient part-time instructor" and said he expected some changes. Brian left still visibly upset.

To some, the cost of remaining in this type of working relationship would have been too high. To Brian, rightly or wrongly, it wasn't and he stayed, made the expected changes, and adjusted to them. We should try to answer the following questions about this incident. Remember, there is probably nothing Brian could have done in this situation to change the chairman's behavior, he only had control over his own. Of course, appropriate communication behavior on his part might have led to a more pleasant situation for him.

1. Did Brian focus his communication on behavior rather than personality?
2. Did he focus his communication on observable behavior rather than inference?
3. Did he focus his communication on the here and now rather than the there and then?
4. Did he focus his communication on alternatives rather than specific solutions?
5. Did he provide only the needed amount of communication rather than the amount he wanted to give?

What if we rewrote Brian's part of the communication according to these rules. Do you think it would have changed the situation to the better for Brian?

All the concepts we have covered in other dyadic relationships can be appropriately applicable to the working relationship. Is it so unrealistic to believe that a working relationship can contain the elements of trust, honesty, and freedom? We think not. We see no reason why we cannot at least make an attempt to reach the third and fourth levels of communication by openly expressing our ideas and feelings. Of course, if we put our job in jeopardy by suggesting a radical new procedure, criticizing the boss's pet plan, or expressing frustration with our work load, we may decide against this approach. Perhaps the job may not be worth the price of such limitations. Perhaps we can be one of the modern leaders who approaches others, not merely in order to increase productivity and reduce resistance to authority, but to utilize and maximize the unique individual talents of each person in the work situation.[32] We can consider the suggestion that not only would task orientation and goal achievement not be obstructed by this approach, it might even be enhanced.[33]

The dyadic relationships we have discussed are certainly not exhaustive, but they are those in which we will most likely be involved for the rest of our lives.

## Summary

This chapter was devoted to a discussion of relationships between two people—dyadic relationships. Probing as they do the deepest levels of communication, it is wise to choose them well. With this in mind, we suggested that we could enter such a relationship by (1) advertising ourselves honestly, (2) limiting the relationship to similar interests, and (3) allowing the other his freedom. Assuming that the goal of a dyadic relationship is personal happiness and growth we suggested that in removing ourselves from an untenable situation we ask (1) what price we are paying to stay, (2) what it would cost us to get out, and (3) what we could do once we are out.

In speaking specifically about communication, we identified five points of appropriate focus in dyadic relationships: (1) on behavior rather than personality, (2) on observation rather than inference, (3) on here and now rather than there and then, (4) on exploration rather than advice, and (5) on amount of information needed rather than on amount available to give.

We then looked at four specific dyadic relationships in which we will be engaged, in one form or another, for the rest of our lives; family, friendship, partnership, and work.

We pointed out that family relationships were, in reality, a number of one-to-one relationships and needed to be treated as such. We suggested that such time-worn problems as the "generation gap" could be ameliorated by the application of certain principles and *our* use of the approach usually offered solely to parents.

As do others, we found friendship difficult to define but settled for "a special kind of love, minus sex." Again, we applied the principles

---

32. See Raymond E. Miles, "Human Relations or Human Resources?" *Harvard Business Review,* July–August 1965, pp. 148–56.
33. Robert R. Blake and Jane S. Mouton, "Managerial Facades," *Advanced Management Journal,* July 1966, p. 31.

for getting in and out of such a relationship and making the most of ones in which we are engaged.

We began the discussion of marriage by immediately substituting the term "partnership" which we feel is more reflective of present day dyadic relationships of this type. We spent some time in discussing the appropriate way to get into this very important relationship by (1) eliminating role conversation, (2) introducing authentic reservations, and (3) exploring differences. We then moved to an exploration of marriage, and shared some ideas about the desirability of and the way to "fight" constructively. We ended this section by identifying the six most mentioned elements in an ideal partnership: commitment, communication, individual identity, role flexibility, change, and end experience.

In viewing work relationships we talked from what we considered to be the point of view of being an employee. Though a bit more difficult than other relationships in this regard, we found there were beneficial ways in which the principles discussed could be applied.

# 12

# Small Group
# Experiences

Increasingly we are engaging in interpersonal communication in small group settings which are arranged by someone with content and/or relationship goals in mind. A great deal of small group behavior also takes place as people cluster together to engage in conversation, and these groups are formed in a natural way without any organized preplanning. Everything we have said to this point about interpersonal communication can apply to the small group settings in which we find ourselves. Thus, we must integrate what we have explored about interpersonal communication into our focus on and participation in groups.

Treatments of intrapersonal communication, interpersonal communication, language/meaning, and dialogue are especially relevant for facilitating small group communication. We can review the route from self-awareness to self-actualization; techniques such as those in transactional analysis and rational-emotive theory; and such guides to clarity as the "map is not the territory," "words are not things," and "have you checked that out?" This information will serve as a necessary foundation for a study of small group communication.

# What Is a Small Group?

It may seem insignificant to ask: What constitutes a small group? How many persons ought to be included in one group? However, the size of a group *is* significant because individual growth and productivity, as well as the content and/or relationship goals for the group as a whole, will depend in part on its size.

A group which is too small for intended purposes may produce little if any significant outcomes. On the other hand, a group which becomes unwieldy because of its largeness can encourage participants to be inhibited or lazy about making contributions which can be of benefit to themselves, to other individuals, or the group as a whole.

Most books dealing with small group communication indicate what the ideal range is for a formal or informal small group, and communicologist Vincent DiSalvo summarizes: "A small group is defined as three or more individuals who are engaged in face-to-face interaction with one another in such a manner that each person influences and is influenced by each of the other individuals."[1] DiSalvo suggests the upper size of a group is around twenty, "and the ideal size of our group would be between five to seven members."[2] At times the range and depth of a group need to be expanded because of the group's mission; at other times intimate, intensive, and personal goals are best solved by a small group size. Moreover, small group communication, generally speaking, includes two major kinds of groups: intensive small groups (encounter), or problem-solving small groups (task-oriented). Two examples can illustrate these views about the size and kinds of groups.

Those in the field of education continually serve on permanent and *ad hoc* committees. These committes are usually small groups charged with task-oriented responsibility. When a committee has a broad and general problem area to deal with, such as the preparation of an instructional critique, an entire college in a university's organization, a group of about ten members (perhaps one person from each department in the college) seems necessary. On the other hand, in intensive or growth-oriented groups the intimate and spontaneous communication is often stifled when the group includes more than seven or eight members. In the growth-oriented group experience, the larger group becomes less likely to encourage certain participants to

---

1. Vincent DiSalvo, "Small Group Behavior," in John J. Makay, ed., *Exploration in Speech Communication* (Columbus, O.: Charles E. Merrill, 1973), pp. 108–41.
2. Ibid., p. 113.

become active. However, when such a group is smaller all individuals are free and perhaps *compelled* to contribute to the flow of ideas. When problem-solving groups have broadly based goals to achieve, four or five participants may be insufficient for the job to be undertaken.

## Communication Goals

Individuals who participate in small group experiences usually have self-oriented goals as well as group-oriented goals; the group-oriented goals often are more apparent and common to all. Debra, for example, was a young woman who did something quite common; she became active in a small group charged with the responsibility of determining policies and directions with which to guide a local Planned Parenthood Chapter. Clearly the group had specific content goals centered in raising money for development and operations, the development of educational programs, seeking new membership, and providing general input to their entire Chapter. She also knew that a basic reason for her group participation was to develop stimulating interpersonal relationships with others in the group. She indicated to friends that suburban homemaking was less than satisfying so she needed to meet and transact with others like herself if she was to find life satisfying. The general purpose, then, of the group was to complete tasks and solve problems, while group members were also probably active in the group behavior for satisfying human relationships.

What about us? Do we join groups or accept committee assignments only to complete tasks and solve problems? Or do we wish to build friendships, to grow personally, and to just enjoy the company of others as well? Recently an attorney was invited to serve on a core faculty for a Doctor of Ministry candidate. The candidate, an ordained minister, and five core faculty members met every two or three months over a two-year period to guide and evaluate the candidate toward his goal of earning the advanced degree. But was this content goal their only reason for getting together for several hours each meeting? No, because the lawyer admitted periodically that he especially enjoyed the growing friendship he shared with the others; they in turn affirmed each other by admitting a similar attitude.

Obviously there are group experiences which tend to focus primarily on content goals, while any relational ones are side benefits. On the other hand, group experiences may be primarily aimed at relationship goals, with content matters being at best secondary.

Whether a group aims at one kind of goal or the other, and regardless of its size and nature, usually someone provides leadership. Therefore, we will recognize primary responsibilities and functions which are characteristic of leadership in small groups.

## Leadership

Have you ever participated in small group communication and felt ill-at-ease, frustrated, or angry because the communication interaction seemed boring, confusing, unproductive, or nondirectional? We all have, and sometimes we have accepted our negative feelings because they were the honest, although unsatisfying, results we received from taking the risk of participating in a leaderless group. Intensive groups often, but not always, operate without an assigned leader or facilitator. In contrast, problem-solving or task-oriented groups most often have a designated or assigned leader. Whether a group has a designated leader or not, an active and fluent small group setting can reveal leadership traits and behaviors in any number of members of the group. In these situations, participants assume leadership functions. Recently a course in group leadership was admitted to the offerings of a department of communication at a midsize eastern university. During the entire quarter no one in the class is designated or elected to lead the groups in the class activities. Though frustrated at first, the struggling students soon realize that the functions of leadership can naturally emerge within the life of a group. More commonly, however, when people in the world beyond the classroom meet as groups, one or two persons are assigned the responsibility for providing the leadership.

The responsibilities and functions of a leader, whether designated, elected, or self-appointed are many and varied. To simplify as well as clarify them, we can examine a partial and useful list:[3]

1. A leader can establish a format for the group; he or she may do this with the help of group participants.
2. A leader can "get the group going" in pertinent and productive directions.

---

3. Gerald M. Phillips, *Communication and the Small Group,* 2d ed. (Indianapolis: Bobbs-Merrill, 1973), p. 68. See additional detail in Michael Bargoon, Judee K. Heston, and James C. McCroskey, *Small Group Communication: A Functional Approach* (New York: Holt, Rinehart, and Winston, 1974), chapter 10, "Leadership in the Small Group."

3. A leader can assume responsibility for keeping the group "on the track" and focused at group goals.
4. A leader can make clarifying summaries when they seem necessary to group progress.
5. A leader can assume responsibility for keeping group communication from being one-sided.
6. A leader can seek to relieve high tensions which result from heated controversy in the communication of the group.
7. A leader can ask relevant questions to draw information out of participants for group consumption and response.
8. A leader can attempt to keep a group "alive" insuring that no group member remains passive in the small group setting.

Although small groups can be classified into a wide variety of categories, for our study we will use two major headings of group experience which take into account the wide variety of special groups: intensive group experience and problem-solving experience. Intensive groups, a contemporary approach, are generally associated with humanistic ideas and techniques, and problem-solving groups, though written about most frequently in traditional ways, can also be humanistic. It is up to the members of the group to determine whether a humanistic orientation is to be incorporated.

## Intensive Group Experience

A fast growing body of literature is developing which describes the process of intensive group experiences. Perhaps most prominent is information about encounter groups. Although some of this literature questions (may even attack) the process and effects of encounter in human growth and development, evidence abounds to support and advocate encounter for the development of healthy individuals.[4] The encounter group as intensive group experience is far more humanistic than is the formalized problem-solving group. Those largely uninformed about encountering have at times charged such groups with being "touchy-feely" groups. This sort of labeling shows a lack of knowledge and understanding of a genuinely humane and responsibility-building approach to small group communication. Many of us

---

4. Morton A. Lieberman, Irvin D. Yalom, and Mathew B. Miles, *Encounter Groups: First Facts* (New York: Basic Books, 1973); Robert T. Golembiewski and Arthur Blumberg, eds. *Sensitivity Training and the Laboratory Approach* (Itaska, Ill.: Peacock, 1970).

already possess at least a general notion of encounter for this intensive group experience has spread throughout our country and includes an untold but vast number in our population.

We study encounter groups in this chapter because as Carl Rogers has written they "lead to more personal independence, fewer hidden feelings, more willingness to innovate, more opposition to institutional rigidities. Hence, if a person is fearful of change in any form, he is rightly fearful of encounter groups. They breed constructive change. . . ."[5] They serve largely relationship goals but can serve content goals as well.

One encounter group was formed to help eight persons use reality therapy to make themselves highly responsible individuals. Though their experiences together brought them into deep friendships with each other, and each learned about himself or herself from the reflections of others in the group, each person also developed a realistic personal plan for fulfilling his or her basic needs in responsible ways. Judi, for example, not only felt good about her new relationships with others in the group but she increased her self-esteem and developed a way in which to remain a student in college. She struggled in self-sufficiency, and she shifted her occupational goal from English education to pharmacy.

Encounter groups cover a spectrum ranging from the T-group with emphasis on developing human relations skills, to the sensitivity group (not unlike the T-group) which helps build team efforts in business and industry, to the organizational development group with a primary aim toward growth in skill as a leader for each participant. As encounter groups they emphasize personal growth and the development and improvement of interpersonal communication and relationships through an experiential process.

Psychologists Morton Lieberman and Mathew Miles and psychiatrist Irvin D. Yalom, like other writers, are aware of the widely varied forms and functions of encounter groups, but they clearly identify the common features of encounter groups:

> Intensive, high contact, group experience; they are generally small enough (six to twenty members) to permit considerable face-to-face interaction; they focus on the here-and-now (the behavior of members as it unfolds in the group); they encourage openness, honest, interpersonal confrontation, self-disclosure, and strong emotional expression. . . . The specific goals of the groups may vary from

5. Carl Rogers, *Carl Rogers on Encounter Groups* (New York: Harper & Row, 1970), pp. 4–5.

reducing juvenile delinquency to reducing weight . . . generally the overall goals involve some type of personal change—change of behavior, of attitudes, of values, of life style.[6]

# Group Phases

The intensive group usually goes through an early phase in which each member gets to feel reasonably comfortable with the other members of the group. Matt, for instance, joined an "open and on-going" group when it began its fourth meeting. The six others who had attended since the first meeting seemed relaxed and friendly toward each other, they seemed to feel they were all members committed to the group. Matt was nervous and hesitant about joining but he had interpersonal problems he hoped the group would help him work out. Moreover, his initial remarks in the group prompted one woman to tell him he was welcome in the group but he would have to work hard to gain her acceptance of him. Others offered different comments. After two weeks Matt enthusiastically looked forward to group and attended regularly until he was finished with what he felt he needed to work on.

A second phase in an intensive group deals with power, influence, and authority. Members of a group led by a trained facilitator usually look to this individual as the person in charge, the one who possesses most power, influence, and authority. The members often see this person as "the healer" and themselves as needing to be healed. Professional status can cause persons to assign more power, influence, and authority to some members rather than others. Two examples serve to illustrate these points. During the first meetings of one group Carol would always look at *one* of two psychologists in the group and ask if she could say something. Bill, the one she asked, would respond by saying, "Are you asking for my permission? You don't need authorization from me to ask for or to give something in the group." Carol eventually took the responsibility herself for deciding what to say and when to speak. Fred was a college professor in a group which included seven others. Only the trained facilitator had a college degree, two of the women were students at the university where Fred was employed, one man was an auto mechanic, another a retail clerk, a sixth a clerk typist, and the seventh an "odd job" semi-retired man. For several weeks most members of the group seemed to assign special power,

6. Lieberman, et al., *Encounter Groups,* p. 9.

influence, and authority to Fred simply because these traits seemed to go with the one who possessed the most education. Eventually Fred and the others worked to change this, so each seemed to feel his or her own power, influence, and authority and those of others in a well-distributed way. During the life of the group the seven under the guidance of the facilitator still acknowledged the psychologist to be most powerful, influential, and authoritative, but she did not inhibit their dialogue.

A final stage which seems to be very important in the intensive group experience is the affection group members develop for each other. They become close, even though they might be from diverse occupations, age groups, education and income levels, emotions/ beliefs, attitudes, and values. One group, for example, decided to end their weekly meeting with each member hugging each other member. This was a way of displaying and experiencing open and honest affection. The same group discovered one of its members had a birthday on the day of their next meeting, so they spontaneously decided to spend one of the two hours they were to meet by having a birthday party for Claire. The group had a warm and rich experience at their party and Claire confessed it was her first birthday party since she was a very small child. Predictably we can expect intensive small groups to pass through these phases during their lifetimes.

What sort of format would this group follow? The response to this question about a format for encounter is two-fold: (1) often no pre-established format is used, and the group goes where its members find themselves taking it in their search for personal growth; (2) a format can be generally planned by members who, in advance, decide on a matter or personal problem they want to work on to grow with the group. The members who do not set goals in advance of a group meeting, however, have nothing to do with setting time allotments in a format.

An intensive group usually has a leader who is often referred to as a facilitator.[7] For example, the Columbus (Ohio) Community Mental Health Center has an "ongoing" encounter group with two facilitators who are psychologists with particular expertise in transactional analysis and Gestalt psychology. They serve as guides in probing the group members and in the application of TA and Gestalt psychology in the group's life. Rogers, whose work with similar groups has been highly extensive, identified twenty trends or tendencies in the encounter

---

7. Carl Rogers, "The Group Comes of Age," *Psychology Today,* December 1969, p. 27.

group process. Twelve of these tendencies are especially appropriate to our study.[8] In order to have an idea of what goes on in intensive groups we need to remember the key ideas presented in the previous chapters are descriptive of human behavior within such groups. Now we shall focus on the process patterns, or trends.

1. *Milling around*—When individuals come face-to-face with group participation when there is no tightly structured format there is a milling around until persons begin to focus and direct themselves toward aims and goals. One group facilitator begins this focus after several minutes of general chatter within the group, by asking, "Who wants to work?" After a short period of silence, someone begins and encountering soon results.

2. *Resistance to personal expression*—Some often hesitate to reveal their real and genuine ideas and feelings until they feel they can take a risk and trust themselves and each other. Remember what we studied about dialogic communication.

3. *Description of past feeling*—As communication proceeds and disclosure assumes a large part of this discussion, participants share freely of past feelings which are responsible to some extent for bringing them to group.

4. *Expression of negative feelings*—For a number of speculative reasons, some of the first remarks offered by group members toward themselves, each other, or the facilitator may be negative. Perhaps this is because members test whether or not the group is a place where they can take risks. They may expect more initial direction, they may enter the group with hostility inside of themselves, and/or they may possess low self-esteem.

5. *Expression of personally meaningful material*—Once individuals recognize the group is theirs, and will only be as helpful as each wants to make it, they can become quite self-disclosing. It is not unusual for people who join a group to take several meetings before entering into the communication of personally meaningful material. For example, once a woman was especially withdrawn her first time in a group, she was clearly hostile the second meeting (even calling the activity in the group dumb and probably of little help), and then early in the third meeting she opened up and began to

8. Rogers, "The Group Comes of Age," details the twenty trends and his book on encounter groups explains thirteen, pp. 14–34.

share her problems with others. She took the risk and found it was well worth it!

6. *The expression of immediate interpersonal feelings in group* —A common experience in the encounter is the explicit bringing into the open of feelings experienced in the immediate moment by one member toward another. For example, a member of a group spoke so often of the same hang-up that another member said, "Marge, I really like you as a person. I think you're neat. I understand your problem. But now I am bored with it. Why be so preoccupied?" Another decided to move around the group and to respond to each member in a nonverbal way. Stopping at each member she patted a head, shook a hand, or gave a hug. When she arrived at the last person, she waved her arms in disgust, turned about face and walked as far away as possible. The expression of "here and now" feelings led to meaningful "here and now" dialogue.

7. *The development of healing capacity in the group*—Rogers states, "One of the most fascinating aspects of any intensive group experience is to observe the manner in which a number of the group members show a natural and spontaneous capacity for healing in a helpful, facilitating, and therapeutic fashion with the pain and suffering of others."[9] Admittedly students in speech communication classes are not expected to seek "healing" in a way they might in a group facilitated by a university counseling service or a community mental health center. However, in a dialogic group environment the spirit of caring does exist. Members of any intensive group can find others with whom to share frustration, insecurity, and pain, and the caring in response to self-discolsure contributes to healing the wounds in individuals.

8. *Self-acceptance and the beginning of change*—When a communicator in an encounter group realizes he must learn to accept himself, that this involves a mature and forgiving personal value and grace, his inner being and outward behavior can change. This idea is supported in all the humanistic psychological literature, including such material as Rogers' client-centered theory, Ellis' rational-emotive theory, Glasser's reality theory, and Perls' Gestalt theory. Jess

9. Rogers, *On Encounter Groups,* pp. 21–22.

Lair's *I Ain't Much Baby But I'm All I've Got* is a fascinating book about self-acceptance, and subsequent change.

9.  *The cracking of facades*—Defensive behavior is typical in encounter groups as it frequently is in daily life. As the Johari Window used in chapter 9 showed, one can erect such a strong facade that his or her smallest dimension is the known-to-self and known-to-others, when this dimension ought to be the largest. A popular song begins with the lyric, "Smiling faces, smiling faces, sometimes they don't tell, the truth . . . tell lies and I've got the proof," and the singer describes in song how facades are erected and can be removed. The intensive group experience is an excellent way in which to crack facades in the spirit of dialogue. An invitation to this behavior can be seen in the words written by a member of an intensive group: "I'm trying to get to know you. I want to be your friend. But this is very difficult. It is not at all easy."

10. *The individual receives feedback*—Obviously, a real advantage of the intensive group experience, as compared with typical public speech behavior or much general conversation, is the great deal of data each group member collects about how he appears to others (interpersonal growth). The Johari Window includes a dimension of known to others but unknown to self. Feedback in an intensive group can significantly reduce this dimension in the personalities of group members. If the feedback is offered in the spirit of dialogue, whether negative or positive, it can be highly constructive. One student found the most useful information about himself in years, in just *one two-hour intensive group experience.*

11. *Confrontation*—As Rogers states, "There are times when the feedback is far too mild to describe the interactions that take place—when it is better said that one individual confronts another, directly 'leveling' with him."[10] Confrontations can be both positive and negative, but most often they result in positive feelings within and among the members of a group. For instance, in a confrontation between two members of a TA group, one young woman sharply lashed out at the group facilitator because she felt the group was not very helpful to her. Her angry *child* shouted in anger and

10. Rogers, *On Encounter Groups,* p. 31.

frustration at the facilitator's *parent.* His *adult* ignored her *child* and responded to her *adult.* A third person's *parent* sought to defend the woman's *childish* anger and spoke to the facilitators's *parent.* Then the facilitator's *parent* spoke to the third person's *parent,* and eventually the young woman's *child.* Thus, complementary transactions eventually took place, the feelings were honestly out in the open, and everyone profited from the experience.

12. *The basic encounter*—Rogers made an important point about these trends when he stated, "Running through some of the trends . . . is the fact that individuals come into much closer contact with each other than is customary in ordinary life. A university professor, for example, appears to be one of the most central, intense, and change-producing aspects of group experience."[11] A university professor was in a group comprised of persons from far less educated and less affluent segments of the community, and he found his initial feelings to be somewhat hostile—after all, he was a university professor with a doctorate and the others were men and women with minimal education and financial means. After working with others in the intensive group his entire outlook toward the group members (and others outside the group similar to the members) changed significantly. The view of the members of the group toward the professor changed as well. A caring and dialogic relationship developed to bridge the phony gap and often, when the group met, I-Thou relations (as described in chapter 7) existed.

Intensive groups, then, are largely unstructured, though often under the guidance or leadership of a trained facilitator. They can be most valuable to persons who are in pursuit of relationship goals, though content goals can be among the aims. Frequently the basic intensive group, the encounter group, is handled by a leader who not only provides typical functions of leadership, but who guides a particular psychological approach within the group life (e.g., Gestalt, rational-emotive, transactional analysis, or reality therapies). The trends identified by Carl Rogers describe the major process patterns found in intensive group communication, and the group usually passes through phases of getting comfortable with each other; dealing with power, influence, and authority; and developing affection among members.

---

11. Rogers, *Encounter,* p. 33.

# Problem-Solving Groups

Problem-solving, or task-oriented, groups hold a traditional place in the research, literature, and instruction in the field of communication.[12] The emphasis and directions in this kind of group may be described as being more *logical* than *psychological*. This is because problem-solving groups are far more interested, generally, in content goals rather than relationship ones. This does not mean, however, that humanistic benefits are not among the outcomes of problem-solving groups. Indeed, a humanistic approach to interpersonal communication combined with traditional views of ways in which a group can solve a problem can achieve significantly more results than one which avoids humanistic concepts and behaviors.

The problem-solving group is committed to discovering more information and ways of dealing with a problem than would be available to one person facing the problem alone. Research in small group communication confirms the notions that the combined efforts of a small group are more effective in solving problems than the efforts of one or two persons. The accuracy and the quality of the final group product is increased because the group is more likely to be comprehensive and creative than the individual or dyad, and is more likely also to eliminate inferior contributions to the problem-solving efforts, while integrating useful ones.[13] Humanistic skills, when used in problem-solving groups, can significantly help the group to avoid or overcome interpersonal obstacles.

A huge national corporation purchased a former motel with considerable conference facilities. The motel was converted into a training center for management employees of the corporation. Part of the training given to managers includes basic interpersonal skills (as described in this book), part of the training includes intensive small group communication to encourage dialogue and the building of good human relations. The men and women are put into small groups which seek to solve important problems typically faced by the company. Because the training in interpersonal communication precedes the problem-solving setting, the results, according to training evaluators, are far more satisfying and effective to individuals in the group and the corporation's needs as well.

---

12. B. Aubrey Fisher, *Small Group Decision Making* (New York: McGraw-Hill, 1974); William Smith, *Group Problem-Solving Through Discussion* (Indianapolis: Bobbs-Merrill, 1965).
13. DiSalvo, "Small Group Behavior," p. 118.

The problem-solving group is not best described in terms of trends similar to those characteristic of the intensive group. Certain conditions and patterns of analysis reveal the nature and functions of the problem-solving group. We can say the problem-solving group is likely to accomplish more positive outcome in terms of both content and relationship goals if it becomes dynamic and cohesive. A dynamic group is one which is very much alive, with each member making frequent, direct, and constructive contributions. If the group is cohesive its members have a commitment toward "working together," though perhaps possessing differences of opinions. A cohesive group encourages co-operative efforts to bring about sought after aims.

As the group works toward its goals it will deal with problems external to the group and problems arising out of working together on the primary task. The first kind of problems can be identified as adaptive-instrumental problems while the second kind are called socio-emotional problems. The group must deal with these two kinds of problems and strive to remain dynamic and cohesive. Certainly an awareness of these problems with a commitment and efforts to resolve them seems to be a requirement for effectiveness and satisfaction.

In problem-solving groups there are certain factors which can give communication a *chance* to be effective. In humanistic terms, the most important of these is the dialogic attitude. Having a dialogic attitude means, in this context, that the participants are seeking the best answer to the problem being attacked by the group, and the search involves use of the conditions and characteristics of dialogue. In addition to dialogic attitudes, the group can agree to the following conditions:

1. Everyone genuinely seeks an answer to a commonly shared problem.
2. Everyone works toward the *same* content goal.
3. There is a lack of concern about what may be the particular solution as long as it is the *best answer.*
4. Participants have a *detachment* from their own proposals.
5. Individuals bring *information* to contribute, and offer it freely.

The problem-solving group has two major problems even if the members have dialogic attitudes. These problems are to find an appropriate format and to agree on the answers to the issues in it.

What is a format? One view is that a format is an outline of topics which are to be considered by the group. This is an acceptable, though very broad, explanation. For some groups, such as board meetings or executive committee meetings, a preplanned format can be provided. In this sense, format means *the list of issues on which there is disagreement, and which if settled to the satisfaction of all participants should remove the barriers to agreement.* The task of participants in small group problem solving is to find where the disagreements are on each issue faced by the group and to state these disagreements as issues. Then they become the format for the particular problem. If the group process reveals additional disagreements, the format can be changed to include the new issues.

It is essential to effective problem solving to be able to find the points of disagreement on issues and to proceed using sound interpersonal skills to resolve them. A format of issues may sometimes be constructed in advance. Perceptive persons might do this and consider it a part of their preparation. The early stages of the group would then be devoted to choosing from all of the contributions the issues which the group accepts as the real obstacles to agreement. Some possible issues would be thrown out if everyone seemed to be on one side. Listening to each other might call previously unrecognized issues to mind. For example, if a group of physicians were in favor of euthanasia and sought to make it a permanent policy in medicine and health care, the issue of whether or not persons had the right to decide for themselves about ending their lives may not be an obstacle to agreement among these professionals. If so, they would quickly set the issue aside and turn their attention to others about which there was considerable disagreement.

If a format has not been prepared in advance, the early stages of the group's life may be a random presentation of views. Someone, perhaps a leader, can keep track of the issues as they appear, and the session can be limited to time necessary to locate points of disagreement; no attempt will be made in these moments to resolve the disagreement. It is not uncommon for a group to meet several times to locate these points. A staff of managers in a large manufacturing company was asked to define and describe the duties of a vice-president they would work under. They met weekly for one month, three hours per meeting, working on locating points of disagreement about what each believed a vice-president's responsibilities were. These meetings were followed by others to resolve the points of disagreements and to prepare the report of the group.

If the group determines what the issues are it can take each one and seek some agreement on it. One popular way of approaching this task is to:

1. Mentally elaborate (reason) on the issue as a group
2. Summarize the diverse viewpoints
3. Resolve disagreement by clarification and matching of reasons for holding views
4. Summarize the issue and go to the next.

The emphasis is on finding the disagreement and resolving it as efficiently as possible. The answer will not always be right, but this format increases the probability that it will be at least a solution that the group can make work. The process doesn't always seem efficient, it is only hoped that it will be more efficient than having no plan at all.

Problem-solving groups can operate at maximum levels of efficiency and accuracy if they are guided by a pattern of analysis. A number of patterns are available for groups to rely on but the most traditional one, the reflective thinking pattern, can produce highly satisfying results if a small group *actually* utilizes it for maximum yield or results. Recent experimental studies suggest that the reflective thinking pattern is useful but newer patterns of analysis may yield more accuracy and effectiveness. No particular pattern of interaction is going to guarantee best results, for results are as much dependent on member participation and the nature of the problem as they are on the chosen pattern of analysis. Here is an outline developed around the reflective thinking pattern. This pattern of analysis has worked effectively in small groups for generations. It can be used in problem-solving groups.

I. What is the nature of the problem?
   A. What are the facts of the present situation?
      1. How can the present situation best be described?
         a. What is going on?
         b. Who is involved?
         c. What kinds of difficulties exist?
         d. When did the problem develop?
         e. Have we presented enough factual information to make the nature and scope of the problem clear?
   B. How serious is the problem?
      1. Is the problem extensive?
      2. Is a change urgent?
      3. Why is the problem important now?
   C. What are the causes of the problem?
      1. What is the history of the problem?
      2. What conditions brought it about?

D. What forces are at work to change the present situation?
1. What solutions have been tried?
    a. How extensive have they been?
    b. How successful have they been?
2. Is there need for additional attempts to solve the problem?
3. What will the probable results be if no action is taken?
E. To what extent does this group agree on a course of action?
1. On what matters do members agree?
2. On what matters do members disagree?
3. What are the controversies that must be worked out?

*Goals*

II. What standards, criteria, or goals must any solution to the problem meet?

A. What kind of a world do we want to live in?

B. What ideals must a solution satisfy?

*Possible Solutions*

III. What courses of action are possible?

A. What is one possible solution?
1. What is good about this possibility?
2. What is bad about this possibility?

B. What are other possibilities?
1. What are the good points about them?
2. What are the bad points about them?

C. Which solution should this group choose?

*Application*

IV. What steps should be followed in putting this solution into effect?

V. How can we evaluate the results of the application?

A group faced with a shared problem can benefit greatly from this pattern of analysis if they actually use it. Some problem-solving groups follow a sound reflective thinking pattern and conclude with highly effective results while others begin with this analytical approach but soon abandon it after taking stages out of sequence, ignoring some stages completely, or frustrating themselves by getting into long, largely irrelevant discourses about "the way things ought to be," before the nature of the problem has been examined sufficiently. They move into cummunication centering around a statement such as, "You know what we really ought to do?" The group gets side-tracked, time is wasted, and productivity is minimal. These events of frustration and poor productivity also can result from misuse of other similar patterns of analysis for problem-solving groups.

A specialist in small group communication, Carl Larson indicated that while early problem-solving operated on the assumption the reflective thinking pattern was both highly appropriate and desirable for success in problem solving, there was reason to question this assumption. His interest was in distinguishing characteristics of "effective" and "ineffective" groups.[14] One way to make this distinction would be in terms of accuracy of a group's solution to a problem. A significant dimension on which accurate and inaccurate groups differ is the *form of analysis* which their problem takes. Larson sought to find out whether variations in forms of analysis would produce associated variations in the accuracy of small groups. He discovered that problem-solving patterns did aid groups in effectiveness, but current problem-solving patterns appeared to be more productive than the traditional. Larson's study used the reflective thinking format (not as detailed as we have outlined it) and two other patterns of analysis: the simple question format and the ideal solution format.

*Single Question Format:*

1. What is the single question, the answer to which is all the group needs to know to accomplish its purpose?
2. What subquestions must be answered before we can answer the single question we have formulated?
3. Do we have sufficient information to answer confidently the subquestions (if yes, answer them, if no, continue below)?
4. What are the most reasonable answers to the subquestions?
5. Assuming that our answers to the subquestions are correct, what is the best solution to the problem?

*Ideal Solution Format:*

1. Are we all agreed on the nature of the problem?
2. What would be the ideal solution from the point-of-view of all parties involved in the problem?
3. What conditions within the problem could be changed so that the ideal solution might be achieved?
4. Of the solutions available to us, which one best approximates the ideal solution?[15]

14. Carl Larson, "Forms of Analysis and Small Group Problem-Solving," *Speech Monographs* 36 (November 1969): 452–55.
15. Ibid., p. 453.

Patterns of analysis can be further examined by focusing on a study reported by communicologist John K. Brilhart.[16] We know that often in problem-solving groups the pattern or system to be employed is indicated and facilitated by the appointed or elected leader. If a group has a weak leader who does not effectively communicate and guide its movement, then there is often a high degree of probability the group will experience more frustration than necessary and waste valuable time. How can a leader communicate a pattern of analysis to the other group participants? Brilhart faced this question and examined three techniques a leader can employ: use of a visual aid in advance, an oral explanation in advance, and an oral step-by-step explanation. Brilhart found limited support for the notion that a designated leader should announce the discussion pattern in advance. Perhaps most significant is the finding that in this case a majority of participants found the use of a visual presentation on a chart identifying the reflective thinking pattern more helpful than oral presentation, and either oral or visual presentation more useful than announcing each step once a group had arrived at it. The influence on the group was due in part to the use of trained leaders and sound record keeping of group progress.[17] In any event, the tradition of a clear pattern of analysis finds support in terms of both use of a pattern and sound leadership.

## Summary

This final chapter allows us to focus specifically on the small group experience in interpersonal communication. The small group, ideally, consists of five to seven members, and may be either an intensive or a problem-solving group. Intensive groups are concerned mainly, though not entirely, with relationship goals, while problem-solving groups aim largely at content goals. The intensive group and the problem-solving group usually have a designated leader, though one is not always necessary.

Leaders function to facilitate the growth and progress of the group toward goals. The basic functions typical of leadership can benefit most groups.

The basic intensive group is the encounter group which focuses on the here-and-now and which is largely unstructured. Within the group persons are encouraged to be open, honest, self-disclosing, and

16. John K. Brilhart, "An Experimental Comparison of Three Techniques for Communicating a Problem-Solving Pattern to Members of a Group," *Speech Monographs* 33 (June 1966): 168–69.
17. Ibid., pp. 176–77.

not afraid of confrontation. Carl Rogers provides a description of the basic trends of intensive small groups.

The problem-solving group focuses likewise on the here-and-now but is far more structured with an aim toward solving a problem shared by members of the group. A group with members trained in interpersonal communication and the intensive group experience is more likely to be successfully productive than an untrained group. The reflective thinking pattern is an effective format for most problem-solving groups. Modified variations of this pattern have also proved effective in group problem solving.

A small group experience is a good way to "get it all together" in understanding interpersonal communication and developing interpersonal skills. Therefore, we should try to gain a good deal of group experience.

# Bibliography

Aiken, L. "Relationships of Dress to Selected Measures of Personality in Undergraduate Women." *Journal of Social Psychology* 59 (1963): 119–28.

Anderson, Kenneth E. *Introduction to Communication Theory and Practice.* Menlo Park: Cummings, 1972.

Bach, Geoege R., and Peter Wyden. *The Intimate Enemy: How to Fight Fair in Love and Marriage.* New York: Avon, 1968.

Bach, George R., and Ronald M. Deutsch. *Pairing.* New York: Avon, 1970.

Barker, Larry L., and Robert J. Kibler, eds. *Speech Communication Behavior: Perspectives and Principles.* Englewood Cliffs: Prentice-Hall, 1971.

Barnlund, Dean C. *Interpersonal Communication: Survey and Studies.* Boston: Houghton Mifflin, 1968.

Blake, Robert R., and Jane S. Mouton, "Managerial Facades." *Advanced Management Journal,* 1966, p. 31.

Berne, Eric. *Games People Play: The Psychology of Human Relationships.* New York: Grove, 1964.

_____. *Transactional Analysis in Psychotherapy.* New York: Grove, 1961.

Borden, George, Richard D. Gregg, and Theodore Grove. *Speech Behavior and Human Interaction.* Englewood Cliffs: Prentice-Hall, 1969.

Brandon, Nathaniel. *Breaking Free.* Los Angeles: Nash, 1970.

———. *The Disowned Self.* Los Angeles: Nash, 1971.

———. *The Psychology of Self-Esteem.* Los Angeles: Nash, 1969.

Brilhart, John K. "An Experimental Comparison of Three Techniques for Communicating a Problem-Solving Pattern to Members of a Group." *Speech Monographs* 33 (June 1966): 168–69.

———. *Effective Group Discussion.* Dubuque: Wm. C. Brown, 1967.

Brooks, Keith, Jack E. Douglas, Carroll C. Arnold and Robert S. Brubaker. "The Study of Speech Communication." In John J. Makay, ed., *Exploration in Speech Communication.* Columbus: Charles E. Merrill, 1973, pp. 4–18.

Brooks, William D. *Speech Communication.* Dubuque: Wm. C. Brown, 1972.

Brown, Charles T., and Paul W. Keller. *Monologue to Dialogue: An Exploration in Interpersonal Communication.* Englewood Cliffs: Prentice-Hall, 1973.

Browne, Harry. *How I Found Freedom in an Unfree World.* New York: Macmillan, 1973.

Brown, Roger. *Words and Things.* Glencoe: Free Press, 1958.

Buber, Martin. *Between Man and Man.* New York: Macmillan, 1958.

———. *I and Thou.* 2d ed. New York: Charles Scribners, 1958.

Burke, Kenneth. *A Grammar of Motives and a Rhetoric of Motives.* New York: World, 1962.

Burgoon, Michael, Judee K. Heston, and James C. McCroskey. *Small Group Communication: A Functional Approach.* New York: Holt, Rinehart, and Winston, 1974.

Carson, Robert C. *Interaction Concepts of Personality.* Chicago: Aldine, 1969.

Clark, Tony, Doug Bock, and Mike Cornett. *Is That YOU Out There? Exploring Authentic Communication.* Columbus: Charles E. Merrill, 1973.

Compton, N. "Personal Attributes of Color and Design Preferences in Clothing Fabrics." *Journal of Psychology* 54 (1962): 191–95.

Cooley, Charles H. *Human Nature and Social Order.* New York: Charles Scribners, 1922.

Crable, Richard E. "A Situational Approach to Purposeful Nonverbal Communication." In John J. Makay, ed., *Exploration in Speech Communication.* Columbus: Charles E. Merrill, 1973, pp. 299–314.

Davitz, J. R. *The Communication of Emotional Meaning.* New York: McGraw-Hill, 1964.

DiSalvo, Vincent. "Small Group Behavior." In John J. Makay, ed., *Exploration in Speech Communication.* Columbus: Charles E. Merrill, 1973, pp. 104–41.

Eisenberg, Abne M., and Ralph R. Smith. *Nonverbal Communication.* New York: Bobbs-Merrill, 1971.

Ellis, Albert, and Robert A. Harprer. *A Guide to Rational Living.* Hollywood: Wilshire Book Company, 1961.

Ellis, Albert. *Humanistic Psychotherapy: The Rational-Emotive Approach.* New York: Julian, 1973.

Fotheringham, Wallace C. *Perspectives on Persuasion.* Boston: Allyn & Bacon, 1966.

Ginott, Haim G. *Between Parent and Teenager.* New York: Avon, 1969.

Glasser, William. *Reality Therapy: A New Approach to Psychiatry.* New York: Harper & Row, 1965.

Goble, Frank. *Third Force: The Psychology of Abraham Maslow.* New York: Pocket Books, 1971.

Golembiewski, Robert T., and Arthur Blumberg, eds. *Sensitivity Training and the Laboratory Approach.* Itaska: Peacock, 1970.

Hall, Edward T. *The Silent Language.* Greenwich: Fawcett, 1959.

Hall, Robert A. *Leave Your Language Alone.* New York: Linguistica, 1950.

Hart, Roderick P., and Don M. Burks. "Rhetoric Sensitivity and Social Interaction." *Speech Monographs* 39 (June 1972): 75–91.

Harris, Thomas A. *I'M OK—You're OK: A Practical Guide to Transactional Analysis.* New York: Harper & Row, 1967.

Haultsby, Maxwell. "Systematic Homework in Written Psychotherapy." *Rational Living* 6 (1971): 16–23.

Hayakawa, S. I. *Language in Thought and Action.* 3d ed. New York: Harcourt, Brace, Jovanovich, 1972.

Hill, Archibald A. *Introduction to Linguistic Structures.* New York: Harcourt, Brace, and World, 1958.

Howe, Reuel L. *Partners in Preaching: Clergy & Laity in Dialogue.* New York: Seabury, 1967.

_____. *The Miracle of Dialogue.* New York: Seabury, 1964.

Johannesen, Richard L. "The Emerging Concept of Communication as Dialogue." *The Quarterly Journal of Speech* 57 (December 1971): 373–82.

Johnson, David W. *Reaching Out: Interpersonal Effectiveness and Self-Actualization.* Englewood Cliffs: Prentice-Hall, 1972.

Johnson, Wendell, and Dorothy Moeller. *Living With Change: The Semantics of Coping.* New York: Harper & Row, 1972.

Johnson, Wendell. *People in Quandries: The Semantics of Personal Adjustment.* New York: Harper, 1946.

James, Muriel and Dorothy Jongeward. *Born to Win: Transactional Analysis with Gestalt Experiments.* Reading: Addison-Wesley, 1971.

Jourard, Sidney. "An Exploratory Study of Body-Accessibility." *British Journal of Social and Clinical Psychology* 5 (1966): 221–31.

————. *Disclosing Man to Himself.* New York: Van Nostrand Reinhold, 1968.

————. *The Transparent Self: Self-Disclosure and Well-Being.* New York: Van Nostrand Reinhold, 1964.

Knapp, Mark L. *Nonverbal Communication in Human Interaction.* New York: Holt, Rinehart, and Winston, 1972.

Knower, Franklin H. "What Do You Mean—Communication?" In John J. Makay, ed. *Exploration in Speech Communication.* Columbus: Charles E. Merrill, 1973, pp. 19–26.

Lair, Jess, and Jaqueline Carey Lair. *"Hey God, What Should I Do Now?"* Garden City: Doubleday, 1973.

Lair, Jess. *"I Ain't Much Baby—But I'm All I've Got."* New York: Doubleday, 1969.

Larson, Carl. "Forms of Analysis and Small Group Problem-Solving." *Speech Monographs* 46 (November 1969): 452–55.

Lieberman, Morton A., Irvin D. Yalom, and Mathew B. Miles. *Encounter Groups: First Facts.* New York: Basic, 1973.

Laing, R. D. *The Divided Self.* New York: Pantheon, 1960.

————. *The Self and Others.* New York: Pantheon, 1969.

Langer, Suzanne K. "The Origins of Speech and Its Communicative Function." In James W. Gibson, ed., *A Reader in Speech Communication.* New York: McGraw-Hill, 1971, pp. 87–93.

Lazarus, Arnold A. *Behavior Therapy & Beyond.* New York: McGraw-Hill, 1971.

Levant, W. P. "Antagonistic Functions of Verbal Pauses: Filled and Unfilled Pauses in the Solution of Additions." *Language and Speech* 6 (1963): 1–4.

Lee, Irving J. *Language Habits in Human Affairs: An Introduction to General Semantics.* New York: Harper & Row, 1941.

Makay, John J., and Thomas C. Sawyer. *Speech Communication Now! An Introduction to Rhetorical Influences.* Columbus: Charles E. Merrill, 1973.

Makay, John J., and William R. Brown. *The Rhetorical Dialogue: Contemporary Concepts & Cases.* Dubuque: Wm. C. Brown, 1972.

Mases, Paul. *The Voice of Neurosis.* New York: Grune and Stratton, 1954.

Maslow, Abraham. *Motivation and Personality.* New York: Harper & Row, 1954.

_____. *The Further Reaches of Human Nature.* New York: Viking, 1971.

_____. *Toward a Psychology of Being.* 2d ed. New York: Van Nostrand, 1968.

Matson, Floyd W., and Ashley Montague, eds. *The Human Dialogue: Perspectives on Communication.* New York: Free Press, 1967.

May, Rollo. *Man's Search for Himself.* New York: New American Library, 1953.

Mayerhoff, Milton. *On Caring.* New York: Harper and Row, 1971.

Mead, George H. *Mind, Self, and Society.* Chicago: University of Chicago Press, 1934.

Mehrabian, Albert. *Silent Messages.* Belmont: Wadsworth, 1971.

Miles, Raymond E. "Human Relations or Human Resources?" *Harvard Business Review,* July-August 1965, pp. 148–56.

Miller, Gerald R. *An Introduction to Speech Communication.* 2d ed. Indianapolis: Bobbs-Merrill, 1972.

Moray, Nevell. *Listening and Attention.* Baltimore: Penguin Books, 1969.

Myers, Gail and Michele Myers. *The Dynamics of Human Communication: A Laboratory Approach.* New York: McGraw-Hill, 1973.

Ogden C. K., and I. A. Richards. *The Meaning of Meaning.* New York: Harcourt, Brace & World, 1923.

O'Neill, George, and Nena O'Neill. *Open Marriage: A New Life for Couples.* New York: Avon, 1972.

Otto, Herbert A., and John Mann. *Ways of Growth: Approaches to Expanding Awareness.* New York: Viking, 1968.

Pei, Mario. *The Story of Language.* Philadelphia: J. B. Lippincott, 1949.

Perls, Fritz, Ralph F. Hefferline, and Paul Goodman. *Gestalt Therapy: Excitement and Growth in Human Personality.* New York: Dell, 1951.

Perls, Fritz. *Gestalt Therapy Verbatim.* Toronto: Bantam, 1969.

Phillips, Gerald M. *Communication and the Small Group.* 2d ed. Indianapolis: Bobbs-Merrill, 1973.

Powell, John. *Why Am I Afraid to Tell You Who I Am?* Chicago: Argus Communications, 1969.

Reich, Theodore. "Friendship and Love." In Robert Cummins, *Friendship.* Winona: St. Mary's College Press, 1971.

Rogers, Carl. R. *Becoming Partners: Marriage and Its Alternatives.* New York: Dell, 1972.

_____. *Carl Rogers on Encounter Groups.* New York: Harper & Row, 1970.

_____. *On Becoming a Person: A Therapist's View of Psychotherapy.* Boston: Houghton Mifflin, 1961.

Rogers, Carl R., and Barry Stevens. *Person to Person: The Problems of Being Human.* Lafayette: Real People Press, 1967.

Rogers, Carl R. "The Group Comes of Age." *Psychology Today,* December 1969, pp. 27–31, 58–61.

Rosenthal, Robert. "Self-Fulfilling Prophecy." *Readings in Psychology Today.* Del Mar: CRM Books, 1967, pp. 466–71.

Rubin, Theodore I. *The Winners Notebook.* New York: Collier, 1967.

Ruesch, Jurgen and Weldon Kees. *Nonverbal Communication.* Berkeley: University of California Press, 1972.

Sanford, Aubrey C. *Human Relations: Theory and Practice.* Columbus: Charles E. Merrill, 1973.

Scheidel, Thomas M. *Speech Communication and Human Interaction.* Glenview: Scott, Foresman, 1972.

Schutz, William C. *Here Comes Everybody.* New York: Harper & Row, 1971.

*Social Psychology: Explorations in Understanding.* Del Mar: CRM Books, 1974.

Stevens, Barry. *Don't Push the River (It Flows By Itself).* Lafayette: Real People Press, 1970.

Stewart, Charles J., ed. *On Speech Communication: An Anthology of Contemporary Writings and Messages.* New York: Holt, Rinehart, and Winston, 1972.

Stewart, John. "An Interpersonal Approach to the Basic Course." *The Speech Teacher* 21 (January 1972): 7–14.

————, ed. *Bridges Not Walls, A Book About Interpersonal Communication.* Reading: Addison-Wesley, 1973.

Sullivan, Harry Stack. *The Interpersonal Theory of Psychiatry.* New York: W. W. Norton, 1953.

Tillich, Paul. *Morality and Beyond.* New York: Harper & Row, 1963.

————. *The Courage to Be.* New Haven: Yale University Press, 1952.

Trager, G. L. "Paralanguage: A First Approximation." *Studies in Linguistics* 13 (1958): 1–12.

Tosi, Donald J. *Youth: Toward Personal Growth, A Rational-Emotive Approach.* Columbus: Charles E. Merrill, 1974.

Toulmin, Stephen. *The Uses of Argument.* Cambridge: The University Press, 1958.

Vernon, W. D. *The Psychology of Perception.* Baltimore: Penguin Books, 1962.

Watts, Alan. *The Book: The Taboo Against Knowing Who You Are.* New York: Vintage, 1972.

_____. *The Wisdom of Insecurity: A Message for an Age of Anxiety.* New York: Vintage, 1951.

Watzlowick, Paul, Janet Beavin, and Donald D. Jackson. *The Pragmatics of Human Communication.* New York: Taplinger, 1972.

Wilson, Colin. *New Pathways in Psychology: Maslow and the Post-Freudian Revolution.* New York: Taplinger, 1972.

# Index